For my Mother and for Miranda, Robin and Jason

Acknowledgements

This book would not exist without the help and encouragement of a small army of supporters. Apart from the fellow pilgrims whose lives at that time provided the story, my gratitude to so many of my friends is boundless.

In particular I should like to thank my editor at Schiel & Denver, Simon Hornby for his wisdom, patience and above all for his enthusiasm; as well as Marie-Hélène Cuckow who valiantly worked through the first draft and made thousands of corrections and Jason Tarver who has critically read and re-read the manuscript more times than it was fair to ask. Deep gratitude is also due to Roberto Induni, Terry Munyard, Praveen Greedharry and Shujata Laptajan for their unstinting support and encouragement, as it is to Richard Kidd, and his mother Barbara, for their thoughtful advice. Thanks, too, to Pauline Hoskins who first made me believe in this story, and to Debbie Schiesser who first encouraged me to write it.

Profound thanks are due above all to David Dry RIBA without whose inspiration, enthusiasm and talent the manuscript might well have remained forever at the bottom of the wardrobe.

Contents

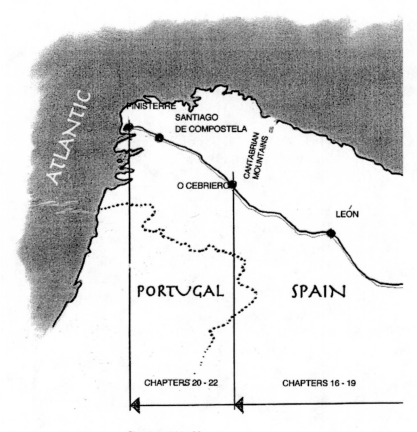

Chapters 11 to 22
Kilometres walked: 882
Days travelled: 28
Cantabrians: Altitude 1325 metres

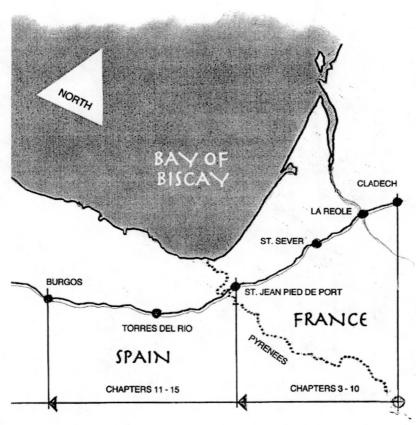

BAY OF BISCAY

NORTH

CLADECH

LA REOLE

ST. SEVER

BURGOS

ST. JEAN PIED DE PORT

TORRES DEL RIO

FRANCE

PYRENEES

SPAIN

CHAPTERS 11 - 15

CHAPTERS 3 - 10

Chapters 3 to 10
Kilometres walked: 700 approx.
Days travelled:16
Pyrenees: Altitude 1440 metres

I had been told from the first that the cottage was on the ancient Pilgrims' way to Santiago de Compostela.

Chapter One
How It All Began

It was fifteen years since I had first seen the cottage abandoned at the edge of a field, on top of a French hill, encased in brambles as if it guarded the Sleeping Beauty. But guarding, closer inspection revealed, only straw, a quantity of antique farm machinery and a fireplace of rustic magnificence.

Fifteen years. From a chain in the chimney hung a huge blackened kettle which, for twelve of them, had provided hot water for washing clothes, crockery and bodies indiscriminately in a tin tub on the hearthrug. In summer the shower was a pulley slung from a branch of the apple tree which hauled bags of water, heated by the sun, to a point just high enough not to have to duck too far. The children visited, acknowledged its romantic appeal - and hurried home to England.

I had been told from the first that the cottage was on the ancient pilgrims' way to Santiago de Compostela; and undeniably, if you gazed at it from sufficient distance it was possible to see, between two parallel lines of treetops to one side, an impenetrable and apparently interminable thicket of brambles which was certainly ancient. And definitely defunct. This path, so popular a millennium ago that it was trodden by thousands of people a year, had all but disappeared due to disuse over the past two or three centuries; it only really regained its popularity as a pilgrim route towards the end of the 1980s. Not that the destination meant anything much to me at the time, but pilgrim routes are always interesting. They must have been the main travel arteries of ancient times; the ways along which news spread and people migrated.

In time, I too migrated. What had been a holiday retreat became a permanent home and life settled into a peaceful, fairly solitary routine of survival; tending vegetables, lugging wood and recycling candles, in between short spells in England fulfilling the teaching contracts which paid for renovations. And slowly the late twentieth century, if not quite the twenty-first, began to work upon the atmosphere of the place, bringing with it comforts and conveniences never dreamed of

1

by the original incumbents who slept with their beasts before the fire, drying herbs and eventually tobacco from the rafters over their heads.

Other things changed too. The relationship I had brought with me, to share this idyll until death did us part, collapsed almost immediately beneath the strain of primitive living surrounded by a foreign language; and for a time, as life spiralled out of control, it seemed as if the whole idea had been a dreadful mistake. One night, in a fit of melancholic abstraction, I put a smouldering log back in the log basket, before I went to bed, and woke to find the entire ground floor engulfed in flames. On another occasion I carefully steered the car round a blind bend on the wrong side of the road. The resulting head-on collision destroyed both vehicles involved, and landed the other driver in hospital. Things did not look good.

In time I had met Bernard, an exceptionally kind Frenchman who looked like a taller version of Pablo Picasso and who, incredibly, seemed actually to like the idea of spending his time smoothing my path through life in his country. He taught me French after a fashion, introduced me to his vast circle of friends and was particularly brilliant when it came to sorting out the minefield of French bureaucracy, not to mention criminology. Bernard was an extremely useful person to know in any case; having lived all his life in the same small town, as well as having run a popular brasserie for over a decade, he was an invaluable source of gossip and influence. That he had friends in just about every walk of life meant that, no matter what the problem, he could usually find someone to sort it out. Having cycled all over the region as a boy he knew the countryside well too - knowledge which, from time to time, proved invaluable to visiting film crews in search of locations.

Once, on my birthday, he had arrived to pick me up telling me mysteriously to put on strong shoes and bring a couple of candles. Parking the car in the middle of nowhere, he had scrambled up a wooded bank and disappeared into the side of a hill. Following with difficulty, I had found myself in a tunnel, a little less than two metres high and sharply perpendicular, which had been hewn out of solid rock more than eight centuries before.

This passage had climbed steadily for a couple of hundred metres, turning this way and that, lit only by the light of two tiny flames (a torch beam might have disturbed the bats) and had been exactly as he had found it forty years before. Once, there had been light from a well shaft about halfway up, he whispered, but that had been covered over by the local authorities after feuding families took to dropping bodies down it.

The ancient stone steps had spiralled round and up, emerging eventually into an impossibly romantic ruined castle, swathed in ivy and hidden by trees. It all seemed vaguely familiar, and I began to wonder if I had seen it in a dream until I remembered a film I had seen several years before. One of the scenes had been shot just where I was standing. It was Bernard who had alerted the crew to the existence of this perfect location, and he had wanted me to see it, he said, before it collapsed completely or was developed for tourism.

"Everything changes." He added sadly, rubbing at some graffiti on a pillar.

The landscape closer to home had changed too. In the fifteen years since I had bought the house thickets had been razed and ancient footpaths reopened. Returning from England one summer morning, I found to my astonishment that the brambles and scrub alongside the house had completely disappeared; in their place an enchanting woodland walk stretched its dappled way through the trees.

Often, as the year progressed, I gazed down that path and imagined what it would be like to follow it all the way to Santiago. From time to time I tried walking along it for a whole day to see how far I could get before nightfall, setting off cheerfully towards the rising sun. It was several weeks before a neighbour pointed out that, with Spain and Santiago well to the west of Europe, I was going in completely the wrong direction. Oh well. To the west the path was less pretty and disappeared completely before I'd gone very far. This was not surprising - after all, several centuries had passed in which the countryside might have changed completely from the one my mediaeval forebears would have known. A glance at a map showed that it could be connected to other paths to form a reasonably direct route. At least at first. Perhaps in their time it would all have been one path. Perhaps in their time they would have set out along it to walk to Santiago - perhaps, even in my time, it was still possible.

I was fifty-six then, and for several years my life had oscillated schizophrenically between basic survival on one side of the channel and a demanding job, training sharp-suited executives, on the other. I wasn't necessarily looking for a way out, but there was something about the single-mindedness of a pilgrimage, coupled with the excitement of exploration, which seemed very appealing - a way to draw a line under past failures and prepare for the future in a new spirit.

Man's thirst for adventure is a fact of life, but to satisfy that thirst by discovering unknown locations nowadays seems to need the backup of an extensive (and expensive) network of support, or at the very least the camera crew of a minor television company. Simpler by far to look at history, and a route along which ordinary people embarked by the thousand in its mediaeval heyday. Plenty of people do it still, but nowadays there are traditional starting points and transport systems to get you to them. Paul Theroux believes that 'Travel is transition. At its best it is a journey from home, a setting forth...' and this is doubtless what my mediaeval forebears would have believed too. They would have closed the door and stepped straight out onto the path to Santiago - there would have been no other way. They would have set out, possibly penniless and probably without ambition but for salvation in another life.

Though it wasn't always like that. Pilgrimage in the credulous, superstitious days of the Middle Ages served a great many purposes in this life, never mind any other. Paradoxically, it was used both as a means of escape from the arm of the law and as a sentence imposed by law. Presumably, in imposing a pilgrimage on a criminal, the courts had in mind that they would be rid of his presence for some considerable time (if not forever) whilst possibly reforming his character into the bargain - a sort of mediaeval version of Community Service. It isn't such an archaic idea either, in Belgium it continues to this day.

Not that everyone who was sentenced to walk to Santiago necessarily did it. There were plenty of people, priests in particular, who would undertake the journey for you for a fee, and pilgrimage by proxy seems to have been considered perfectly acceptable in those days. They don't appear to have come cheap though. According to a sliding scale of charges which had evolved by the end of the Middle Ages, Santiago was on a par with Rome, costing £12, no small amount at the time. India was worse, it cost £60 to get out of going there.

It was, perhaps predictably, the Irish who started the whole thing off with their priests imposing pilgrimages to Rome as penance for sins admitted during confession. Perhaps it was also the Irish who began the idea of carrying stones in ones pack to represent those sins. There can't be many backpacking journeys where pebbles make up part of the luggage but, until you get to the Cruz del Ferro in Galicia, pebbles - the heavier the better - are an essential part of this pilgrimage.

These penitents, too poor to buy their way out of their punishment, probably made up the bulk of pilgrims during the bumper years of the eleventh and twelfth centuries, but they were by no means alone. Plenty of people made the journey out of piety, out of curiosity or out of a search for healing. There is a rather endearing story of a Frenchman who arrived in Santiago in the tenth century, to ask for a cure for impotence; apparently his wife had so far failed to conceive after several years of marriage. To his immense joy he found when he returned, after two years, that the miracle had already been accomplished. A ready-made family of two were waiting for him.

Central to the whole concept of redemption-by-pilgrimage, though, was the clocking up of relics visited. It was, presumably, possible to document the cures that were produced by touching the bones of a saint. Nobody seems to know quite when touching them came to be viewed as a step on the road to heaven, but it was well before the fourth century.

Here again, there was a sliding scale of points awarded. The closer the saint had lived to the time of the crucifixion the higher their body-part rating, in credits to be put towards salvation - in Saint James's case, of course, he was closer than most. But although his body was supposed to be in Santiago, bits of him were found all over the world; his arm might have been in Flanders but his hand was walled up in Reading.

The presence of these relics hugely increased the popularity, and no doubt also the wealth, of the monasteries which displayed them. And the whole thing was self-perpetuating because, certainly on the way through France and Spain to Santiago, as relics were sought out more shrines were built to house them. Thus evolved the rambling, twisting route which zig zagged across country between shrines, enabling pilgrims to clock up credits towards redemption by touching their macabre contents as they went along. Nor was it only bones which were revered; bits of the cross, bits of shroud, bits of clothing, phials of blood - even phials of water purporting to be the tears of Christ - all these were viewed with an awe which would have made Sotheby's look like a car boot sale. At some point an enterprising monk must have remembered a by-product of circumcision, because hundreds of mummified 'foreskins of Christ' started popping up all over Europe.

Inevitably there were conflicts of interest. In Toulouse, for instance, they claimed to have had the body of Saint James long before it was supposed to have been found on a Galician hillside. This presumably would have wrecked a very lucrative legend before it had even got under way, had not someone put Pope Calixtus' name to a document insisting that the Toulouse relics were the fakes. The wonder is that no-one appears to have questioned his opinion at the time.

Not that Saint James had all that big a following in Spain, early on. When Santiago de Compostela was conquered and plundered, in the tenth century, the contemporary writers didn't even give him a mention. But in France he was much more popular. Ever since the Bishop of Le Puy en Velay made a pilgrimage to Santiago, in 950, the French have followed suit in their thousands. Le Puy is still the favourite starting point for anyone setting out from France, and they were far and away the best represented nation on the Camino when I was there. In fact there is a theory that the growth of the entire Santiago cult was due largely to the presence of French soldiers in Spain during the Middle Ages.

In the Middle Ages, moreover, most of the English royal families were French by birth. The Abbey at Reading, for instance, was founded by Henry I who was the son of William the Conqueror. The two kings who came after him, Stephen and Henry II, were the respective Counts of Boulogne and Anjou, and it was Matilda, daughter of Henry I, who made the well-documented pilgrimage to Santiago bringing back to Reading the famous hand of St. James.

With these connections it was hardly surprising that in England, as well as France, the idea caught on. Two centuries later, in 1434, nearly two and a half thousand English pilgrims are recorded as having set out for Spain, travelling by sea. Presumably there would have been still more who made the journey more cheaply through France. For, as I began to research my possible path, I discovered that there were several routes by which the English travelled. Many took the easy way, by ship to Corunna with only a relatively quick hop to Santiago at the end. Others took in Canterbury before embarking across the channel, following the route down through Normandy to Paris then Orleans, and so on. Still more might have gone by way of Mont St. Michel and followed the coast down to Biarritz, continuing all along the northern coast of Spain until they met up with the lazy ones disembarking at Corunna. That coastal route is still known by its old name of the Camino Ingles - the English Camino. Mont St. Michel too is still a popular starting place, and the reason for all the little statues of Saint Michael one finds competing with those of Saint James along The Way.

And what was the basis in fact, of the legend for which they made such a long and risky journey? Not much, really. Saint James is supposed to have gone to preach in Spain after the Ascension. Since the apostles were known to have travelled widely at the time that much may very well be true though it is not documented that he had much success. Even the legend only credits him with seven disciples. They, apparently, followed him back to Jerusalem where he was beheaded by Herod Agrippa in AD44, becoming the first of the apostles to be martyred.

His disciples rescued his body (by some accounts with its head miraculously re-attached) and took it down to the coast at Jaffa, where they found a boat mysteriously waiting for them. By some entirely superhuman power they were whisked, in only a week, all the way to the Bay of Padron on the coast of his old evangelistic territory. Before they could lay him to rest, though, his disciples had to tame a couple of wild bulls, and then hitch them to a cart strong enough to haul a tomb of solid marble up twenty-five miles of hills, to the place where he was finally buried.

And that was that for about six centuries until, in a miraculous vision, a hermit saw stars falling on that particular hillside and scurried off to tell the Bishop. The ensuing investigation uncovered a tomb with three anonymous bodies inside - unquestionably those of the saint and two of his disciples. A chapel dedicated to Santiago was immediately built on the site, and the place took the name of Campo Stellarum - which in time became Compostela - Field of Stars.

It didn't take long after that to build up a host of miraculous anecdotes around these remains, which were woven and promoted with consummate skill by an ecclesiastical spin-doctor who could have been a role model for Alistair Campbell or Donald Rumsfeld.

For by then Spain had been overrun by Islam. And the ferocious zeal with which the Moorish conquest had taken hold would seem to have stemmed from their unquestioning devotion to a figurehead - Mohammed. What the Christians needed was a figurehead, one to whom they could not only relate, but who would inspire them to fight back. And so Beatus the Monk (later to be made Saint Beatus for his pains) launched a massive public relations exercise, which in no time at all presented the saint as the saviour of the Spanish people. Notwithstanding that he was reduced to a skeleton somewhere near the coast he was to be found, according to the propaganda, on a white horse in the thick of battle slaying Moors with a blazing sword. In time, the legend of Santiago Matamoros (St. James the Moor Slayer) became associated with over forty different battles. And it worked. After eight centuries of occupation the Moors were finally driven back, though in reality Spain owed less to Saint James than it did to Charlemagne who, realising the threat to the rest of Europe, came over the Pyrenees to help.

But the propaganda had taken hold, and in the twelfth century it proved to be very helpful indeed to the authorities of Santiago de Compostela. Replacing the humble chapel with a magnificent cathedral had plunged the city deeply into debt, and a long-term input of cash was urgently needed. So they used these stories to justify a tax which can only be described as a masterpiece of audacity. On the strength of these clearly fanciful accounts, the whole of Spain was compelled to pay the city a percentage of the profit from all corn and wine it had produced, since the infidel had been driven out by the 'intervention' of the ghost of Saint James. It's hard to imagine that they could have got away with it in the first place, but even more incredible is the length of time they managed to keep the fraud going. This infamous tax wasn't finally abolished until 1834.

And on the strength of that legend, myth, cynical public relations exercise, load of poppycock - call it what you will - pilgrims from all backgrounds made what was possibly the most dangerous journey of their lives. For whichever way you look at it, setting aside gullibility, financial gain, moral or even legal coercion, there is no doubt that at the heart of this pilgrimage was a bedrock of utter devotion. Devotion to the saint, to God or to something deep inside themselves, it didn't matter - every pilgrim who set out must have been expecting to encounter the unknown, and to be changed in some way. For that journey in the Middle Ages, would have been like climbing into the capsule of a space shuttle nowadays, without the benefit of an astronaut's training. They must have had enormous reserves of trust in something to have done it at all.

Some of this could have been to do with the spiritual qualities associated with the path, which go back further than the legend. Legend alone, one imagines, would have been hard-pressed to justify

Santiago's meteoric rise in popularity - by the twelfth century it had overtaken Rome to become second only to Jerusalem in importance as a pilgrim destination. The most likely explanation is that it was a route which already carried an inherent mysticism from pagan times, to which the Christian legend was simply bolted on.

The fact that many pilgrims from the start continued to Finisterre, a sacred place in the days of Celtic Sun Worship, would seem to bear this out. And it was the Finisterre connection that gave to this pilgrimage the emblem of the cockleshell - the original pilgrims used to lug them home with them as proof that they'd arrived. It wasn't only ordinary people who did it either. Some of the best known figures in history have made the pilgrimage, from Chaucer to St. Francis of Assisi, from Hannibal and all his elephants to Napoleon, from Charlemagne to King Ferdinand and Queen Isabella of Spain.

In 1999 the actress Shirley Maclaine walked the Camino and recorded her experience in a book. Two years later so did the writer Tim Moore. His pilgrimage seems to have been more of a bacchanalian tour of Spanish bars, with a donkey in tow. Shirley Maclaine's was a journey through her previous incarnations, with an angel for company. For her, clearly, the stars were the drivers of the spiritual energy along The Way; according to her it was all something to do with ley lines connecting the earth to the energy of the stars, in particular the Milky Way. I didn't understand any of this, but I did know that above my field at night the sky was an awe-inspiring mass of stars, and that there was a powerful feeling of serenity there. Were the two connected? Did this serenity come from the path which ran past the cottage? And did it continue all the way to Santiago? Well, there was only one way to find out, walk it and see. And so the idea became a plan.

Not that I was expecting to repeat Shirley Maclaine's experiences. Practically the whole of her book is devoted to accounts of trances and dreams of past lives. When she was transporting herself back to the Middle Ages, and discovering that she had been Charlemagne's mistress, I wanted to give her the benefit of the doubt. But a large chunk of the story is devoted to her embryonic development, in a crystal tank of golden liquid surrounded by flying saucers. Here I had to give up. It wasn't that I didn't believe that she had experienced it all in some way - for why would anyone bother to make it up? It was just that I couldn't give it any credibility myself.

So, religion, stella worship, mysticism or just plain curiosity. Any of these could have inspired a pilgrim who might have been living in my house in past centuries, and prompted them to start out. It was that inspiration I wanted to find. In the months ahead, my pilgrim forebears would have much to answer for.

... you will see a little yellow arrow pointing off onto an enchanting shady path through a wood.

Chapter Two
To Walk Out One Midsummer Morning..

I also blame Laurie Lee. When he wrote 'As I Walked Out One Midsummer Morning', his definitive account of a penniless wanderer's journey through Spain, he must have woken a wanderlust in more than a thousand hearts. I have never forgotten my wonder at the sheer romance of walking away from home one day, and not turning back - no trains or ticket queues to work ones way through, no airport delays and strikes to blunt ones enthusiasm. Just to set out and walk. And keep on walking.

But Laurie Lee had a violin. He had the means to earn a living as he walked, and although that is not really the point of a pilgrimage it is certainly a consideration. It seems that in the Middle Ages it was not unusual for pilgrims to break their journey, sometimes for long periods of time, in order to earn enough to continue. One of the most fascinating things about the church sculpture all along the route is the way that individual styles can be seen again and again, showing pretty clearly that these, possibly pilgrim, sculptors worked their passage as they went along. It was as well that they did. Originally, the grander architecture of Spain had owed its allegiance to Islam; when the Moors were finally driven out they left behind a population largely ignorant of the skills needed to build great monuments. Had it not been for these foreign artists and artisans passing through, it's arguable that many of the cathedrals and churches of the pilgrims' way would never have been built at all.

Certainly any pilgrim would have committed many more months to their journey than would most of their descendants today. The state protected their property for a year and a day, but no longer than that because it was by no means certain that they would return. Whole villages would accompany a pilgrim for the first few miles, before waving him on his way with considerable grief as well as encouragement. Quite apart from the many who died en route, a substantial number of them simply chose not to go back home. Villafranca for instance, on the edge of Galicia, is so named because of the number of French pilgrims who settled there - possibly because, if you were unable to continue, you could still get all your credits towards salvation in Villafranca, so long as you called at the 'Door of Forgiveness' in its church of Santiago. And you wouldn't have to make the punishing climb over the mountains into Galicia. It must have been a tempting place to stop. Nowadays the journey is expected to take around a couple of months, depending of course on where you start. But even with economies made here and there, it doesn't take an accountant to work out that travelling continuously for that length of time won't be cheap.

The expense is certainly mitigated, though, by the many organisations which offer free, or much reduced, accommodation in refuges along the Camino as well as on some of the major routes which approach it. In so doing they are following a tradition begun by the Knights of Santiago, which was an offshoot of the Knights Hospitaller, an Order which itself had grown out of the Knights Templar, who provided shelter for pilgrims to the Holy Land in the wake of the Crusades. The Santiago Order built hospices all along the Way of St. James, where they provided food, shelter, medical care and spiritual guidance to pilgrims far from home. Most of the original hospices are in ruins now, if they can be seen at all, but modern versions of them are being opened all the time.

There's just one snag - access to these refuges, and other benefits besides, depends on the ownership of a 'Credentiale', or Pilgrim Record. This is a sort of Union Card, which you get stamped at places along the Way to prove you've actually been there, and on your own two feet - or two wheels though horseback is also allowed. A credentiale can be obtained from various churches, once you are actually on the Way of St. James in Spain, or at any of the popular starting points. But what if you intend starting out from a house in the middle of France, on an obscure path which peters out after a couple of miles, leaving you to plot a course across country until you stumble onto one of the major pilgrim routes? Well, then you need to find someone to issue you with one before you go.

The time had come to visit the Confraternity of Saint James in Blackfriars, London. This is the society which has done so much to restore and promote the ancient pilgrims' way, and which also exists to advise and support the pilgrims who set out from England. It has its counterparts too in other European countries, though I didn't know this until I arrived at the Confraternity's office. This was not as simple as it sounds. First, it was necessary to find the place. It gives, as its address, the Blackfriars Rd. In fact - and only after considerable searching - you will find it there, but behind a church hall just past the bridge. My first attempt landed me in a yoga class. It was fortunate that I was escorted from there right to the door because, left to myself, I might well have missed the tiny plaque announcing the offices of 'CSJ'.

The effort was made worthwhile though, when the door was opened by the organisation's secretary, the encyclopaedically informed Marion Marples. She sat me down in the wonderland of information which is the Confraternity's library and gave me her full attention, rather like a doctor acting for the Ramblers Association. There was much she needed to explain. I learned, for instance, that to talk of a Pilgrimage is not the same thing as to talk of a Camino - 'camino' is merely a Spanish word for a path - as is 'chemin' in French. To talk of 'ones Camino' is simply not done; one is only in possession of ones Pilgrimage. Such is the etiquette of The Way of St. James.

Two hours later I emerged, a fully paid-up member of the Confraternity, with a stack of books under my arm together with a sheaf of papers several inches thick which mapped the 'new' route of the Voie de Vezelay. This famous path, which comes down from Germany via Belgium, had seemed to me to be the most direct of the old pilgrim arteries to the Pyrenees. It wasn't too far away from me either, according to the books I had so far read which basically advised me to follow the GR654 cross-country footpath. But I had reckoned without the myopic detective work of the Confraternity's French counterpart, Les Amis de St. Jacques. Their research conclusively rubbished my easy route. They, it appeared, had discovered the absolutely definitive path taken by the ancient pilgrims, and it was much further west. Oh well.

I also carried an application form for the precious credentiale. The idea is to get this record stamped at every overnight stop along the way, as well as in bars, churches or mairies (town halls) in any towns you pass. In addition to being a passport to a free or at least a cheap bed, it provides an interesting and at times impressive record of the distance you've walked. The Guide issued by the Confraternity of St James cautions against a too heavy preponderance of stamps obtained in bars, however, in case it makes you look frivolous since

13

qualifying for your certificate, once you have reached Santiago, will be a serious matter.

This guide - a list of do's and don'ts for pilgrims, which incorporates the whereabouts and opening hours of all the Spanish refuges - also suggests that you get a stamp before you leave, to mark your starting point, from your local mairie or church. Bernard having been brought up a Catholic, catechism and all, suggested that if I were going to ask my local priest for a stamp I ought really to go to Mass to find him — to strengthen my credibility, as it were. So, the mayor of my village having professed complete ignorance of the whole business of credentiales, I set out for the church in the nearest town one Sunday before my departure. The priest must have heard of them. I had never been to a catholic Mass before - but it wouldn't be a big deal I thought, a mere matter of joining the three or four other members of the congregation, popping up and down when they did, and presenting my credentiale to an eager-to-please clergyman at the end.

Accordingly, I sauntered up to the porch just before eleven o'clock in the morning, and entered the church. And it was packed. Whatever attendance crisis the church may be experiencing, it evidently wasn't experiencing it in this town. What was this? Was there some special service for children, which involved the attendance of hoards of admiring extended family members? Squeezing myself onto one of the last seats available, I looked around. The mixed congregation didn't seem to present much evidence of large family groups, or of infantile adulation come to that. A whiteclad, circular priest entered whilst the largely geriatric choir and orchestra were well into what was billed on my service sheet as the Ouverture du Celebration.

Slowly he bowled down the aisle, answering questions and umpiring disputes between his tiny acolytes. On one occasion this involved a good-humoured smack-on-head, but more often a gentle pinch-of-chubby-cheek. It was impossible not to be distracted by this pastoral pantomime but at last, candles carried high with immense concentration, the juvenile procession moved back to the entrance of the church. A hush fell on the congregation in anticipation of their return, a couple of minutes later and to the peal of trumpets, leading in a string of gold clad priests amongst whom even I could recognise a bishop.

The service which followed was long and elaborate. It seemed to have attracted a cross section of the entire community. Two black-clad youths with shinily gelled hair, whom I would have hesitated to leave in charge of my car, seemed to be taking a major part. The old twelfth century church, largely undecorated but for a murky fresco and some simple stained glass, seemed to be regarding the whole show rather wearily, as if it was all a bit much. Though when one of the youths with the gelled hair climbed to the lectern and, in a voice low with sincerity, offered a prayer for the soul of Pope John Paul II, it was genuinely touching.

So I'd gone and picked the end of the period of mourning for the dead Pope to ask for my pilgrim stamp. Well, it could have been worse - it could even be rather good, I could imagine the scenario which might take place in the church porch when I introduced myself to the assembled clergy afterwards. I picked the kindliest looking of the bunch as my target. I would ask him for my stamp and he would, of course, be so impressed by my zeal that he would lead me to the bishop. What could be better than to have ones Pilgrim Union card not only stamped but blessed, by the ecclesiastical shop steward.

At last the service came to an end and the priestly procession made its way back down the aisle and out into the sunshine. Clutching my pilgrim credentials, I made my leisurely way outside - only to find that they'd all scarpered. Not one holy hand to shake and to thank me for making the effort to pray for the old Pope's soul, not to mention mark my card. They'd probably nipped round the corner for a drink. It was beginning to feel like something out of Monty Python.

But fate was about to step in to delay my departure in any case. Having been striding up and down hills for months on end, in an effort to get fit enough to take on a thousand mile trek, I had decided to raise the pressure. I would go to the Alps for a few days in March, to get used to real uphills, and snowy, slippery ones at that. Bernard, who wanted to see his daughter, would come too, but just before we were due to set off disaster struck. It was carelessness really. Rooting around in the wood shed one morning, I fell over the lawnmower and impaled my breast-bone (or my sternum as I was to learn to call it) on an iron spike. Apart from swearing floridly at the pain I didn't give it too much thought, but when much later I found that I was unable to lift even the kettle to make a cup of tea, I began to worry. How much heavier would a rucksack be? From her office in London my friend Steph wailed down the phone.

"Perhaps your body is telling you it doesn't want to go! Had you thought of seeing a doctor?" No, it hurts enough already. "Or of giving up, perhaps?"

After a week of sleepless discomfort I was ready to agree with her and bin the whole idea. But the Alps are pretty in the snow, so I went along all the same. And there Bernard's daughter took over. Marching me off to see a friend of hers, she explained that he was an Osteopath. And a Buddhist. The Buddhist bit was promising, they don't believe in hurting any creatures, do they? Even humans. And can there be any better combination than the skill of a masseur and the mind of the Dalai Lama?

Massaging and prodding oh-so-gently, Stephane remarked in his dreamy, meditative voice, that perhaps this was a test of my determination to do the Camino. So he wasn't telling me not to go then? No, not so long as I kept my back straight and my shoulders relaxed. But I ought not to haul my rucksack off the ground for the time being, and it might not be a clever idea to bivouac for at least the first week.

Ah. So it would have to be the comfort of hotels rather than the hardness of the forest floor, and carte blanche to rest my rucksack on anybody's garden wall. Well, I could manage that. If only I could manage the pain of carrying it at all. I had intended to sleep out under the stars, from time to time, but there didn't seem to be much point in shutting them out with a tent which would also add weight. So I had bought (at staggering expense) the lightest, simplest bivouac bag I could find. This is a sort of heavy duty, waterproof sleeping-bag which covers everything else and keeps you dry if it rains. Tents, though, do offer some protection even if it's only psychological, whereas bivouac bags leave you exposed to everything elemental, animal or human which might pass by you in the night. I'd begun to worry about that as time went on, and could only hope I'd get used to it. For the moment, though, the problem was postponed.

A far more immediate concern was the weight that even reduced the paraphernalia associated with sleeping in the open would add to the rucksack, especially since it would be redundant for the time being. But I couldn't leave it behind, I might need it later on, so what to do? And then my younger son, Jason, announced his intention to come to stay in the cottage, just when I would be away. This presented a dilemma because I would miss him, but it also presented a solution because, if I hung on for a further week's recovery now, I would have been walking for only a week by the time he arrived and would have got no further than La Reole. I had discovered, during my practice walks, that a day's walking roughly equated to half an hour in a car, and a three and a half hour drive to meet me would definitely be a possibility. So it was sorted; I would set off with a lighter pack to start with, and he would bring the heavy stuff, after I'd had a week to build up the stamina to carry it. I'd be able to spend some time with him, and then continue the journey with all my equipment. And now, with only weeks to go to departure, advice came in from all directions.

"Put your money in your knickers," said Claire-from-down-the-road. She'd been inter-railing in Naples and knew what she was talking about when it came to security. In fact I was to find, once I reached it, that security wasn't much of a problem on the Camino. Belongings were left on bunks, mobile phones left to charge in corridors and bathrooms, rucksacks left standing open and I never saw that trust abused. I remember one evening flicking my sleeping bag over my belongings to hide them before I went out, and feeling that I had deeply insulted my fellow pilgrims who wouldn't have dreamt of touching anything which didn't belong to them. Disconcertingly, it was only as I drew close to Santiago - arguably the spiritual heart of the Camino - that I began to see signs on the walls of refuges warning of theft. But that was all a long way in the future then.

"If you're going to walk all that distance, why not walk somewhere beautiful?" Asked Frank, a retired doctor who spent his winters in the next village, and his summers in a remote log cabin in the wilds of Washington State.

Ah, Frank, if only you could have seen some of the beautiful places through which I walked. Frank had driven along some of the Camino route in a car. He had passed pilgrims walking by the road, he said, clearly, it was a very dull trek. What motorists like Frank don't know is that possibly only a few hundred yards further along, if you are approaching it at a walking pace, you will see a little yellow arrow pointing off onto an enchanting, shady path through a wood. That is the beauty of the Camino.

Peter-the-Gay-Hiker-from-Guildford, who had done this sort of thing loads of times and was planning a trek through the Andes, was more practical. If I was going to buy a decent rucksack, he counselled, I would need to test it out with all my stuff inside it.

If there were an award for the most patient shop assistant of all time, there is a young man working in the Guildford branch of Black's who ought to be seriously considered for it. Almost a quarter of the entire floor area of the shop was covered with my tatty belongings by the time I had finished packing, unpacking and repacking a dozen prospective packs. The one I eventually chose was technically only a Day Sack, and the packing would need to be precise in order to get everything in, but I knew that if I chose one big enough to give me plenty of room I would only fill it with more stuff - and more weight. According to the Confraternity Guide, the absolutely vital thing is to keep the weight below ten kilos. This is almost impossibly light, and involves long hours spent climbing on and off the bathroom scales with one piece less of sticking plaster here, a smaller bottle of shampoo there, and virtually no books at all. Plodding through France and Spain though, I lost count of the times I thanked God and Saint James that I'd done it; especially on the hills. All the same, I did miss the books.

An essential item of equipment, so the Confraternity Guide told me, would be a stick. I hadn't been in the habit of walking with a stick - but then I hadn't been in the habit of walking with a ten kilo pack either. Apparently a stick will take up to twenty-five percent of the strain. That was a consideration. But what sort to take? History dictated that it should be two metres long with an iron spike for warding off bandits and dogs. But mediaeval pilgrims were more limited in their choice than I was, and though I wasn't sure about the dogs, bandits surely wouldn't be a problem nowadays. Modern, telescopic walking poles don't come cheap though, not the good ones. Besides, I already had a stout hickory staff, brought from America by my daughter Miranda, years ago. It would certainly look the part, and it would be comforting to take something of hers along with me. But what if I lost it? With two months walking ahead this seemed to be a definite possibility. Was it wise to take along the extra baggage of emotional attachment?

Besides, not being telescopic it couldn't be hidden away in a rucksack if I was trying to look cool - cropped, bleached hair and a backpack could, at a pinch, be passed off as alternative. Leaning on a wooden staff would definitely mark one out as a member of Old Mother Time's coven. Perhaps if I had the rest of the costume - missing teeth, ratty hair, signs of incipient leprosy - I could have accepted the image. But I wasn't quite there yet. Not quite.

I was not to know, then, that all the coolest pilgrims still carry the stoutest, heaviest wooden staff they can find. Carry it, in fact, like an emblem. But in the end the dilemma was solved by the arrival, during the delay caused by the sternum injury, of a present from my brother; a lightweight, telescopic, aluminium walking pole, thoughtfully chosen and carefully packed. It would never have arrived in time had I not been delayed, so I took that as a sign and packed it. The telescopic factor turned out to be invaluable.

Returning to England for the last time before the walk, I had one last visit to make. Since moving into sheltered accommodation my mother's world had shrunk significantly. Once a hugely sociable person, with a passion for travel, her confidence had been so eroded by successive bouts of depression that she now discouraged all but a very few close visitors and had reduced her adventures to one outing a week - for a cup of tea at the local garden centre. Reluctant to make her feel even more isolated I had put off even discussing the pilgrimage. But now, rather to my surprise, she was excited by the whole idea - though she was more than a little dismayed by the lack of books. A prolific reader, and always the first person I turned to for advice on new titles, she had a wealth of suggestions to make all of which had, regretfully, to be rejected.

"But there will be so much to see," she consoled me. "You probably won't have any time for reading anyway - you'll be much too busy observing everything." If only she had been right.

She had travelled all over Spain at various times in her life, and knew the major towns of the Camino very well.

"But it will be completely different for you," she said. "You will be walking. You will see so much more." She could hardly wait for me to come back and share it all with her.

"Phone me whenever you can and let me know where you are!" She called as she waved me goodbye.

This brought me to the final luggage decision and one item with which I had had, initially, no problem at all in deciding to leave behind: my mobile phone. It seemed to fly in the face of the whole pilgrim thing, which was about breaking away from dependence on technology and reaching back to a quieter time, where the only voices one would hear would be birds - and other pilgrims of course. Besides, the Confraternity Guide had advised against it, on the grounds of weight and the paucity of signals. There'd be extra weight in the charger too, and in the adaptor. I found it odd, though, that it was the first question everyone asked when they knew I was planning to make the pilgrimage. Everyone. And that my answer in the negative was met with universal dismay.

"But what if you get lost?" Everyone asked. "Or fall down a ravine and break your neck?" (Much good would a phone be then.)

"*But what if we need you?*" This one from the children.

Ah now, that was the Achilles Heel of the whole thing. I was already carrying a sizeable pebble to represent my sins, I didn't need to add to them by being an irresponsible parent. In the end, I found myself slipping it almost unconsciously into my pocket just as I was leaving. Divine Intervention, or Technology Dependence? Only time would tell.

The evening before I was due to leave, the rain which had been falling all day moved on and the sky cleared. It was one of those lovely, soft springtime evenings which are still close enough to winter not to be taken for granted, when the lightness in the air is a delight. I leaned against the doorpost looking out into the garden which was golden with daffodils. The sun had just set and a full moon was already shining through the branches of the apple tree, but even so the air was full of birdsong. It was as if they were determined to get full value out of the lengthening days. I asked myself, not for the first time, why on earth I was making this pilgrimage. Why I was leaving a place so beautiful, and where I felt so secure, to walk alone for months on end across countryside of which I knew nothing, for a purpose I did not understand.

Oh come on! It wasn't as if I were going to the South Pole, or the centre of the Equatorial Rain Forest. And how long was it all going to take? A matter of weeks not months, let alone years. But I was not alone in my misgivings, for had not Laurie Lee confessed to a certain disappointment, when he realised that nobody was going to run after him to persuade him to come home, as he set out alone towards an unknown destination? And when, in the 1970s, the writer and broadcaster Edwin Mullins had set out to follow the - in those days largely obsolete - path through France to Santiago, in a car with his wife for company (and presumably a comfortable advance from his publisher) even he went through several periods of ambivalence towards the book for which he was making all the effort. Fortunately they didn't put him off, because his superbly researched book 'The Pilgrimage to Santiago' remains one of the most delightful studies of the architecture along all the various arteries of the Pilgrims' Way.

Besides, as I reminded myself, there had been the Night of The Shooting Stars six months before, when I had lain out under the clear sky intending, with every one I saw, to make a wish for one or other of the children. Instead, as each bright filament traced its way overhead, the thought had risen unbidden that I 'wished' to go to Compostela. Even then, it would seem, my subconscious mind had made its decision.

Mind you, had I known how large a part of me would change after I had walked the Camino, and how straightforward it was not going to be, I might have paid more attention to my misgivings and might never have set out. But then I wouldn't have discovered how profoundly the Camino can alter ones horizons - or how a chance meeting with three strangers would shape the whole experience.

Nor did Bernard tell me then that one of his friends, who earns a good living as a clairvoyant, had told him that I would find the walk almost unendurably difficult, and that before I finished it something would have happened to change my life forever. Some things it is better not to know.

Besides, he didn't believe her anyway.

… I came upon a jewel. The tiny twelfth century church of St. Christopher, patron saint of travellers…

Chapter Three
.. *Or Even One Mid-Spring Morning*

And so the day came, when I found myself standing by the front door, my rucksack on my back, looking out at the drizzle. I had said all along that I would not go if it was raining. And of course the week before, the weather had been glorious. But there had been enough delays. It was mid April, and with Miranda's wedding imposing a mid-June deadline at the other end, it was now or never. And anyway, it wasn't really raining. Not yet.

So, taking a deep breath I closed the door and set off along the path through the wood, feeling rather like Frodo going off to save the Shire. But Frodo had friends - all I had for company were my already complaining body parts. And Frodo had Gandalf the Wizard to sort out his problems - not only Gandalf, moreover, but Gandalf as portrayed by Ian McKellen. Now, if I had Ian McKellen for company...

And so I plodded through the wet leaves. In the seventeenth century an Italian, Domenico Laffi, wrote about his pilgrimage through France to Santiago. As they crossed the Spanish border he and his companions had turned, apparently with tears in their eyes, to take a last look towards home.

"Goodbye," they had said to the view, "God knows when we may meet again." At a bend in the path, I turned for a last look at my house. I knew how Laffi must have felt.

One of the downsides of starting out from home was that the countryside was not only familiar in appearance, it was in distance too. It was impossible to avoid making comparisons between travelling times on foot and on wheels. Having left home at eight-thirty in the morning it was not until lunchtime that I passed the first town, a mere ten minute hop away by car. It was all a bit discouraging. To make things worse, my bladder was adding its complaints to those of my feet and chest. In his book Tim Moore mentions the 'stop-and-drop approach to public urination' - easy for him, I thought. Not for the first time I reflected gloomily on the uneven way these anatomical features had been divided at the time of

Creation. Men had it all so easy. Female gender and middle age had made this more than a matter for idle consideration. It was predictably a man who, writing in the Confraternity Bulletin, had recommended drinking the best part of a litre of water before setting out each morning; for a man, of course, passing that amount of liquid over the next couple of hours would pose no problem.

Now the need was becoming pressing. Oh, for a nice thick wood! But passing a closed looking house with crumbling shutters and a thick shrubbery bordering the road, I noticed a gap in the hedge. The place was clearly unoccupied. Practice in this business had dispensed with the need to remove my rucksack which made a huge difference I thought, as I squatted down - and saw, between the trunks of two low trees, not only an open front door but a small, amiable looking dog trotting out into a patch of watery sunshine. O-mi-god! What if it saw me and began to bark?

Dragging my waistband and my rucksack behind me, I stumbled scarlet faced into the road, mortified to think that I had just relieved myself in an inhabited garden, narrowly missing the embarrassment of coming face to face with its owner. It was almost enough to compel me to go through the whole process again. In another place. This being France, I should have known that fading shutters were no reliable indication of abandonment. But then, this being France, they possibly wouldn't have done more than shrug; the inhibitions of an English upbringing tend to leave their mark. It could have been worse, though. Shirley Maclaine, in a similar situation with her knickers round her ankles, had been approached by autograph hunters.

At least for the moment it wasn't raining - thinking of the mediaeval pilgrim in whose hypothetical steps I was walking, I watched an immensely heavy cloud moving across the western sky. Far away I could hear the faint rumble of thunder as ripples of lightning flashed across its blackness. As it moved away southwards I felt as my pilgrim forebear might have done standing at this height, watching with relief as the Moorish army bypassed him and moved on to attack someone else. Though, in my case the invading hordes were meteorological ones.

The path wound on past the town and its satellite villages, eventually dropping down into the woods. And all the time, as I walked, I was accompanied by the calling of cuckoos, their flat cadences perpetually falling through the air like mourners at a feathered funeral. They had disappeared by the time I was passing the airfield though, because they probably knew what was coming.

Up on that desolate plateau, shorn of trees and any other shelter, presumably in the interests of planes coming in to land, the Meteorological Moors came back, attacking in force. The deluge which followed would have capsized Noah's Ark, and I discovered at first hand why many walkers do not favour ponchos over anoraks. They may be quick to put on, but in a really heavy downpour they deposit all the water onto the fronts of your legs. Worse, if there happens to be a gale blowing at the time, they either whip up at the front and blot out your vision with a wet slap in the face, or they blow over your head from the back, leaving your rucksack to get soaked. Of course there are full length ones you can buy, which make you look like a hunchbacked Wee Willy Winky stumbling along over the hems, but I didn't know about these at the time. I thought of the pilgrim who, writing in the Confraternity Bulletin, had described his trek through France as 'a marvellous month's walking'. There was really very little that was marvellous about this, and if it was going to continue for a month I was going home. Masochism, even with spiritual uplift (and this wasn't) can take you only so far. Peter-the-Hiker, who must have been checking the weather on the internet, sent a text:

"MY DARLNG. HAVE SPOKEN TO THE NEW POPE. HE WILL STOP THE RAIN!"

I replied rather sourly that he hadn't, and received a sequel:

"VATICAN APOLOGISES. NEW POPE STILL LEARNING."

Three hours later I trudged wetly and miserably into Montferrand, and splashed into the reception area of its only hotel. The 'Lou Peyrol' is run by an Englishwoman whose French husband is the hotel's superb chef. A bath, and a dinner of duck with girolles followed by walnut gateau, made up for a great deal. You can eat these things when you are walking all day because you can pretend you are going to burn off the calories tomorrow.

Undressing later, in front of a full length mirror (never a good idea after a substantial meal) it occurred to me, gazing balefully at my rolling midriff, that I had better do just that. A final reason for making this pilgrimage had been to lose weight - I had heard of pilgrims losing as many as 18lbs. Regular walking practice might have trimmed my legs, but the result only looked like a barrel on sticks. To complicate matters further I had bought an outfit for Miranda's wedding in a sort of sludgy pink ('Dusky Pink,' had insisted the saleslady) and in a moment of ridiculous optimism and supreme vanity I had bought a size smaller than usual. Well, I had reasoned, with the amount of practice walking I was doing I was bound to lose weight. In fact, with the amount I had been eating after each walk, I had been bound to put it on - it was probably two sizes too small by now. If I had had doubts about the colour when I bought it, as I fell asleep that night I was far more concerned about the fit.

~

Waking to the sounds of the farmyard opposite, I focused miserably on the grey light seeping through the shutters. Not much change there then. Not, that was, until I opened them and found the village on the hillside opposite washed in luminous early sunshine. A further text came through:

"GIVEN UP ON VATICAN. INCA SUN GOD WILL ACCOMPANY YOU TODAY!"

Oh, the wonders of modern technology.

An hour later, climbing up beyond the village I came upon something very rare in France. A footpath banned to off-road motorbikes. Motocross seems to be an ever-growing culture throughout the countryside. Every Easter (and Easter had just passed) there is a huge race across the whole of the valley and its surrounding hills, using the Grand Randonee cross-country footpaths - presumably to economise on track space. This makes walkers' lives hell, since many of the paths are rendered all but impassable on foot after the motorcycles have been by, particularly after heavy rain when they become torrents of mud, slippery on the downs and impossible on the ups.

But here was a quiet, unchurned, relatively dry woodland walk, which rose gently through the sunshine, the trees seeming veiled in green gauze as their pale leaves began to open. Suddenly life was good and pilgrimage an excellent idea.

Emerging from the wood I came upon a jewel. The tiny twelfth century church of St. Christopher, patron saint of travellers, stood alone in the middle of a field, its ancient wooden door looking more like the entrance to a sheep-fold. Pushing it open I found the inside covered with fading, crumbling frescoes. English Sarah had said something airily last night about a church with "a few nice little fresques," but I had been too wet, and too fed-up, to take much notice. The interesting thing though, was that the subject matter didn't seem to be particularly ecclesiastical. Rather, it seemed almost pagan. In its time, presumably before the Thirty Years War arrived to ruin it, this must have been a mini Sistine Chapel. Very mini. You'd have had a job to squeeze in a congregation bigger than a couple of dozen. The cemetery too was absolutely packed to bursting - definitely flying room only there, and had been for some time to judge by the dates on the tombs. It was rather comforting to think of my pilgrim forebear pausing here (how many centuries ago?) perhaps to say a prayer.

Blithely following the red and white markers of the Grande Randonee footpaths a couple of hours later, I was feeling extremely pleased with myself. This network of paths which stretches across Europe forms the basis of latter-day pilgrim routes, and I had seen on the map that I would have to change from one to another a few times in order to keep going in the right direction. Even the most complicated changes had not gone wrong - or not yet. Plunging to the bottom of a long wooded ravine and praying that I wouldn't have to climb back out again, I came to another divergence of the paths. Nothing on the map corresponded with this. There was no alternative, it would have to be the compass. My practice walks having almost always ended with Bernard having to use his local knowledge to carry out a Search and Rescue operation, my friend Sue had not only given me a compass but had arranged a day's instruction with Gary-the-Orienteer so that I would know how to use it. Tall and gangling, with formidable reserves of energy, Gary had gone loping off across the Sussex Downs with me puffing in plump pursuit, my sole ambition being to keep him somewhere in sight.

"Right, where are we then?" He would demand, stopping suddenly and shoving the map under my nose. It was no good. Try as I might, unless the sea was visible somewhere in the distance I hadn't a hope of getting my bearings. The sun was no help, it spent the entire day sulking behind the clouds. Still, practice does tend to make, if not perfect, at least a lot better than before and by the end of the day I began to feel that I had at last begun to memorise the technique. And now? Oh God. It said I had to climb a near-perpendicular path at an almost ninety degree angle to the one I'd just come down. Well, at least it wasn't raining.

Gary's instructions had not been confined to the use of a compass, though, and trudging upwards I thought them over. The best piece of all had been to take warm, lightweight and above all waterproof gloves - walking through icy rain warm hands make all the difference in the world to your morale. Eyeing my clothes doubtfully he had told me to go and buy some loose, light, cotton trousers.

"Take your jeans by all means, if you want to, but don't walk in them. You are going to get wet, and cotton dries faster than denim. Skin dries faster than cotton for that matter, so walk in shorts if you possibly can." He had also told me not to rely on the compass alone (just as well under the circumstances) but to use all the landmarks the map provided and, should I see a signpost in the distance, to make for it straightaway in order to check my bearings. Panting at last to the top, there indeed was a signpost in the distance, which told me in no uncertain terms that I was going in completely the wrong direction. Well, at least going back was downhill - as the compass was consigned in disgust to the bottom of the rucksack.

The only other option was to cross the river. There was a line of stepping stones which looked promising, but the trouble was that it had been raining yesterday and now the water, in full spate, was whooshing over them leaving them several inches below the surface.

I just knew, as I stepped onto the first of them, that this could only end in disaster. But when I slipped off the third, to land on hands and knees in freezing water with a scream from my sternum, I was still shocked and demoralised enough to want to cry. On the far side the bank and the track beyond it were a gleaming mass of wet mud, so there was no alternative but to squelch on up the hill in wet socks. I didn't need to see the tyre marks to know who had last been through - heaven only knew when this path had last seen anything resembling a pilgrim.

I remembered a remark made by my elder son Robin, when he was nine and we had just forded a swollen stream in a downpour, in the Lake District.

"When the water's been in your boots for a bit, you don't notice it any more, do you?" He had said. Slipping and gasping upwards, I put his theory to the test - and found that I couldn't agree.

Eventually the path dried out and I arrived at a grassy, cushiony bank under a tree. Here I could change my soaking socks and give my feet a rest and a good long one too, they had earned at least an hour. Brushing an ant off my leg I pulled out the yoghurt I had saved from breakfast. Savouring the joy of rest and food I brushed away another ant, and then another - golly they were big. Where were they all coming from? I looked around, I looked up and finally I looked down, and discovered that the cushiony tufts were the top of an anthill. By the time I had shaken these monsters out of folds in clothing and creases in skin there didn't seem to be much point in settling down again, and so the trudge continued, arriving eventually at a deserted village where I had hoped to refill my water bottle. In Spain I was to find that almost every village on the Camino has a water fountain, spouting clean cold water, larger towns have several. In time I was to value those water fountains more than any other provision along The Way. There is nothing like that system in France, but I had been told that most cemeteries have a drinking-water tap and this was certainly true. Moreover the sun was warm on the tombstones and my feet positively purred with relief at the feel of dry socks.

I imagine that under most circumstances cemeteries are relatively peaceful places to spend a few idle minutes, but as I continued my pilgrimage they tended to feel more and more like home. This is not as macabre as it sounds; I was in limbo then and every step brought new experiences and surroundings. Cemeteries at least have the virtue of a certain familiarity, so it was little wonder that they seemed to become places of shelter as the weeks passed. And it wasn't only passing pilgrims who found shelter there; some weeks later, and much further south, I was resting on a tombstone when I noticed a blade of metal protruding from behind a cypress tree. Looking closer I found it to be part of an enormous aircraft propeller, like the ones you see in films of the Second World War. And so, indeed, it was.

The inscription told the story of the young pilot buried there, who had lived in Kent and had died of his wounds after being shot down near the village. It was achingly poignant to think of the villagers finding this young man, in limbo and far from home, taking him from his aircraft, nursing him and finally burying him among their own families on that quiet hillside, chaining his propeller to the headstone as a lasting memorial to his bravery. He was only twenty-two. Now, however, a glance at the map told me that five hours' walking I had carried me less than six kilometres, not even a third of the day's distance. If I wanted to reach a town with a hotel before dark I would have to abandon the woods and follow the roads. Well, at least they would be small roads.

It's really amazing how even the tiniest, twistiest roads feel like motorways when you are moving at 2mph. It was not only cars whizzing by either. A bevy of cyclists sped past, looking for all the world as if they were training for the Tour de France. One of them managed to hiss a belated "Bonjour!" from under his elbow as he passed, head down in fierce concentration. The other never relaxed his gaze by so much as the flicker of an eyelash. And here on the hard white road the sun was hot.

As I stopped and took off my rucksack to fish out my sunhat, more Tour de France Wannabees whizzed by. Tanned and supple, in their sleek lycra bodysuits, they didn't even appear to break sweat - they were even chatting. They were certainly not going to acknowledge (if they even noticed) a damp and sticky geriatric in a heap by the roadside.

The main road by contrast, when I reached it, was as straight as the Romans had left it and every bit as busy as it must have been in their time. Stepping blithely out onto it I jumped smartly into the ditch as an enormous lorry thundered by laden with tree-trunks. Scrambling out, I was blown back in again as a tanker careered past in a cloud of diesel fumes. This didn't match anything my pilgrim forebears would have experienced - all they would have had to worry about would have been cow-pats and cartwheels.

But the hotel, as I approached it across the town square two kilometres later, was sufficiently grey and gloomy to have lowered the spirits of any of Domenico Laffi's French contemporaries. Its narrow, musty entrance looked as if it had been there for centuries - as did the ancient man in the cubby-hole which served as a reception desk, who appeared to be the only person alive in the building.

Creakily he led me upstairs, and together we negotiated a deserted corridor of wobbly floorboards to my room, where he inquired wearily whether I would be eating dinner.

It was strange, but I didn't mind about being on my own when I was actually walking, whereas the idea of sitting alone in a deserted hotel dining room felt unaccountably forlorn. Tomorrow would be different because Bernard would be meeting me at Castilionnes to say goodbye; it was salutary to think that he would have less than an hour's drive to get there, whereas by then I would have been walking for three days. At the present rate of eighteen kilometres a day, it would take me a lot longer than my allotted sixty-seven days to reach Santiago. I had better get fit rather quickly.

At any rate, that evening I eschewed the 'careful' cuisine I had seen advertised by the entrance, and ignored the whining of my empty stomach. Instead, I followed my damp, aching feet to bed and went straight to sleep.

I climbed up and through a wood gushing with yellow mud, until I came upon something singularly sinister.

Chapter Four
By Highways and Byways

Coming down to breakfast in the morning I climbed over a large, battered holdall in the passage. I had not been the only guest then. After getting my credentiale stamped at the Mairie, I saw the holdall again, this time attached to its owner, a large man with a weatherbeaten face and the world weary expression of an itinerant labourer. Sighing heavily, he hauled it onto the wall of the pretty, covered Halle in the town square, pulled out a can of beer and asked if I was walking to Santiago, the first person to recognise the cockleshell emblem sewn onto my rucksack. He had been twice, he said, over the Somport Pass via Jaca - the difficult way. Weren't they all? I wondered. Now he was travelling east and then to Marseilles. And then? He shrugged. Maybe find work on a ship - who knows? He might have come from another age. A Steinbeck age.

As I prepared to move on, he called out across the square, "Ultreya!" ("Go with courage!") One of the very few times I was to hear that traditional greeting. I walked on, feeling less lonely then. Shirley Maclaine had been advised to walk alone, but she at least had her previous lives and alter egos to keep her company. Tim Moore had his donkey. Walking with only one's body parts for company, talkative though they might be, was proving to be limiting to say the least. And talkative they were - my legs complained constantly, so did my feet, and my shoulders grumbled that the rucksack felt heavy. Everyone had said that walking through France would get me fit enough to tackle the Pyrenees. Well, it didn't seem to be. But nature has a way of compensating, and my weariness today was accompanied not by the mournful cuckoo but by the rippling song of nightingales. Every bush and thicket along the road seemed alive with never-ending music. Standing still and listening for several minutes, I thought of Hans Christian Anderson's story of The Little Nightingale, and how the Emperor of China had listened night after night to that glorious sound. Later I realised that I didn't have to stop to listen, because as you walk their song follows you long after you have passed the spot, in fact until you reach the next bird's territory. You miss all this in a car.

The road that day wound through farms and hamlets, dreaming timelessly in the sunshine. But as the afternoon wore on the air grew warm and close, and a sound suspiciously like thunder rumbled in the distance. If there was to be a storm, I devoutly hoped (please God and for that matter please Saint James in whom I'm not sure I believe but I could just be persuaded...) that it would hold off until I reached Castilionnes.

Climbing, eventually, the last sharp hill to the ramparts of the old town I walked round them at least twice before I found an hotel. I passed two coach-loads of men of assorted ages, shapes and sizes, absorbed in what was clearly a vast and nail-biting tournament of Petanque, the national game of rural France. Silent, and with total concentration, they watched as each ball rolled slowly to its mark before arguing volubly and passionately over the umpire's decision. Just beyond them I came to a flight of steps which opened onto a garden. The brochure of the Logis de France, in flowery prose, had talked of 'nature's treasures', which were to be found in this garden. It invited one to pause and listen to the splashing of the fountain - well, perhaps it was too early in the year for the fountain. The hotel itself boasted ten rooms of 'character', which in the case of mine was accurate, if one defines the French use of the word as an indication of rather dingy paintwork and utilitarian furniture. The ceiling could certainly have done with re-decoration, though given its distance from the floor one could understand the delay. The stepladder must still be under construction.

The windows though, were splendid. Enormously tall, nearly as high as the room and made of stout, heavy oak, with huge, cast iron handles which required both hands to turn them. The light in the room was dimmed by a pair of majestic shutters which, as I pushed them, swung gracefully open. It was as I leaned over the balustrade to look down into the street, that the first serious drops of rain began to fall. Round One to Saint James.

~

It was becoming clear that saving money and weight, by going without maps from now on, had not been a good idea. Nicholas Crane, when he made the journey described in his book 'Clear

Waters Rising', knew the value of large scale maps which showed all the footpaths; he used so many that he had had to send parcels of them ahead to await his arrival at the various embassies and post offices he passed on the way. Mind you, he had walked from Finisterre to Istanbul, way behind me to the East - to Nicholas Crane my journey would have been like popping out to buy a pint of milk.

Anyway, having decided to make do with a list of towns to follow, the only route possible the following day was along another major Roman road. With scarcely a bend between Castilionnes and Lauzun, there wasn't much to slow down the traffic, but fortunately it was Saturday which meant few cars and even fewer lorries. And the landscape was lovely; lush fields of spring grass bordered the route and still the nightingales poured their song, which washed back as the sound of each car faded in the distance. After only an hour I walked into Lauzun. It's a pretty town, much beloved of the British, with a carefully tended public garden divided by a picturesque waterfall. Here I bought my longed-for pain au raisin. I had awarded my stomach the daily treat of one pain au raisin, which I tried to put off eating until I had walked for a least an hour, and this was the perfect place.

On the road out of the town I caught up with a boy of about seventeen who was hopefully holding out his thumb. I stopped to wish him luck, and he asked where I was walking.

"Miramont," I replied. It wasn't more than a few kilometres up the road.

"On foot?" He gasped. Well, if I could do that so could he. We would walk together, he said, replacing his thumb in his pocket and crossing the road. Where was I going after that?

"Santiago de Compostela."

"ON FOOT?" Clearly, he was reconsidering the wisdom of spending the afternoon in the company of a lunatic. I tried to pretend that the tone was one of admiration.

He was going to Miramont to work in the shelter for homeless people there, and soon after this exchange decided to go back to hitching - perhaps he found it too early in the day to be dealing with a potential client. He didn't have much luck though; car after car passed him by without so much as dropping speed. He had done this thousands of times, he said plaintively, and he'd never had any trouble getting a lift before. I pointed out that it was possible that people thought he was walking with his grandmother, and that they

35

would have to take me along as well. It wasn't entirely flattering that he agreed so wholeheartedly and immediately dropped behind to allow me to go on ahead over the hill - evidently in more ways than one. It worked though. Two minutes later I heard an engine slowing, then a car door slam, and next moment he was whizzing past me without a backward glance.

As my watch moved towards midday, the traffic increased. An awful lot of people seemed to be going for lunch in the smart restaurants of Lauzun. The French are a funny lot, especially the women. Every female driver who had passed me, since I had begun this walk, had stared hard at me as if I had recently arrived from an unrecognisable planet. Noses pressed to their windscreens the only expression their features registered was one of baffled astonishment. No, I lie - the day before, one had looked at me with something I would like to think was admiration, but it could just as easily have been compassion. It may have been early in the year and the weather might not have been exactly conducive to walking, but surely a lone, female hiker is not so unusual a sight as to warrant these blank stares of amazement. Perhaps if I'd been on a bike and wearing a lycra body suit it would have been different, but this was no fun at all.

A small and beguilingly quiet road led off to the right, but was it worth following without a map? Oh, what the hell - I had time. So I followed it for about twenty minutes, until it ended in front of a farm where a gnarled old man was tying small trees to stakes in an orchard.

"Could one pass?" I asked, my French still hesitant.

He surveyed me in silence for a while, though whether he was working out the question or the answer was not entirely clear.

"If you like." He replied at length.

"Then the road continues?"

He looked round at his house, and considered this imbecility for several minutes.

"No, it stops here."

"But there is a path?"

Another pause.

"Yes." But where, was not obvious.

"It will be muddy perhaps?"

He turned, and surveyed the full circle of the horizon.

"Well, we've had a lot of rain."

This was beginning to sound like one of those teaching tapes for elementary level French Conversation.

36

"Would it be better if I went back to the main road?"

A gallic shrug.

"It will be shorter."

"But the traffic is very heavy."

He nodded slowly, taking in my appearance from toe to shoulder. I had been slightly wary of talking to elderly male strangers ever since the days of my practice walks, when I had regularly come across an octogenarian farmer who used to engage me in animated, if incomprehensible, conversation. Nodding blithely and uncomprehendingly in response to a monologue one day, I had found myself swept into a passionate and malodorous embrace - somewhere along the line I had apparently accepted an offer of marriage. It had become necessary to change the routes of my walks for quite a long time after that. But if this man had had the same idea he had clearly thought better of it.

"It will be."

"And I have time,"

He weighed this up carefully, chomping on his gums, before coming to a decision.

"Then I will show you."

At last! I gave up trying to understand the next suggestion he made as he had turned away towards the house, rolling a little on his bandy legs. Leading me round the back, he showed me into a yard where there were two kindly looking horses. Oh good, he was going to lend me a horse. I had a momentary vision of Myself Matamoros flying past Miramont, Duras, Monsegur and all the rest at a gallop, and arriving in Spain in record time, slicing Moors to pieces as I went - but no. He was only going to point out that beyond the yard was the track.

"Now," he said, turning to me, and his tone said, "Listen carefully." I could follow the track, but it would become very muddy. It looked to me as if it already was. But, if I walked down there, at the bottom of that field of wheat, I could follow some tractor tracks which would be less muddy. They would lead to a road which would lead to a bridge which would lead to a hill which would lead to a crossroads... and there I'd be. He held out his hand, it was leathery and comforting. He started to wish me good day but changed his mind and wished me courage instead, which was less comforting.

But it worked. I couldn't imagine how the path could have been muddier than the tractor tracks, but I got there. At the crossroads,

37

since I was obviously getting good at this, I took another tiny road which again petered out into a track. I climbed up and up, through a wood gushing with yellow mud, until I came upon something singularly sinister. On a telegraph pole opposite the entrance to an isolated farmhouse someone had erected a huge cross, about three metres high, like a crucifix except that, instead of the body of Christ, a dirty jerkin flapped its tatters in the breeze and a crudely modelled head hung from the top, suspended by a rope round its neck. In a neighbouring village to mine, when a dispute had become bitter, people who were judged to be turncoats had woken to find crucifixes hung with jerkins erected outside their front doors - but this was the first time I had seen this particularly macabre version. Standing there in the dripping rain, looking at the head dangling from its noose, I felt suddenly chilled and uneasy in the silent wood, and it was a relief when the path emerged eventually onto a small road which, a signpost told me, led to Miramont.

By the end of that day I had passed only half a dozen cars, far fewer than I had expected when I had set out in the morning. The oddest thing of all was that as I strolled along the top of a ridge, the whole of Aquitaine laid out before me, I had the feeling that I was not alone. In her book, Shirley Maclaine talks about an angel which accompanied her, smelling of vanilla. Well, I couldn't smell anything that I couldn't very easily trace to a passing bush, and I wouldn't know what an angel's presence feels like. This was just a lovely, soothing sense of companionship, of all being well with my world. Perhaps it was the pilgrim forebear in whose steps I was hopefully treading. Perhaps it was just relief that finally I knew where I was going.

I walked through a village where the owner name on every single letterbox was unmistakeably an English one. This area was the scene of considerable activity during the Hundred Years' War, and it was perhaps a village like this which had prompted a local politician to observe dryly, a few years ago, that the invasion which the British had failed to achieve with their armies in the fourteenth century had been accomplished through their cheque books by the end of the twentieth.

Trudging on up a hill towards a hamlet I came upon an old man (every farmyard seemed to have one) in a huge black beret, sitting on a wall at the side of the road. He had only one eye, and the wide smile with which he returned my 'Bonjour!' was all but toothless as he held out a hand to invite me to sit beside him. Why was I walking? He wanted to know. And was I making this pilgrimage alone? I was? Good heavens! Then what did I do for a lover? If this question - dropped so early into a passing conversation - took me by surprise, his next one was even more startling.

"Are you any good at making love?" He asked, waggling his eyebrows up and down at my rather prim reply that, as a pilgrim, I wasn't thinking much about it at the moment.

"If the weather was better we could have made love here." He offered, indicating with a sweep of his arm the soggy field behind him and leaning heavily towards me as his eyebrows increased their pace - the image loomed large and inescapable. To change the subject I asked him where he lived and he pointed cheerfully at the farm across the field, adding for good measure that his wife didn't like making love. His eyebrows, as well as the rest of him, were now bouncing up and down with such enthusiasm that I thought it prudent to move on. As I rose to go I said, with what I hoped was impressive piety, that when I reached the end of my pilgrimage I would think of him.

"No," he said, smiling slyly, "When you next make love you will think of me!" His name was Eugene and he was ninety-four. When I turned to look back from a bend in the road, he was sitting with his head slumped on his chest, asleep in the drizzle, evidently worn out by all the excitement. And so I came eventually to Miramont, not tramping along a diesel choked highway, wearing pristine trousers, but strolling down a leafy byway in trousers caked with mud from the ankle to the knee, and having turned down what was probably the best offer I would get for several weeks.

Madame Szpala's bed and breakfast establishment was clean, light and comfortably, as well as prettily, furnished. Warm and cosy, and a great deal cheaper than the Hotels of the Logis de France, it was an auspicious introduction to the world of Chambres d'Hôtes. Madame herself, brisk and chic, insisted on making me a chocolat chaud before, patting her varnished hair and arranging her cashmere cardigan more precisely about her shoulders, she sat down to begin her interrogation. Discovering my destination she shrieked with incredulity and threw up her hands, rushing into the garden to summon her husband. Were they going to try, between them, to dissuade me from going? Not a bit of it. Monsieur, it seemed, was a keen cyclist and it was Madame's idea that he could give me detailed instructions on all the best routes to take, from here to La Reole on the Garonne. They would have been very helpful too, I expect, if they hadn't been so detailed that I forgot all but the first two. He was concerned that I would go a kilometre or two further than I need, if I didn't listen extremely carefully. Though, as Madame tartly remarked, if I were going to walk all the way to Santiago de Compostela, what difference would a kilometre or two make, here or there?

Before I left next morning I went to Mass again, in a further attempt to get an ecclesiastical stamp for my Credentiale. This time I was not going to wait for the priest to make his way back down the aisle. I would pounce, the moment the service was over, before he'd even left the sanctuary of the altar. Accordingly, as the small congregation turned to leave, I grabbed my stuff and elbowing my way through the pious coming the wrong way, rushed up the aisle. And he'd gone. This time he'd slipped out of the back door through the vestry. It was beginning to feel like a conspiracy.

Back at Madame Szpala's, to collect my rucksack, she insisted on taking a souvenir photo before pointing me in the right direction with hugs, kisses and solicitude. Had I got a raincoat? And a phone? And enough to eat? And would I remember to watch out for the cars? She waved until I turned the corner at the end of the road.

The route, as it turned out, was quiet and virtually car-free. It rambled on over hills and into valleys, passing through hamlets with stunning views over the Lot-et-Garonne. Tomorrow I intended to join the Voie de Vezelay, so this would be my last day of wandering the countryside in search of the Way of Saint James. Had I been Edwin Mullins, in a car, I would have wandered further and seen more. But Mr. Mullins wouldn't have heard the nightingales from his car, or smelt the waft of damp May blossom as it drifted across his path. But now this very minor road (as Monsieur Szpala had described it) was beginning to feel unusually well endowed with cars - all of them in a considerable hurry. I seemed to have missed out rather a lot of his instructions and, after a while, had to accept sadly that I had found my way back onto the main road again, this time to Duras.

I passed a Dutch couple on a bridge, sitting on folding chairs, sipping tea from a flask and gazing at the river. They had been watching me approach from a long way off, and had long ago decided that I couldn't possibly be French. Not walking; not with a rucksack; not in April. They gave me a chair and a cup of tea, and assured me that, though I might be lonely now, I would find many friends once I was on the Camino. Evidently they had assumed that loneliness would be a problem, but it was only then that I realised that the loneliness had passed. They had travelled along some of the Camino route in their car, and while I drank my tea they told me about the places they had seen. Eventually I waved goodbye, and set off again to face another main road of speedway straightness, this time careering into Duras.

Except that it wasn't. I passed a sign warning that after Auriac sur Dropt, coming up just ahead, the road would be closed for repairs. The through traffic had been diverted onto a minor road. So I found myself walking into Auriac all alone, on a deserted five metre wide footpath, the countryside of Gascony stretching away on either side. I felt a bit like Clint Eastwood entering a frontier town in a Spaghetti Western. I was just celebrating this freedom and testing my sobriety by walking along the white line in the middle of the road, when the blare of a loud horn from behind reminded me that Auriac is not entirely bereft of visitors, and that those who do visit do so at speed. Apart from that, even a prolonged shower couldn't dampen the pleasure of walking on smooth tarmac, in tranquil solitude. Passing through Auriac, which was every bit as shuttered and silent as a frontier town, I found myself engulfed by a glorious perfume. Not an angel; a lilac hedge after rain. Seductively it billowed round, defying me to move on and leave it behind. I was missing all these flowers blooming in the garden I had created at home, but I was being more than compensated by those in the gardens of other people.

One of the advantages of Chambres d'Hôtes is that the proprietors are usually interested in spending time with their clients. But although Madame Chaugier and her husband invited me to join them for soup and a salad, I felt the need for some energy-boosting pasta and I wanted to have a look at Duras. So Madame, whose name I discovered was Marie Christine, drove me into the town through another shower, insisting that it would be no trouble at all to come back and fetch me. The old part of Duras is a compact little bastide which stands high above the immense plain of Aquitaine. The impressive looking castle was closing when I arrived, so I passed the time before the restaurants opened by exploring the maze of tiny alleys which inter-weave the town, many of them apparently unchanged since the middle ages.

It was a surprise to find that the town had actually been pro-English during much of the Hundred Years' War. In fact the Lords of Duras were among the delegation which went to England just before war broke out, to offer their loyalty to Edward III - loyalty which must have seemed a bit misplaced when he forgot to send the troops he had promised, to support them against the rest of France. It's really a wonder that their descendants don't resent the British more.

The rain cleared whilst I was eating, so I decided not to disturb the Chaugiers and walked back, my shadow lengthening in front of me along the closed road, only to find them waiting up. Marie Christine came running to the door to invite me in to share a tisane, and we sat and drank tea made from their own lime flowers, whilst her husband - who had been a farmer until multiple sclerosis had forced him into a wheelchair - described the way the countryside had changed since he had been born in the house next door. The problems were the same as Britain's really; the rise in agri-business, the sale of farms as holiday homes, the exodus to the cities. They were a youngish couple, not more than early forties, and yet Michel had lived all his life in the same small area. Nowadays he ran the bed and breakfast, whilst Marie Christine worked as an analyst in a laboratory near Bordeaux, testing all the new wine before it goes to the suppliers. No wonder she only drank tea in the evenings.

I breakfasted with Marie Christine before she left for work the following morning. And what a breakfast! She had obviously gone to immense pains - heaven only knew how early she had got up. It was unique among all the breakfasts of my pilgrimage, as much for its quantity as for its quality. The groaning, white clothed table was dominated by an enormous basket of fresh fruit, which in turn was surrounded by baskets of bread, baskets of toast, and dishes of home cured prunes all soft and glistening. There were homemade fruit tarts, cakes and yoghurts, together with homemade jams and a huge pat of locally made butter - there was barely any room left for the teapot. She insisted on wrapping up a selection of everything for me to take as a picnic.

I left their house with regret, and great affection. Such kind, gentle people. Fate hadn't dealt them the best of hands, but they had made the most of their situation, and had lost neither their generosity nor their sense of humour.

...leading all the way to the twelfth century church of St. Sulpice.

Chapter Five
The Way of St. James

I might be heading south, but I had no choice that morning but to walk west, back in the direction of Duras. It was frustrating to be unable to cut across country, but there are only two bridges over the River Dropt and I'd left the other one far behind, the other side of Auriac. I thought of all those mediaeval pilgrims at the mercy of the currents, or of the ferrymen, and realised what a difference bridges must have made when they were first built.

In the twelfth century a Frenchman, Aimery Picaud, wrote the first known guide book for the pilgrims of Saint James. He was scathing about the dishonesty of the ferrymen, in particular those of the Basque country. Actually, he was pretty negative about every region on the route, with the glowing exception of his native Poitou. In Gascony, the region through which I was now passing, he liked the wine but he thought the people were a load of loud-mouthed, scruffy sex-maniacs who were permanently drunk. On the other hand, he also said that they were hospitable to the poor and homeless, and I could vouch for that.

There seemed to be a dearth of minor roads between Duras and Monsegur, so turning south I tramped along the main one which, as the rain and the traffic grew heavier, became more and more tedious. Leaping in and out of ditches was adding distance, as well as time, to the morning. Strawberry fields stretched flatly away on either side - obviously no pee stops here, and that problem was becoming acute again. I had bought a map in Duras though, and it showed a footpath coming up on the left hand side which ought to lead across a field and into a wood. I considered this as I plodded through the rain; there would be mud in a wood, and wet boots, but weighed against a barrage of wet traffic it didn't seem such a terrible hardship. It would certainly be worth a try - if only for peeing camouflage.

It was muddy, and wet; but I could hear the birds again and life was back at a walking pace. There were compensations too for the extra time it took - the croaking of frogs in a pond, the scent of flowers after rain, or coming round a corner and seeing a horse chestnut tree, majestic with blossom. There was camouflage as well - or so it seemed until it was too late. Crouched in an inadequately sparse patch of scrub and trying to avoid the prickles below and behind, I heard voices. Peering through the branches I saw two men walking along the footpath I had just left, guns slung carelessly across their shoulders. I had heard enough stories of people being mistaken for animals and shot by hunters in the woods of France, to make me freeze, holding my breath, until they had passed. I was just beginning to relax when the dog came bounding up, barking wildly. Shrinking back instinctively (from my crouching height it was enormous) and with the weight of the rucksack still on my back, I overbalanced and sat down heavily on a patch of stinging nettles. The men whistled and the dog raced away, leaving me wedged in a bush with a smarting bottom.

Damp, grubby and more than a little demoralised, I winced up the final hill into Monsegur, the last stronghold of the Cathars, the sect which had defied the established catholic religion of France towards the end of the fourteenth century. One could see why they had fallen back on Monsegur; standing high above the surrounding countryside, the citadel must have tested the determination of the most zealous of enemies - even the Inquisition. As I crossed the town square, two men put down their pastis and stared at me with open mouths. Whatever must I look like?

I had hoped to stop in Monsegur, but apart from a foot-resting break there wasn't much point. It was lunchtime, the town was closed and I'd long ago consoled myself with Marie Christine's picnic, so I wasn't really hungry then. But a look at the map made it clear that the minor roads from there to La Reole were going to form a very large loop, and that I could only be sure of joining up with the authentic pilgrims' path at a point where it crossed the main road further down. Following the small roads, I might miss it altogether. So I dropped down the hill past the football stadium and took shelter from a downpour beneath the spreading branches of a magnificent copper beech whilst I thought this through. Taking a deep breath as the rain eased, I decided to brave the long, straight trunk road of the D668. Well, it was only four kilometres, it would only be for a little while.

That 'little while' turned out to be two hours. It didn't help either that during another monumental downpour all the lorry drivers in Gascony seemed to want to race each other into Monsegur for lunch - I lost count of the times I was blown into the ditch. But eventually the rush hour passed and things quietened down, the traffic count dropping to nearly zero as all those speeding snouts got buried in the trough.

And suddenly, I had arrived! There, on the corner of the junction with the road to St. Sulpice, was the post with the yellow top which the instructions from Les Amis de St. Jacques had told me to look out for. And there was the next, and the next, leading all the way to the twelfth century church. I had made it! I had found the old chemin de St. Jacques - The Way of St. James. All the wandering, the searching, the lousy compass reading were over. Never again would I have to gaze at the terrible, muddy verge of the D668. From now on I would not be alone, either. I would be guided by the maps and instructions of the Amis, as well as presumably the waymarks of these yellow posts. Waymarks which, it had to be said, did bear a striking resemblance to the ones which are usually employed to mark circular, local walks. But now that I was on the path to Compostela, I thought blithely, surely the waymarks would have been commandeered for that.

I would have friends too - I would meet other pilgrims, and walk along having conversations with proper voices, not just my complaining limbs. No longer would I be the only lunatic walking through France in a soggy April. Had my rucksack not been so heavy, I might even have skipped along the glistening tarmac. I felt as euphoric as if I had reached Santiago already - a foolish notion since I still had at least forty-six days and well over a thousand kilometres left to go.

It was raining again in earnest, so I dived into the church porch and sank onto a very ancient, pilgrim-like bench, savouring the pleasure of sitting somewhere dry, for once, and watching the rain get worse. I passed the time by packing away all my old maps, and my compass, at the very bottom of my rucksack. My reading glasses too - I wouldn't be needing any of them again today, now that I had these yellow posts to follow. As the sky cleared it was time to follow Saint James. And almost immediately I was lost.

The trouble was that my understanding of the Amis' French instructions didn't tally with the yellow posts. Moreover, if I followed the posts I seemed to be turning north again, instead of continuing south. Well, the line on the map did twist and turn a lot, and in any case the rain had made the slip of paper with the instructions on so limp that it was virtually impossible to read -

certainly without glasses - so I had little choice but to follow the posts. And what a lovely walk this was; how good to know I was on the real Way at last, the path that Chaucer might have walked, or Goethe, or any of the thousands upon thousands of pilgrims from the countries to the North, who might have made this journey down the centuries.

After an hour or so, striding happily over the top of a hill and down the other side, I could see the D668 below. This was not a problem, the map showed that I'd have to cross it. Then I noticed that one or two buildings looked familiar. Then there was no mistaking the view. I was looking at the entrance to the football stadium. There was the tree under which I'd sheltered... hours ago. Oh please, oh please no. But I had. I'd followed those yellow-topped posts right back into Mon-sodding-segur.

Plodding on mechanically I stared hard at my surroundings, willing them all to change into something I didn't recognise - preferably the outskirts of La Reole where I would have been by now if I hadn't taken Saint James's stupid path. The only solution seemed to be to start off round the circle again and at that moment I could have sat down and cried, really howled, if I hadn't already been so wet. Then I stopped, unable to face that road again, and turned, storming back up the hill, fury lending a speed to my feet that secondhand piety, or even the appreciation of nature, had so far failed to do. Pounding along, I rained down curses on Saint James and his blasted Amis, who couldn't even mark a map properly, let alone give decent instructions or put a post in the proper place - my own stupidity, of course, was too painful to think about. Saint James could stuff his useless map. I would take the road to La Reole. Not the D668 though, the minor road which at that moment seemed to run parallel to it. The trouble was it didn't for long, but all the same I marched furiously along it as it looped up and over ridge after ridge, like the closing sequence of a Roadrunner cartoon.

Several times I arrived at unmarked junctions with absolutely no indication of which way to take. By then I had developed a theory about this if you have absolutely no indication of the way to go, always take the uphill option, not only because the higher ground might enable you to get your bearings (it usually doesn't) but because, if you turn out to be wrong it's so much less discouraging to retrace your steps going downhill. There's only one flaw - nearly all uphills have downhills on the other side, so if you don't make the right decision quickly you'll still have to trudge back uphill and the whole strategy will be shot to pieces. I found this out the hard way more than once; and through it all the rain poured, the wind whipped and my feet made never a murmur. But in one of my legs I began to feel an ominous pain.

By the time I limped into La Reole that evening, I was becoming worried. The last time my legs had felt this bad I'd lost sight of my ankles for three days. And the room I'd booked from the phone box in St. Sulpice choosing at random from the Amis' list of accommodation - was two kilometres outside the town. On the other side. Hobbling past numerous hotels, their windows glowing invitingly with lamplight; gazing glumly at pristine dining rooms with gleaming tables, where comfortable diners were tucking into platefuls of food, I came at last to a grimy truckers' night-stop. The surly barmaid clomped ungraciously up the wooden stairs ahead of me. Indicating, with a curt flick of her head, the shower and toilet down the other end of the corridor, she pushed open the door to one of a series of tiny rooms (cells might have been a better word) with two small beds in it and nothing else. Certainly no air. I began to protest that, when I had phoned, she had promised a large bed and a 'toilette'. Shrugging, she replied that this was all there was and I could take it or leave it. I took it. I calculated that I had walked forty kilometres that day.

There is a tradition among Francophiles that, if you want a really good, reasonably priced meal, you will find it in the truckers' cafes (the truckers apparently being among the most discerning gastronomes in France) but this did not appear to be one of them. Moreover, a woman eating alone in this one might as well have been in a zoo. Having swallowed what I could of a tough steak and limp salad, and endured the unblinking stares of my fellow diners for as long as I could, I hobbled back up the noisy staircase and locked my door. Later that evening the occupants of the other rooms arrived. From the wheezing, coughing and suppressed giggling, as well as from assorted bumps and creakings, it appeared that my room was sandwiched between those of an asthmatic lorry driver of considerable girth, and a call-girl doing a brisk trade. It was no comfort at all to reflect that she had probably been given the 'large bed' I'd been promised.

Well, a problem shared is a problem halved, they say, and it would all feel better after a grumble to Peter. His reply to my text carried all the hallmarks of carefully considered advice:

'MY GOD! FORTY KILOMETRES IS TWENTY-SIX MILES. I'M ENTERING U 4 THE LNDN MARATHN MY DRLING SO GET LEG BETR ASAP. SUGGST SELL BODY 2 LORY DRIVR 2 PAY 4 RM.'

Advice I ignored.

But tomorrow would be another day, and a rest day at that. Jason would be coming to meet me in any case, to bring my bivouac gear, and my rapidly swelling leg suggested that it might be an idea to cadge a lift through the Landes, to save a bit of walking. Obviously I desperately needed to rest, and I certainly couldn't rest here.

Gloomily, I surveyed the situation. The leg was not the only problem. The prospect of wandering in the Landes with an inadequate map, incomprehensible instructions and evidently no waymarks at all was not inspiring. But why were there no waymarks? Dear God, the Arles route had famous waymarks, and so did the one from Le Puy, so why not the one from Vezelay? If I'd stayed on the Grande Randonee footpath, as I'd originally intended, I'd have had red and white markers all the way to the Pyrenees. But the Amis de St. Jacques, who had made such a song and dance about their research into this historic route, hadn't put up even so much as a cockleshell to guide trusting pilgrims. So much for authenticity, I grumbled bitterly.

The bar beneath my room began to come to life again before six o'clock in the morning. Even through the muffling of my earplugs, the crashing of furniture and the shrill voice of the barmaid penetrated floor and sleep in a way the traffic had been unable to do. Soon afterwards the trucker next door got up and clomped noisily down the stairs, coughing as he went. Now fully awake, my first thought was that my pillow smelled of vomit, and that a cat had recently peed in my room. Disgust with my surroundings was swiftly overtaken by the recollection that I had been shut up in my room, all night, with my boots. Tim Moore had complained of being kept

49

awake all night by the smell of someone's boots, and it was embarrassing to think that someone other than me might smell these - though it did cross my mind that it could possibly be turned to my advantage; how pungent would they have to be, I wondered, before they entitled me to a private room in a crowded refuge.

Gingerly, I felt my leg. The ankles were still there. I could move the foot, but - Ouch! Peeling back the bed clothes was not encouraging. There was a livid red patch on the front of my shin. I knew that I hadn't bumped my leg, so if this was a bruise it was coming from inside. Peering through the shutters, moreover, I could see that the sadistic weather system had produced a brilliant day - just perfect for strolling through the Landes. Oh hell. I lay down again until nine o'clock, when everything seemed to have gone quiet, then got up and went downstairs to ask, in what I am certain was perfectly intelligible French, when I would need to vacate the room. The surly barmaid, after staring at me blankly for several minutes, held up ten fingers and shrieked 'Dix!' Well, maybe she had a language problem.

When the car came round the corner I was waiting in the sunshine. Jason jumped out and hugged me.

"I can't believe you've walked all this way! God, what a dump - let's get you out of here!" His friend, Amber, came running across the car park shouting as she ran.

"It's alright! We're here! We've come to save you!" I could feel tears of relief pricking my eyes and, hobbling towards her, was overwhelmingly tempted to give up altogether. What stopped me was not Saint James, nor the faith of my family and friends, it was the thought of that anonymous Dutch couple I'd met on the bridge before Duras - people who had seen the cockleshell on my rucksack and offered refreshment to a pilgrim in the time-honoured way, and who had smiled at me with such frank admiration in their eyes. They would never know that I had packed it all in almost the very next day, but I would.

So, slinging my rucksack into the back of the car and professing not to notice the smell of my boots, Jason and Amber swept me out of the car park and off to Bazas. In the Cathedral Square I ate the best chips I have had anywhere in France, or in England for that matter. The day was glorious and we had a car; after a long discussion it was decided that they would drive me for an hour, and then put me down wherever we ended up. The road through the Landes being a dead straight line, this meant that they got me all the way to Mont de

50

Marsan. I was not to see those sandy forests again, in fact, until three years later when I walked through them with a tent - for old times' sake.

Today though, it was disorienting, after a week on foot, to be whizzing along at speeds I had been cursing only yesterday. Actually, it wasn't the speed itself that felt weird, it was seeing a signpost telling me that somewhere was eleven kilometres away and realising that it wasn't going to take the rest of the day to get there. Walking was a different world.

The buildings overhang the river in the precarious way that villages overhang the ravines of Northern India.

Chapter Six
Ignes

If you've got to be marooned somewhere, Mont de Marsan is not a bad place. That is, if you can ignore the French predilection for squeezing the most hideous, modern buildings between ancient masterpieces of architecture. It has the busy atmosphere one would expect of a junction between two major routes to the South. It has a pilgrim refuge too, but, just as I had declined to get my Credentiale stamped in the cathedral at Bazas, because I felt I was officially cheating by arriving by car, so I felt diffident about using genuine pilgrim accommodation until I was able to arrive on foot. So I checked into the Hotel Richilieu.

A second rest day in the same place is a frustrating thing. I woke feeling better, and itching to continue. With uncanny intuition, Jason rang my mobile phone to remind me that there would be little point in interrupting the healing process now, by trying to save a few days, only to be laid up later on. Of course he was right. Besides, as he pointed out, St. Sever was a full twenty kilometres away with no accommodation in between, should I need to stop, and under the circumstances bivouacking was still not an option. So, having been forced to turn from pilgrim to tourist, I did what tourists do. I sat and ate in the sun, in the Place de Gaulle, whilst the town walked by - they are not unchic, the Marsanaises. Then, street map in hand, I hobbled off to explore, the tapping of my stick as conspicuous as a leper's bell.

Mont de Marsan is proud of its mediaeval heritage, though, to be honest, there isn't much of it left. Its real beauty lies in its gardens and its sculptures, including some lovely modern bronzes scattered around the town, and in its water. Whenever you move away from the sound of rivers, the sound of fountains takes over. The buildings along the river overhang the water in the precarious way that villages overhang the ravines of Northern India. Standing on a bridge, I watched a couple of roofers wandering about on the tiles above the foaming rapids without displaying a hint of vertigo.

What my mediaeval pilgrim forebears would have done in my situation I don't know, because so little of the town of that period remains. But in Domenico Laffi's day they would probably have spent the entire day praying to St. James, and to Ste. Madeleine, in the baroque splendour of her church with its kaleidoscopic stained glass and elaborately painted ceiling - though the tableaux of Christ's Passion, rather more modern in style, would presumably not have been there then.

Had this twenty-first century pilgrim done that, though, she wouldn't have been able to admire the serenity of the Rodin inspired sculptures of Charles Despiau, on display in the fourteenth century dungeons, nor the laughing children modelled by Robert Wlerick, or the disturbing stone titans of Joseph Csaky. That exhibition would have been worth a visit all on its own. It was salutary to think that, had I been walking through without a hitch, I might never have seen them. Nor would I have paused to sit in the dappled shade of the Jean Rameau Gardens. Yes, if you had to be holed up anywhere in recovery time you could do a lot worse than Mont de Marsan; but all the same, after a week of walking in the countryside it felt claustrophobic to be in a town too long.

I had rested all day, and taken telephonic advice from all quarters almost all of it in the 'stay put' line. But by the time I turned out the light on my second night I really wasn't sure what I'd do. In the middle of the night, though, I woke up knowing that I would go on to St. Sever the next day. I had the strangest sense of being lifted up and set on my way, and the same feeling of companionship that I'd had on the road into Miramont. It was such a strong impression that I almost fancied I could hear the ghosts of my mediaeval pilgrim forebears in discussion round my bed:

"Well, I think she's fit to go."

"I don't know, she's been in a lot of pain..."

"Nah, that was nothing. Look at my feet - all but eaten away with leprosy by the time I got to Mont de Marsan, and I kept going all the way till I died."

"Well, so long as someone goes with her, to show her the way and make sure she rests..."

Because it was amazing the next day - every time my leg began to shout that it really, really needed a rest, I'd turn the corner and there would be something to sit on. Perhaps an enormous boulder, a flight of steps, or a slab of concrete left, for no good reason, in the middle of a wood - an eyesore under any other circumstances but just then seeming to have been dropped by some celestial crane. Everyone around was different too. Two men in a van at a set of traffic lights stared as usual, but in the car behind them a woman smiled and mouthed "Courage!"; a small child on a country road took my hand and led me to see some horses; two women out for a walk stopped and wished me well. And from the edge of a wood on top of a ridge I had my first glimpse, far in the misty distance, of the snowy caps of the Pyrenees.

By the time I reached St. Sever my leg had deteriorated to the point where I could barely put any weight on it. Using my stick as a crutch I hobbled up the hill into the town, following the brass cockleshells set into the pavement, until I came to the old monastery which now houses the refuge.

A cyclist pedalled across the square and dismounted.
"You are a pilgrim?" The question carried the assurance of a statement, and I could only marvel at the speed with which I appeared to have acquired an air of sanctity. For how else would he have known?

"You have a red face." He told me, in heavily accented English. "It is the sun. All pilgrims have red faces." Oh.

With his messianic hair and the intense gaze of his blue eyes, he seemed like someone left behind by the hippie era. He introduced himself as Ignes and, having already installed himself in the refuge, he escorted me to meet Serge, the hospitalier, and to find my bed. Serge was a short, stocky man with a disproportionately large head in which his face seemed to be entirely covered by a wide, smiling mouth. Meeting him in the town, I was to discover, could be a hazardous business since he travelled everywhere by bicycle and had a habit of whizzing round corners, regardless of pavements or the whereabouts of pedestrians, traffic or any other impediment. But, as a first impression of an entire culture, his refuge was auspicious. The original hospice of the ancient Abbey, its upstairs corridors were paved with old terracotta tiles cracked and worn by the nocturnal slapping of centuries of monastic feet. On the plan of the Abbey, as it would have been in the seventeenth century, this part was designated for 'various prayerful activities', and it was not difficult to imagine the monks shuffling along to Mass in the middle of the night.

On either side of the corridor were about eight rooms, each containing a number of beds. On each bed were a plastic covered mattress, a folded blanket which may or may not have contained fleas, and a grubby bolster. I was grateful for my sleeping bag and camping pillow.

While I lay on the floor, my aching legs propped up on my bed, Ignes leaned on the doorpost and talked. He had cycled from Belgium, he said, via Paris, Bordeaux and Bayonne, on his way to Assisi. I couldn't help thinking that it seemed to be rather a long way round. He told me he had cycled the Camino ten times and that the first had been by accident. He had been on his way to Morocco when he had run out of money; seeing Santiago on the map, and remembering that it had a history of some sort, he had decided to cycle there. He had slept in fields and doorways which, most of the time, had been perfectly adequate. One night though, he had realised there was going to be a monstrous storm and had asked in a village whether there was somewhere he could shelter.

"Of course." They had said. "The old refugio. No problem." So an old, old man (as in all the best stories) had shown him into a bare hut with a dirt floor and a tap in the corner, full of the rustlings of nocturnal creatures.

"That's what the refugios were like in those days." Said Ignes. "Proper places. Not like these Five Star Hotels!" Waving his arm dismissively at the grimy beds and bare corridor.

The following morning, emerging from his hut after the mother of all storms, he had found the old man waiting. Ignes had tried to thank him for his help, but the old man had waved that aside.

"It is we who thank you." He had replied courteously. "You are the first pilgrim to stay here for seven years. For us you have brought the Camino back to life."

That had been the first that Ignes had heard of the pilgrimage to Santiago de Compostela. After that he had begged a credentiale from a priest in Villafranca, and had gone on to Santiago, the 3,755th pilgrim to arrive there, at the very end of 1989. Now, he said, there are over 40,000 who arrive each year, and the number is rising. He had cycled all over Spain and Portugal, following the sheep droving paths and sleeping wherever he could. One night, some years ago, he had camped in a clearing and been surrounded by wolves. On another, his tent had been rooted up by wild boar whose watering place he had invaded. I felt even less like bivouacking now.

He talked of the old days on the Camino when everyone travelled with a stove and a cooking pot, complete strangers arriving in the same sheltered spot to make their meals, sharing what they had.

"And we were all European languages then. And no-one spoke the others, so we are talking with the hands and with the feet. And now," he continued derisively, "They all eat in restaurants and bars!" I had been rather looking forward to that bit.

His was a freer spirit, with less to lose, than most people I could think of, myself included. Certainly his pilgrimages had been eventful; he had travelled without plans, guided by events and by conversations with people he had met along the way. He had slept in caves and disused prisons. He had knocked on doors and asked permission to camp in people's gardens. I was sure I'd never have had the nerve, but they had invited their friends to meet him and there had been parties into the small hours. He couldn't remember a time when he had consciously decided to become a Perpetual Pilgrim, it just seemed to be the way his life had worked out; though I had the impression that he might have acquired a more ambitious motive.

"If you make many, many pilgrimages – always in the right spirit – it is inevitable that you will become a saint." He declared. It seemed rather quaint to be sitting there, in the twenty-first century, listening to convictions which had their roots in the fourteenth. He lamented the commercialism of the modern Camino which, following its adoption by UNESCO as a World Heritage Site, had recently been listed among the top ten tourist attractions of Europe.

"A pilgrimage is not a holiday." He declared unequivocally.

"You should do the Camino without money. If you do this - just once in your life money will never be important to you again. Now it is all too comfortable and attracts the wrong people. If they took away the beds and the showers, the Camino would be returned to the true pilgrims."

I could see his point, and I wanted to regard myself as a 'true pilgrim', but I wasn't sure about doing without the showers. I was beginning to get despondent - but it wasn't all gloom.

"The spirit is still there for some peoples. But you must look for them. You will recognise them, as I recognised you." So it hadn't just been my red face then; that was reassuring.

The following morning, before cycling away, he inspected my leg critically.

"Alls peoples who get this, get it in the first week." He pronounced. "But they still get to Santiago. You will get there, but this you must get well. At least three days is needed to repair tendons. Three days."

Holding up three fingers for emphasis. Then he shrugged.

"Remember, the Camino is not about kilometres, it's about the spirit. If it doesn't get better, take a bus for a few days."

Now, all the books I had read had taken pretty negative attitudes to 'cheating'. Shirley Maclaine had been forgiving, Tim Moore less so. The Confraternity Guide simply didn't see fit to discuss it. But here was the original, latter-day pilgrim authorising it with a dismissive shrug of his shoulders. After all, it made sense. I very much doubted whether my mediaeval counterpart would have refused a lift on the back of a passing ox cart, had his leg been in the same condition. What was this cult of masochism, which made it such a sin to continue by whatever means one could? Laziness would have been one thing (though why even that should be of concern to anyone other than the lazy person is a mystery) but this was different. This was a matter of taking the bus or giving up. No contest, really.

So I said goodbye to Ignes from Belgium, to Bernt from Germany, and to Philippe from Arras, and went off to find the St. Sever bus station. And this, I was to discover, was the hallmark of the Camino - last night we had all met for the first time. Arriving by chance in the same refuge, we had eaten together and talked far into the night, to a depth normally reserved for friends of long-standing. I had gone to bed feeling that I had made three good friends, and now we had said goodbye and would never meet again - certainly not Ignes who was on a Camino of his own.

It had been exhilarating to move, in one leap, from a solitary walk to this ebb and flow of companionship which, I was to discover, lies at the heart of the Camino. I was sorry to have to stay behind, but I was not sorry I had made the effort to get to St. Sever.

The original hospice of the ancient abbey...

Chapter Seven
St. Sever

The pharmacist eyed me severely.

"There is only one remedy for this," she said, "And that is rest. For at least a week."

A week? I had only gone in to get some cooling gel, but she had taken one look at the leg and prescribed a completely different product. Slapping it on throughout the day, it seemed to make the swelling puff up even further.

And just in case I might be thinking that things couldn't get any worse my separate, complaining limbs had formed themselves into a coalition. I now had my very own version of the TGWU[1] and it had imposed all-out industrial action. Remembering Peter Sellers in 'I'm Alright Jack', I could well imagine the inaugural meeting where the chief shop steward, Shin, would have given his account of the breakdown in negotiations.

"She won't have it, brothers. I tried. I did my best to negotiate with her all the way from Mont de Marsan. But she wouldn't listen, she insisted on carrying on to St. Sever. So we've no alternative but work-to-rule. We'll do what we have to do, and no more. We'll take her down to get her coffee and her croissant in the morning, and then that's it. We'll go no further until she sees sense." They didn't, either.

So, faced with a long day's idleness, I packed up a parcel of all the things I could possibly do without, to send home. Ignes had pronounced my rucksack 'impossibly heavy', and he was on a bike. I wandered into the eleventh century Abbey, a simple, beautiful building which must have been stunning before its frescoes were all but destroyed, presumably in the Thirty Years War. The floor alone was a gem - its worn, ancient tiles, patched here and there, undulating down the nave.

The following morning my leg was bigger than ever, and my ankle had completely disappeared.

1 Transport and General Workers' Union - the largest and most powerful of Britain's unions which led the general strike which brought down the Labour government in 1976

I decided to dump the pharmacist's anti-inflammation gel which seemed to be working in reverse, the drum-tight skin throbbing painfully through the night. Serge made an exception to the One Day Recuperation Rule which, in cases of injury or sickness, allows pilgrims just one extra night in a refuge - after which they must carry on. He told me kindly that I could stay on as long as I needed to - it wasn't as if I was in anybody's way. This was something of a relief since he had thrown a pretty noisy party the night before, which had ended around three in the morning, so sleep had not been much of an option - less of a problem for me than it would have been for the anonymous Dutchman (according to his entry in the register) who had arrived at some point after dark and left at first light.

I envied him though. It was a beautiful, limpid morning, just made for striding through the countryside - except that I wasn't striding anywhere. Gloomily I began counting backwards along the Camino, to see how late I could leave it before giving up and going home. But I just could not believe that I had come all this way, and devoted so much emotional and mental as well as physical energy to this journey, for to it to come to nothing. The day before, Ignes had been reassuring as, disconsolately, I had watched him loading his bike.

"Rest now. Get it well. You will do your pilgrimage, don't worry." I hoped he was right.

The Saturday market made me homesick. But then, a lot of things made me homesick - baguettes piled on a car dashboard, the smell of garlic cooking in early evening. But the homesickness was only on one level, on another the adventure continued to be exciting and at least, whilst I was forced to stop, I could do something about my hair. Shirley Maclaine had begun to worry about her grey roots when she was close to León - I was still ten days from the Pyrenees and mine had become an embarrassment. I had not been oblivious to those masculine stares, nor had I been able to detect the slightest admiration in them. Perhaps if my hair were shorter, the roots wouldn't look so bad.

For such a sleepy little town, St. Sever had a surprising number of hairdressers to choose from. I picked the trendiest I could find - a fluffy, ringletted blonde with technicolour eye make-up and an equally fluffy, ringletted dog of some Tibetan origin, curled up in a basket of fluorescent hairpieces. The salon displayed a huge selection of punk wigs and I was tempted to buy one for later; I wondered how much it would weigh. After only half an hour, fluffed and shorn,

I walked out into the street feeling as if, in those bleached tufts left lying on the salon floor, I had left behind the last remnants of the person who had walked out of my house ten days before. I began to understand the significance of the hair cutting ritual which nuns go through on admission to their convents; a woman's hair is such a symbol of her personality that it must take a lot of courage to discard it completely.

St. Sever was an encouraging place to be marooned on a pilgrimage. As the residents strolled through the town none of them passed without a greeting, if not a conversation. Being a pilgrim here made one interesting rather than peculiar. All the same, a holiday in St. Sever had not been part of the plan. It was so frustrating that, searching for a meaning to the delay, I began to wonder if curbing my impatience was to be a major lesson of the pilgrimage, perhaps even a pre-requisite to healing and moving on.

Missing the reassurance of Ignes' insight, I went to a phone box and rang a friend who had a mystical turn of mind, to discuss my predicament. He responded with an interesting theory. In past centuries, he suggested, people had believed in heaven as a separate place to which, if one had led a good life and made the odd pilgrimage, one went after death. But if one believed, as he knew I did, that heaven is a state of consciousness achievable at any time, then theoretically the timing and the geography of a pilgrimage were both immaterial; the spiritual outcome would be the same no matter where I ended up. This was interesting because, although he was by no means a catholic, it was a theory I heard echoed weeks later by a nun in León. It was also an idea which I found comforting in my immobile state, though my curiosity reminded me that it would be deeply disappointed were St. Sever to prove my ultimate destination. Clearly it wasn't time to give up yet.

Whilst Serge had been reassuringly laid back about the One Night Rule his wife, evidently, wasn't. As the advance guard of a group of walkers trickled in, she burst into my room demanding to know how long I'd been there. Didn't they communicate? She expressed surprise at my apparent ignorance of the rules, that one day only was allowed for pilgrims to recuperate. Evidently they didn't.

A stocky, aggressive woman, she waved her hand imperiously around the room.

"I shall need every one of these beds tonight!" She declared. "I am expecting a very large group."

61

On hearing that it was her husband who had granted this extraordinary indulgence, her attitude softened somewhat. In a voice of ominous calm she conceded that perhaps she was not 'au courant' with what was going on, as she stomped off to find him, and minutes later an argument carried out at a particularly shrill pitch suggested that she felt she ought to have been. It didn't seem to be going Serge's way at all so, not wanting to repay his kindness with domestic calamity, I went down and offered to move out. They turned as one, their faces wreathed in smiles, and said it was certain that I could stay, then fell to arguing again over which room I could stay in, before I had even closed the door.

The 'very large' group Mrs. Serge had anticipated turned out to be four people, so in the end I never did move out. Or not until I moved myself out the following morning.

The bus from St. Sever to Hagetmau, the next refuge on the itinerary supplied by the Amis de St. Jacques, was run by a private company. This meant apparently that no-one, neither the tourist office nor the company itself, could tell me when it would run next. They only appeared to know that it wouldn't on any of the days I suggested. In the end I took a taxi, priced by the kilometre - eleven kilometres would surely not break the bank. Perhaps not, but I hadn't reckoned with the taxi's return journey on a Sunday, without a return fare.

The refuge, when I found it, turned out to be a small marquee on the edge of the campsite.

Chapter Eight
Pierrot and Dani

I left St. Sever on the first day of May. It was an auspicious day, with Lilies of the Valley everywhere, in the French tradition, and the entire town turned out in its Sunday best for the First Communion of its children. Waiting for the taxi in the park near the cathedral, I watched the gathering and the fussing and the frilling. Two large families converged on the car park at the same moment, and their progress was interrupted for a considerable time whilst absolutely everybody kissed absolutely everybody else - the children receiving double rations.

An elderly couple, seeing my rucksack with its badge, made a slow detour across the park to wish me courage on my pilgrimage and to ask me to pray for them by name when I reached Santiago. I had read that this was common practice in the Middle Ages, but it was the first time anyone had asked me to do it; I began to feel positively special - until I saw the bill for the taxi. Thirty pounds? To save a day's walk? My leg had better recover very soon.

By contrast to St. Sever, Hagetmau had little to recommend it but its church spire and a few shabbily picturesque back streets. It seemed largely to have been rebuilt in some early post war period, its buildings plain and utilitarian. It might well have been too; Mont de Marsan must have suffered badly under occupation during the second world war, to judge by the number of plaques erected there to celebrate the liberation, and it seemed to me highly likely that Hagetmau might have been similarly damaged. It was frustrating to see, as I got out of the taxi, a priest leaning on the balustrade in front of his church. After all the times I had tried to find a priest who would stamp my Credentiale, here was one actually standing still. The trouble was that I couldn't really ask him to verify my pilgrimage when he'd just caught me in the act of cheating. Or could I? But even as I weighed up the possibility, his congregation surged up the steps and he disappeared inside.

Hagetmau didn't seem to offer much in the way of interesting eating, either. In St. Sever I had lived on crêpes, here I spent the afternoon with a yoghurt, under a tree by the river. It was pleasant, though, to lie listening to the frogs and watching the play of sunlight on the leaves. The refuge, when I found it, turned out to be a small marquee on the edge of a campsite. It was just big enough to take six iron beds, with a shower room in a concrete hut alongside. Already installed were two pilgrims, well into retirement years, who I had seen through the open door of one of the dormitories in St. Sever.

I had avoided them at the time, out of embarrassment over my impending taxi ride, but now it appeared that they might have been representatives of an arbitration service summoned by the TGWU. No sooner had they set eyes on my leg than they whipped out their maps and began plotting my possible progress by bus routes.

Vivacious and endlessly kind, Danielle and Pierre insisted I join them for supper round their tiny gas stove. They had a formidable larder. I wondered, privately, how on earth they managed to carry it all. Their attitude to the pilgrimage was refreshing - stop at every café you pass and have a drink, and if you are injured, or just too tired to continue, then take the bus and pick up the path later on. Like Ignes, they were hugely experienced. They had walked the Camino Frances alone five times, as well as all the others at least once. The Camino Ingles, otherwise known as the Del Norte since it follows the northern coast, was the most beautiful apparently, but also the most isolated; and the Via de la Plata, coming up from Seville over the Sierras, was the hardest.

I had been wondering whether to divert to the coastal path in order to preserve the isolation which I was beginning to cherish, especially since Ignes had described the overcrowding on the Camino Frances. Dani's only concern was that it would be very easy to get lost without comprehensive maps, and I had no need to remind myself how easy I found it even with them. Pierrot thought about it a long time before finally deciding that, for all its overcrowding, everyone should do the Camino Frances once in their life, because the centuries of passing pilgrims had left a special atmosphere.

"Carry on this time," he said, helping me to more spaghetti. "But be sure to do the other one sometime, because it is spectacular."

Pierrot had led survival expeditions in the Alps, as well as a search and rescue team, before he retired. So, while Dani fussed around taking the blankets off the spare beds to prop up my swollen leg, he gave me his ten commandments for surviving the pilgrimage:

1) Never pass a café without stopping for a drink (carried out to the letter, this would have impeded progress considerably in some of the towns through which I passed).

2) At the start of the day eat at least one piece of fruit. If possible take several fruits with you, strawberries for instance, or an apple or tomato, to eat during the first hour. (Pain au Raisin, I noticed, didn't get a mention.)

3) Don't always drink plain water, or if you do, put sugar lumps into it. Preferably mix it with fruit juice, or alternate it with Coca Cola, which will give more help to your body.

4) At the end of the day's walk buy a litre of orange juice and drink it down. Your body will be ready to absorb the vitamins.

5) At midday eat meat, including sausisson or something with extra salt in it. In the evening eat pasta, with lots of salt.

6) Never throw away your bread! (Seeing me about to chuck it to a pretty red squirrel.) Bread will always come in useful, even if it's only to soak up water to make a poultice for your leg.

7) Carry biscuits and chocolate to boost your energy towards the end of the day.

8) Try to walk the greatest distance in the early part of the day. Your legs will swell less before it gets hot.

9) Stop for at least half an hour when you are halfway. Take off your shoes and socks and lie down with your feet up.

10) At the end of the day, a glass of wine is good for the heart.

Wanting to prove that I was not a complete ignoramus when it came to walking, I showed him the enamelled camping mug I had brought with me so that I could boil water over a fire. He eyed it with derision.

"That will never work. The enamel will crack over the flames. Now, if you were to empty out a tin of peas..."

They got up at five o'clock the next morning, to make the long trip to Orthez where their son and his family were due to meet them for the evening. As I lay in bed watching them pack I discovered the secret of carrying all that food - their rucksacks ran on wheels. Pierrot had designed and made two handy little trolleys with stout poles, which could be pushed or pulled as the terrain demanded. They reminded me of those old-fashioned shopping baskets with which elderly ladies used to provoke such anarchy by whacking people's ankles in crowded places.

He had cheerfully carried twenty-five kilos, and Dani seventeen, when they had been younger (and there was I moaning about transporting ten) but now their backs would not take the load anymore. It meant that sometimes they had to follow the road rather than the path through the woods, but that was just the price they paid for being able to carry on walking. They were endlessly cheerful and full of life. I kissed them goodbye, genuinely sad to think I wouldn't see them again. Then away they bowled, arguing good naturedly over which way to turn out of the campsite.

As I had jumped out of bed to take their photo, Dani had pointed delightedly to my legs which were now almost the same size. But she had counselled one more day of rest before, 'petit a petit', walking on again.

"Don't worry," she had said, "You will reach Santiago." And I began to feel that perhaps I might. The final day of my enforced rest seemed less tedious than the others. I had stopped whipping myself over the ridiculously avoidable detour at Monsegur. But it was still difficult not to wonder how far I'd be if I hadn't had to stop. Frustration is a useless emotion. Besides, it occurred to me that had I not been injured, and had I not then made that painful walk to St. Sever, I might have damaged myself less but I would have missed an awful lot. Over this rest period, through the people I had met, my entire view of the pilgrimage had changed. The advice I had been given would take me a long way, and the periods of undisturbed solitude had forced me to re-evaluate my reasons for doing it. I knew now that it was more than mere curiosity.

However it may have come about, there is an energy on all the paths which lead to Santiago which is different from anything anywhere else - more powerful, more mystical. I would not learn the full power of the Camino for several days yet, but those pilgrim voices had been right. I had rarely felt so happy in all my life.

So off I went, to buy all the food that Pierre had urged me to take with me, and lugging the carrier bag back to the tent I envied them their sets of wheels. But when I actually set out to rejoin the path next morning it was even worse; my rucksack was impossibly heavy. In the end the whole business turned out to be counter-productive since, after struggling up hills for an hour I simply sat down and stuffed myself with everything in one go, just to lighten the load enough to keep on walking.

Hagetmau's architectural appearance hadn't improved with closer acquaintance, but its people couldn't have been friendlier or more interested in the pilgrimage. In fact the whole world seemed to have changed its attitude whilst I'd been laid up. No longer did everybody look at me as if I had dropped from another planet - the occupants of nearly every car that passed waved or called a greeting, and people on foot invariably stopped me to ask how far I'd come and to wish me 'Courage'. The countryside, too, changed as I walked; it was very much hillier now, with spectacular views.

Despite being early May it seemed to be already high summer. Thickly covered trees cast luxuriant patches of shade over fields knee deep in lush grass and buttercups. The wild Acacia trees were in full bloom so that viewed from above, on the ridges, the forests appeared to be snow capped as they undulated away into the distance.

Looking for a pee stop in a small wood, I found the ground covered with soft cushions of grass. The morning was hot, and propping my feet up on my rucksack, as Dani had advised, I fell asleep to the sound of a thrush. Some time later I woke to a gentle rustling, and turning my head slowly I saw a small deer placidly nibbling the grass not five metres away. Oblivious of me holding my breath and wishing my camera wasn't at the bottom of my rucksack, he grazed peacefully on. I remembered a line by Rudyard Kipling: 'They fear not men in the woods, because they see so few...' Well, not men perhaps but men's sleeping mats certainly. Catching sight of the orange corner of mine, he gave a startled grunt and bounded away. I regretted my intrusion into his peaceful world, but treasured the moment as one of the rewards of walking alone. Here in this wood it felt safe enough to bivouac among the animals who naturally inhabited it, and I might have done so but for a twinge of pain in my sternum as I heaved my pack off the ground. Besides, that evening I wanted to check out a place Ignes had told me about. I was off to see Beyries.

The refuge itself was in a fourteenth century stone tower which would not have looked out of place in a fairytale…

Chapter Nine
Beyries

Ignes had described the place as almost unique on the Camino. He knew of only one other place like it, and that was on the Arles route.

"You have to go," he told me, "just for the experience. At first it will seem that there is nothing and no-one there. But put your sleeping bag down in the village hall and the whole village will come to see you. They will give you food. They will invite you for coffee. The children will make you little gifts."

Yeah, right, I thought. But it was free and here was the sign, so why not? And it was all true. There were about three houses, their gardens full of roses, an enormous village hall and not much else. Some builders working next to the hall directed me to a rather tumbledown house opposite. I half expected the door to be opened by a neanderthal dwarf with a disturbing leer and a few teeth missing. Instead it was opened by Pascal, tall, suave, handsome, who runs a computer software company from home.

Inside the hall, amongst stacked chairs and tables for about a thousand people (where on earth did they live?) were two mattresses laid on the concrete floor. There was a toilet and, plumbed incongruously into the wall between two urinals, a shower hose with a drain in the middle of the floor. Since there was no lock it was advisable to sing loudly whilst taking a shower, in case the builders came in for a pee. Behind the bar was an industrial sized kitchen, splendidly equipped, and an enormous box of groceries for the use of pilgrims. Nor was that all - diving into a large chest freezer, Pascal pulled out an armful of baguettes.

"How many will you need?"

It seemed rather churlish, looking at this largesse, to remark on the absence of milk. But I had my morning coffee to consider.

"Ah, but you will take your coffee with us, tomorrow." Declared Pascal - Ignes could have written his script for him. Then he smiled enigmatically.

"And, speaking of milk, why don't you go and visit the church?" The only link between cows and churches that I could think of was the Christmas story, and that had been an ox. But an hour later, showered and changed (the water was scalding) and with my laundry pegged to the fence outside, I wandered up the hill to look at the church.

Restored in the 1960s, it had a simple grace not often associated with building work carried out in that era. Whitewashed stone walls and modern stained glass opened onto an ancient eleventh century choir, which had only been discovered during the restoration. Just as I was leaving, Lilianne, the custodian of the keys, came out of her farm opposite. Could she offer me a coffee? The milk was from her own cow - so that was the connection. Lilianne's house had been the priest's once, but she and her family had lived in it for the fifty years of her married life. Heating up a pan of milk, with a half-inch head of cream on it, she poured it into a large bowl before adding a dollop of strong coffee and a sugar lump. It was superb. Then she told me her story.

Sent to the village as an evacuee during the war, she had married the son of the family which had taken her in. They had farmed the land in the old way until her husband's failing sight, and an accident which left her disabled, had forced them to hand it on to their son who now specialised in veal production. Since her grandsons were at college learning the modern methods of farming, the old farming life seemed to be gone for good, she observed, in a sad echo of Michel Chaugier at Duras. Hers was a face of extraordinary grace, which must have been very beautiful indeed when she was young. In parting she gave me two kisses, and two fresh eggs for my supper. Half an hour later, her grandson turned up at the village hall with a jug of fresh milk just taken from the cow.

After this, one by one, the other inhabitants of that tiny village came to call. Pilgrims, it seemed, were not frequent visitors so the arrival of this one was of universal interest. Last to arrive was Pascal's little daughter who shyly gave me a key fob she had made for me, and a reminder that I was to breakfast with them the next day. And it was there, over another cup of creamy coffee - so much more like Spanish café con leche than French café au lait - that I heard how the refuge came to be.

Having given up work in a supermarket ten miles away and feeling isolated from her friends, Pascal's wife had sunk into clinical depression. She had become agoraphobic, finding it harder and harder to go out and find another job. It was about this time that the mayor, out for a walk one morning after a terrible storm, had met a pilgrim who had only just survived the night by sheltering under a bridge. With no refuge at Hagetmau in those days, the walk from St. Sever would have been a very long one.

"What sort of people are we?" The mayor had asked the village, "If we live on the Way of St. James and leave pilgrims to the mercy of the elements? We must find some way to take them in." And so the idea of the refuge in the village hall had been born. Pascal's wife had volunteered to run it, but had heard no more until about six months later when a pilgrim had simply turned up at the door asking for shelter. Of course nothing was ready, no money had been allocated and complete panic ensued. But gradually things like groceries and showers had been added, and next year she hoped there might even be a cubicle - with a lock.

This story seemed perfectly in line with the tradition of the ancient Knights of Santiago who had opened refuges in remote and inhospitable places, all over France and Spain, to protect and succour pilgrims. Only the day before, I had passed the deserted site where one had once stood, and thought how welcome it would have been to a traveller toiling uphill through a snowstorm.

The refuge's record of pilgrims was a revelation too. I was surprised to find that I was not the first Englishwoman to have passed by that year. The day that I and my leg were being rescued from the truckers' motel at La Reole, Lise Burchill had stayed in Beyries having walked all the way from Vezelay in the north. And I thought I was being intrepid. Evidently the stair-rods which had soaked me outside Monsegur had hit her too, earlier in the day. She wrote that 'after all the rain' the warmth of the welcome at Beyries would be a treasured memory. Her French was a great deal better than mine, as was her stamina, but then, as Pascal pointed out, she was half Swiss and they are as good with languages as they are with hills. More chastening still was the entry of a lone Frenchman walking from the Vosges to Santiago, and back to Annecy in the Alps. Now that was intrepid.

My stay in that deserted village hall was one of the most delightful surprises of my pilgrimage, and according to all the pilgrims I met as time went on it was indeed unique. But the refuge exists, and is there for any pilgrim who takes the trouble to pass by the village of Beyries. As I left them, the entire family having come down the hill to wave me off at the crossroads, Pascal looked at the darkening sky and frowned. But I couldn't believe that after yesterday's brilliant sunshine there would be serious rain; I was wrong. He knew his region - by midday I was trudging through a steady downpour, the first since Monsegur.

I was making for a church I had seen in the distance where, surely, there'd be a porch in which I could shelter and eat my lunch in relative comfort - perhaps even take off my boots and prop up my leg which had begun to ache ominously again. Climbing at last to the aptly named village of Sallespisse, the midday bell located the church a long way off down a steep hill in the opposite direction to mine. Glumly I sat in a patch of wet mud under a horse chestnut tree, which might have provided shelter had its layers of leaves not been so saturated that they poured as fast as the sky out in the open. Chewing disconsolately, the rain running down my neck as well as into my boots (no chance of taking them off today), I read in the Amis' notes that I should have a spectacular view of the Pyrenees from there. Well, no doubt I would have.

I put up with it as long as I could, and as so often happened, no sooner had I hefted my rucksack and set off again than I came upon a perfect little shelter, round the corner by the cemetery. I should have remembered that French cemeteries are almost always situated as far away from the church as possible; a hangover from the days when bacteria from buried bodies regularly contaminated the springs which supplied drinking water. I decided against undoing my wet straps again and sitting down to rest my feet; a decision for which they made me pay all through that wet afternoon, as I trudged on to Orthez. But there were compensations; at one point the route left the road to follow a grassy track which the Amis' researchers were certain was the exact path taken by the pilgrims of the Middle Ages, and apparently in much the same condition. Quite how they can be sure I don't know, but it was exhilarating to think that I was walking directly in the footsteps of my pilgrim forebears, imagining what they wore and how they travelled.

The remoteness of some stretches of the path, and general wildness of the countryside in those days, would have made it advisable to travel in large groups. Some of these were formed by region - the pilgrims, particularly those from France, singing songs in their particular patois to advertise their identity to other travellers. Nowadays pilgrims do the same thing by calling out greetings in a variety of languages as they pass: "Hello!" "Bonjour!" "Buenas Tardes!" "Guten Tag!" to see which one inspires a response.

Had I been alone and penniless, I think I should have tried to attach myself to the entourage of one of the wealthier pilgrims. Some of these travelled in splendid style on horseback or in carriages, their households with them and, as often as not, their furniture and other belongings piled on cumbersome ox-carts - heaven forbid that one should have to sacrifice ones lifestyle just to make a pilgrimage to Santiago. At the other end of the scale would have been the classical pilgrim of contemporary pictures, his broad-brimmed hat turned up at the front, a simple cloak slung over his tunic. He would have carried only a bag for the food he might beg along the way, with a gourd for water hanging from his staff, and he would quite possibly be walking barefoot - though shoes were often donated by benefactors in some of the larger towns. A Frenchman, writing in the Middle Ages, described these groups as being made up of the 'hyperactive, the lame, the hunchbacked and the disgraced', as well as lepers and maniacs; clearly one would have had to consider carefully before choosing one's companions. Deep in this reverie I almost missed the turning into a tranquil wood. Had it not still been raining, this would have been a lovely place to rest my better shod, but still complaining, feet.

Orthez is a town of time gaps. It has an ancient history of hospitality to the pilgrims of Saint James, though at first sight that doesn't seem to be much in evidence. A group of school children emerging from a coach stared, giggling, at this drenched apparition plodding disconsolately down the hill.

Like so many of its larger counterparts on the Spanish Camino, it appears to be unprepossessingly ugly as you approach. From its nondescript outskirts the path descends for a good fifteen minutes' trudge until, suddenly, you are plunged into narrow streets of cobbled antiquity. The refuge itself was in a fourteenth century stone tower which would not have looked out of place in a fairytale - I could well imagine Rapunzel's hair cascading from its upper window. This tower was protected by a tiny courtyard, which in turn was guarded by an immense pair of studded wooden doors. A flight of stone steps led up to another ancient door which scraped open, reluctantly, across the flagstones of the threshold. A spiral stone staircase led up several floors to a third heavy door, marked with a cockle shell. Well, maybe it wouldn't be exactly straw-on-the-floor but it was obviously going to be primitive. In fact it turned out to be cultural camouflage for a sparkling, state-of-the-art apartment, superbly equipped with everything down to a hairdryer and a cleaning lady. No need even to load the dishwasher.

Here too Lise had passed just ahead of me and, like me, appeared to have been much impressed with the hairdryer. Having the place to myself, the first problem was to decide which of the two pretty bedrooms to sleep in. Each of them had three beds with identical covers to match the curtains and - oh exquisite joy - huge fluffy pillows. I felt like Goldilocks.

All this, apparently, was the result of a labour of love on the part of the Pyrenees Atlantiques branch of the Amis de St. Jacques, who had spent heaven only knew how many weekends hammering, plumbing and sewing just so that cold, wet pilgrims could feel loved and cared for. Of all the regions within the society of the Amis (which, I was beginning to discover, are autonomous and act independently of each other) the Pyrenees Atlantiques seems to have far and away the most enthusiastic members. All along that part of the path I found evidence of their dedication in repaired footbridges and drained tracks, not to mention plentiful waymarks. And, of course, they are the custodians of the gateway into Spain at St. Jean Pied de Port. Two charming ladies from the society arrived soon after I did, to ask for my contribution of eight euros towards the cost of running the refuge, and to make sure I had everything I needed. Both French, one taught English, the other German, and it seemed an exceptionally considerate refinement to provide, on an international pilgrim path, a tri-lingual welcome.

Two hours later, my laundry safely installed in the tumble dryer, I turned the four inch long, iron key in the lock of the ancient door and went out to take a look at the town. Apart from the ruined castle and the tower which housed the refuge, the oldest building I could see appeared to date from around the eighteenth century. There was however a rather magnificent church with an immense organ which, to judge from its pipes, must have sounded magnificent. But I wouldn't be there to hear it the next morning. The walk to Sauveterre would be long, and I would need to be away early.

The simple little church of Hôpital d' Orion. Its huge and ancient porch, which might even have been the original hospice, was evidently built to shelter large groups of dripping pilgrims.

Chapter Ten
Josette

The following morning, the Pilgrims' Way led down to the river through tiny cobbled streets, over the ancient bridge with its guardhouse and up past the beamed overhang of the Auberge St. Loup. This intriguingly named building had been the pilgrim hostal in the fifteenth century, 200 years before Domenico Laffi's time. This, finally, was the real mediaeval centre of Orthez - steep, narrow and almost totally unaltered. It was easy, at that hour of the morning, to imagine the feet of pilgrims-past padding up the hill. Well, it was until you turned the corner into the explosion of morning rush hour traffic on the road out to Sauveterre.

The Way followed the road as it climbed out of the town before branching off onto another grassy pilgrim track. This led to Ste. Suzanne where, in the church, I was going to see my first stained glass window of Saint James depicted as a pilgrim. I would have done too, if the church hadn't been closed in the time-honoured tradition of France and Spain. As I stood gazing impotently at its lock, I heard behind me what sounded like the approach of a flock of starlings. Next moment, the most enormous party of day walkers swept round the corner and into view. There must have been at least fifty of them, all chattering at the tops of their voices. Not much chance of spotting shy wildlife with this lot around - so I decided to prop up my feet in a bus shelter and let them get well ahead. I had heard ominous tales of the overcrowding already on the Camino, and my heart sank a little at the realisation of how much I had come to value my solitude.

Silence having washed back in again, the road continued, climbing and descending hill after hill. A poodle that thought it was a pitbull rushed out of a gateway, barking furiously. My friend Jenny had told me her modus operandi for dealing with French dogs which, she insisted, usually worked. She had been a headmistress and was used to disciplining children - dogs apparently were no different. She claimed that I would know if they meant business by the nasty low snarl they made between barks. If that was absent then I would find that calling out "C'est bon!" In an airy sort of voice, would put them off. If they persisted, or did the snarly thing, she recommended a fiercely hissed "Va t'en!" to scare them away. I tried it now and was immensely gratified to see the poodle stop dead in its tracks, disconcerted that its aggression had so little effect.

A couple of hundred yards further on it was a very different story. The matted mongrel which shot out of the farm gates was clearly not going to be put off by a throwaway line, hissed or otherwise. In fact, had it not been firmly muzzled my pilgrimage might well have ended right there, to judge by the amount of times I felt its snout ram against the back of my leg. It gave me small comfort to remember that I had read that the dogs of France were nothing, compared to the dogs of Spain.

A little while later the path turned off into a small wood and - oh look, you can go to Santiago on off-road motorbikes as well. Still, slippery and muddy as it was it wasn't anything like the running gullies of the Perigord. It was just a pity that it was pelting with rain. I walked through a dripping green tunnel for over an hour, savouring the solitude, and even with the rain it was pretty near idyllic. The scent of Acacias hung like sweet wine on the air, wild columbines lined the path and the ubiquitous thrushes were in full song - apparently oblivious of the downpour.

In the simple little church of l'Hopital d'Orion (so named for its position directly under the constellation) I found an extraordinary atmosphere of calm and rest. It boasted very little in the way of stained glass or statuary, and that was unremarkable - but there was just this amazing peace. Built on the site of the hostal where the Knights of Santiago had welcomed pilgrims centuries ago, it had clearly retained more than merely its original flagstones and the bases of its ancient pillars; it had something about it which seemed to eliminate time and the passing of the centuries. Its huge and ancient porch, which might even have been the original hospice, was evidently built to shelter large groups of dripping pilgrims. I was willing to bet that Ignes would have slept the night there at least once.

Out of the village the path climbed again - and again, to heights which must have given fantastic views had they not been obscured by a wet curtain. There was in fact very little chance of seeing any views, or even of getting reasonably dry, that day. My legs moved in a heavy, waterlogged squelch, and it can only have been the bin-bag lining my rucksack which prevented all its contents becoming as wet as the rest of me. Entering Sauveterre on a wet Ascension Day was another Spaghetti Western experience. The entire town was silent. It might have been deserted. A lethargic looking dog got up to bark, then thought better of it. The hotels were all closed, the bars likewise. It was as if I were the only person alive in this town.

Well, not quite. A solitary man was strolling through the streets as I searched vainly for any of the establishments on the Amis' list. Fat, and irritatingly smug, he very nearly earned himself a supercilious put-down by telling me, through a smirk, that I was going the wrong way for Compostela – I would find it some way beyond the town, he said. Through gritted teeth I replied that I was looking for a hotel which wasn't closed. With what amazing speed did he then transform himself into a hero, a paragon, a veritable incarnation of Saint James himself, when he directed me to the Auberge du Saumon. It was a mile outside the town, he said, but I wouldn't find anywhere closer without paying a small fortune. And, best news of all, it was in the direction of Compostela. What a lovely man.

The Auberge du Saumon turned out to be one of the quixotic delights of my pilgrimage. It was a tiny bungalow which had, at first sight, only two rooms. The front one was the dining room and the back one doubled as kitchen and bar. Whilst a chorus of shrieks and crashings went on in a concealed corner behind a dresser, one could, presumably, sit in front of the huge fireplace in which hung a copper cauldron with the Auberge's accounts stuffed into it, and sip an aperitif whilst pandemonium worthy of Fawlty Towers reigned all around. The 1940s time warp in which it appeared to be stuck was reinforced by the crackly record of French wartime songs, being played at full volume. A quantity of large, dark pieces of furniture made moving around a hazardous business, and every available surface was covered with china or pewter - mugs, jugs and ornaments. The claustrophobic effect of all this was offset by the stream of high volume conversation going on between whoever was tucked behind the dresser and the owner, who bustled constantly to and fro.

Madame (whose name, apparently, was Josette) told me that I could have a room - but it wasn't very big and wasn't actually ready yet. But if I would like to sit at the table whilst she arranged it, and drink a chocolat chaud? Or coffee? Another downpour had begun outside; if she had told me all she had left was the dog's bed I would have taken it, and gladly. She brought me a chocolat chaud, surrounding it rather absent mindedly with three large bowls of sugar lumps, and disappeared. I settled down to watch the rain, warming my hands on my cup.

Eventually she returned and took me to another building round the back, which could have been the setting for a Terence Rattigan play about boarding houses. The door opened into a large room lined with more enormous pieces of black furniture and dominated by a huge table covered with a heavy baize cloth. Leading off it were two tiny bedrooms. She dived into the first, which had two unmade beds spilling onto the floor, to extract from the wardrobe a threadbare towel. This was for me. Then she showed me into the next room. One bed had been hastily made up whilst the other, evidently still unmade, had a bedspread pulled roughly across it. The overall effect was one of barely controlled chaos. The only other things in the room were another enormous black wardrobe, a bidet and a washbasin which had not seen a cleaning cloth in a very long while. The shower and toilet were communal and basic, and likewise in need of a clean; but the shower was hot, and hot water at the end of a wet day's walking absolves a multitude of sins.

At 35 euros a night it would have been robbery, were it not for the wonderful air of cheerful optimism with which she fussed around me. Could she dry my socks? Oh, if I wanted to wash them first would I like her to show me where I could hang them? After I'd showered, done the laundry and been resting my feet for about half an hour, there was a knock at the door. Could she perhaps come in and get some sheets? I hadn't checked out the wardrobe, but now it appeared that it held the Auberge's bedlinen. Apparently some people had arrived whose booking she had forgotten, and she needed to make up the beds next door. Wondering how often I was likely to be disturbed in this fashion I asked her, as she was closing the door, whether there was anything else she was going to need. Back came her face, beaming with gratitude. She could do with a hand to make up the beds and get the room ready, would I mind? I am reasonably certain that you could travel all over France without finding anywhere quite like the Auberge du Saumon. The only prerequisite to a night there, apart from 35 euros, is a sense of humour.

But the dinner was excellent, despite the cries of distress from the kitchen, and the bed was to die for. It was one of those glorious mattresses on which it is impossible to sleep with anyone else but which, if you are alone, envelopes you and reminds you of going to stay with your granny when you were little. Whilst we had prepared the other bedroom, Josette had told me a little of her story. She had inherited the Auberge from her father who had been an enthusiastic fisherman, hence its name. She was single, she said, which was very much less complicated, and she ran the place with the help of just one other person to do the cooking - presumably the panic-merchant behind the dresser. The fishing was not now what it had been in her father's day. He had regularly caught seven salmon in a day, on the river Saison, but it was different now.

Three men had come to stay for a weekend's fishing. I had to admire the way she parried their attempts to find out from her the best places to fish, known only to the locals. Throughout a long conversation, carried on at intervals while she served their dinner, she had compared the virtues of various rivers but given nothing away. But had not her father been a well-known fisherman? They pressed. Surely she must be able to advise them!

"Every fisherman has to find his own place." She had replied enigmatically, bustling away to get the cheese.

The following morning she was full of concern as to whether I had been disturbed when they went to bed, and thought it hysterically funny that I had brought earplugs with me. In fact I had packed several pairs, since they weigh nothing at all, and this was the first time I had used them. I had no idea how valuable they would turn out to be.

Josette proved to be a gem. Not only did she refuse to charge me for my dinner or my breakfast - well I suppose I had done the work of a chambermaid - but that morning she insisted on abandoning her other guests in order to see me across the road and well on my way, with an apple and many kisses, waving until I was out of sight. She was also the only person ever to put a message of encouragement alongside her stamp in my Credentiale. Though I didn't know it then, I would not sleep alone in a room again for a very long time. The next town on my list was St. Palais, where the path from Vezelay meets the one from Le Puy. The Le Puy route, I was to discover, was almost as crowded as the Camino itself, with beds in refuges about as difficult to come by as tickets for the World Cup Final.

The Way soon left the road, cutting down through a wood and out across fields; a mist was lying in the valleys but the blue of the sky was already deepening as the sun climbed higher. On a sunny day you are so much more aware of your surroundings; peering out from under a dripping poncho hood all you really focus on is the mud immediately in front, and quite apart from the need to keep your footing, if you do look up the folds of plastic are likely to send rivers of water running down your nose. Without those problems there is so much to delight the eye, a crown of Acacia trees catching the sunlight or some new flower you haven't seen before. And always, in the mountains, I was accompanied not only by birdsong but by the sound of cowbells and rushing water.

Somewhere along the way that day, I lost a sock. For all Josette's cheerful optimism my spare pair had not dried overnight so, naturally, I had tucked them into the straps of my rucksack to dry as I walked. Suddenly those quiet woodland paths did not feel so friendly after all. On one of them, no doubt hanging nonchalantly from a twig, was the difference between sore feet and comfort in the weeks ahead; a spare pair of socks was a necessity. But although I was annoyed with myself, I wasn't too worried at that point since I assumed that I could replace it in St. Jean Pied de Port; and I soon forgot it when, passing another of those villages which turns out to be a couple of farms and a church surrounded by newly built bungalows, the path branched off along a ridge. For there, in the now not-so-misty distance, were the Pyrenees. It was incredible to think that at last, having walked all that way, I was nearly in Spain.

Stopping in a churchyard to rest my feet on a tombstone, I began to wonder if its incumbent had been a refugee from the Soviet bloc. The hieroglyphs carved into the marble bore no relation to any alphabet I knew. Curious, I began to look around. It was the same on every tomb. Was it Polish? Latvian? And then the penny dropped - I had, all unknowing, arrived in the Basque Country. Given the utter incomprehensibility of the language it was amazing that I had not had to cross a border checkpoint. But sure enough, from then on all the road signs, as well as many others, were in two languages. The Basque language was so totally foreign in fact ('barbarous' had been Aymery Picaud's description) that I could only marvel at the tenacity of the successive Spanish Governments who had refused to grant the region its independence.

St. Palais is a pleasant town tucked into a bowl of hills. There is supposed to be a very good refuge there, run by Franciscans; but I was there at midday and it was too early to stop. As I walked through the outskirts, a couple sitting in their garden called to me and came over to the gate. Where had I come from? Where was I going? My accent wasn't French, what was it? Did I have a family in England? When I mentioned that it was Robin's birthday they rushed inside, returning with a cordless phone on which they insisted that I ring him to wish him Happy Birthday - from them. It was all so different from the derisive stares of the Perigord and the Lot et Garonne where I had started out.

As I left, they warned me that I would have a steep climb out of St. Palais which would become a whizz, or as they put it a "Schooom", straight down into Ostabat. They weren't wrong about the first bit but I was not sure, in the end, that I agreed with them about the second. Puffing up the hill, I noticed that someone with a black sense of humour had put up a homemade sign saying 'Santiago: 850 kilometres'. Just to be encouraging, I supposed. And after the Quartier Gibraltar at the edge of the town the path climbed, and climbed, and climbed.

Out in open country again, I began to notice that I was not alone. Where were all these people coming from? They were not day walkers if the size of their rucksacks was anything to go by, but I hadn't seen anyone the day before. Then I remembered. Of course, this must be the joining of the paths - and now my solitude was definitely over. No longer would I feel that I was part of the wildness of the countryside through which the Pilgrims' Way had passed. And no longer would it be possible to stop for a pee without first looking over my shoulder. A completely new phase had begun and I wasn't at all sure that I would like it; I felt like a hermit crab emerging from its shell, only to find itself in a shoal of sardines. Actually, although I had only seen a couple of people on the path I had taken, as time went on I met more and more people who had come down from Vezelay. Only, they had followed the GR654 footpath, the properly waymarked one, the one which the Confraternity of St. James had assured me was now so utterly discredited that no self-respecting pilgrim would even consider it. Needless to say, they had not got lost.

The French can be a cliquey lot. Puffing up to the brow of the last hill out of St. Palais, I passed a group having a rest. If these were pilgrims it would be as well to be friendly, we might be walking within each others' orbits for a very long time. Breathlessly I gasped out a "Bonjour!" but nobody even bothered to look up - so much for Entente Cordiale, or Entente Anything, come to that. As I reached the top I forgot them, though, for there were the foothills of the Pyrenees all around me. No longer in the distance, misty or otherwise, but right there. It was an incredible feeling, and as I stood there wishing it wasn't such a lousy day for a photograph, a much more cheerful French group overtook me, each one calling out a "Bonjour!" as they passed. Thus, sandwiched between the Cheerful and the Surly French, I began the descent to Ostabat - if only it had been. The climb which followed the small downhill bit might have been easier than the one out of St. Palais, but it ascended quite enough to make any idea of 'schoooming' a joke.

Needing to pee again I had automatically moved to the side of the path and begun to fumble with my belt, when I glanced over my shoulder to see the Surly French only a few yards behind. In a very short time I would get used to this problem but then, after so many days alone, it felt like an intrusion - after all was not this My Path? In my exasperation and embarrassment I promptly took a wrong turn, and thus it was that I arrived late at Ostabat to find the Cheerful French sunning themselves in front of a chalet, evidently the refuge, where there was just one bed left. Mine. The Surly ones had been compelled to walk on still further, to find a hotel which could take them all. Hah.

This group, though, were genially welcoming, and having shown me my bed in the roof space invited me to share their supper. They were my introduction to a version of the pilgrimage which is becoming increasingly popular, especially among the French, the Serial Pilgrimage. For those who have to fit their walking into the narrow timescales of their annual holiday it makes sense to do it in stages. For the past five years, therefore, this little group had managed to set aside the same ten days, as well as bring together the same five people (four men and a vivacious, curly-haired blonde called Fredi) every year and to walk a little more of The Way. This year they would be going as far as Roncesvalles, two days away. In two more years they hoped to reach Santiago. My relief at finding the last bed in the refuge was somewhat blunted by the late arrival of a New Age pilgrim. Ignes would have been delighted to see him with his matted hair, his filthy clothes and his dog on a string. A German, he had walked down from Le Puy, he said, rather than Vezelay. I would have liked to ask him why he had chosen that route, but the language problem got in the way, as did the fact that he was totally deaf. I tried Ignes' trick of 'talking with the hands and with the feet' but didn't get very far. All the beds having been taken, I couldn't see what would be wrong with his idea of sleeping on the balcony. But the hospitalier, when he arrived, was adamant that it would be 'against the rules'. The poor boy looked exhausted and his dog no less so, and I began to feel guilty for having taken the last bed. At least, I suggested, the hospitalier could ring someone in the village who might be able to give him shelter. Accordingly the mayor was telephoned and promised to do something, but the German seemed unconvinced as he trudged disconsolately away up the hill. Several times that evening I wondered if he had found somewhere to sleep.

Ostabat is a lovely little village of the sort one finds all over the Pyrenees, and which I was to see again in the hills of Galicia - the sort that was originally built round a farm in its centre. Returning from the little shop we passed the cattle shed divided from the dusty street by its manger, the animals browsing beside us as we walked. The following morning they were driven out to pasture, the noise of their lowing making early rising obligatory for everyone.

At supper I was warned, by several people, that St. Jean Pied de Port would be heaving with people the following evening. Being the end of Ascension weekend, all the Serial Walkers would be converging there expecting to catch a train home on Sunday. Add to that the usual quota of pilgrims arriving from all over the world on the first weekend in May, and you'd have something approaching St. Peters Square the week the Pope died. The Cheerful French had booked beds in a hotel halfway up the hill to Roncesvalles but it was full by the time I rang, so it seemed that I'd have to leave mine to Chance. I consoled myself with the reflection that Chance had, so far, come up with everything I had needed when I had needed it, so it probably would now. Though I didn't know it then, Chance was about to change completely the pattern of my pilgrimage.

~

I set off at the usual time of eight o'clock in the morning, climbing up past a small hotel from which pilgrims were emerging, spruced and showered, with small day-sacks. Who on earth was carrying their luggage, I wondered, and in what? It was all so very different from the solitary Voie de Vezelay. At the top of the first hill I passed a smartly turned out man already talking briskly into his mobile phone, his diary open on the grass beside his tiny bag.

Further on I walked straight past a fallen tree, on the grounds that it was too early for a rest, and instantly regretted it. My Transport and General Workers Union, who had been lobbying me since St. Sever, complained that I was behaving like Goldilocks now - this rock was too high to sit on, that one was too low. Eventually I gave in and stopped at the next one, savouring my Pain au Raisin whilst, in a farm far below, a pig rooted round in the yard. Mr. Smart passed me, now with Mrs. Smart in tow - her generously proportioned figure sporting a chic line in walking gear. All the same, heavy make up and flamboyant earrings did seem to me to be a little at odds with the surroundings, but probably I was just jealous because no-one else was transporting my rucksack and it was quite heavy enough without mascara. Half an hour later I had my last sight of them disappearing under a sea of wool, as they struggled to video a vast flock of sheep being driven down a village street.

One of the advantages of travelling at a walking pace is that it allows you to watch whole scenarios of nature unfold without having to stop. Passing a field, I watched a body-language conversation taking place between a horse and her foal who seemed to be wanting to get to know a newly-born calf sheltering beside its mother who clearly wished they wouldn't. The foal stood by its mother's side, the calf stood under its mother's chin. The equine party displayed good natured interest, ears pricked forward amicably, the bovine reaction was by contrast distinctly menacing, feet planted squarely beneath a lowered head. I walked on round the second side of the field, fascinated by this stand-off. For a full minute none of them twitched so much as an ear. Then, still eyeing the intruders, the cow tossed and shook her head precisely three times before bending it to nuzzle her calf. The horse took the hint and turned away nonchalantly, taking its foal with it. I could have sworn I saw it shrug.

Dawdling along in this fashion, I was alone on the path by mid-morning when it turned off into a beech wood. A small clearing beckoned. It was too early for lunch and the pain au raisin had gone, but the prospect of lying alone in the dappled shade, beside a gurgling little brook, was too close to idyllic to pass up. I'd probably have to pay for this indolence by sleeping on a bench in St. Jean Pied de Port, but what the hell. So, for an hour and a half I lay content, my feet propped on my rucksack, and watched the sun flickering through the leaves. Moving on I met a pack-laden man unmistakeably a pilgrim but, rather surprisingly, coming the other way. A German, he didn't speak much French and no English and he was walking back to Germany having taken the Via de la Plata, from Seville to Santiago. He had been two months on the road, a much quieter one, he said, than I was taking. After my fortnight on deserted paths I could understand.

His eyes had the bewildered, shell-shocked look of a refugee from some war torn country, and the voice with which he bade me Buen Camino (the first of the millions of times I was to hear that Spanish greeting) carried the low monotone of deep, deep weariness. I should have liked so much to question him further, to ask him all about the places and people he had seen, and what had happened to him there, but it felt as if that would be an intrusion. He reminded me of Coleridge's Ancient Mariner, staring through me with eyes that had seen too much, though he evidently had no compulsion to tell his story. He would have come from St. Jean Pied de Port, and when I got there I understood his look of bewilderment. In fact I probably had it myself to judge by the amount of people who seemed to want to be very helpful, and to speak very gently to me.

The warning I had been given the evening before was no exaggeration. The town was teeming. I had also been told that I would meet other English people there, but the only English I heard spoken was by a family who were having a collective whinge about the prices in the souvenir shops, as they walked back to their car.

Here was the cross marking the spot where Charlemagne is supposed to have knelt and vowed to rid Spain of the Moors with the help of St. James.

Chapter Eleven
Spain

St. Jean Pied de Port is very much a town for tourists of the car-borne variety. Any hopes I might have had of finding a hiking or camping shop, in which to replace my lost sock, were doomed to disappointment. There were plenty of souvenir shops, clothes shops, pottery shops, but not many selling anything that you'd want to lug around in a rucksack for the next month and a half.

Wandering down the main street of the old town I met the New Age pilgrim again. How had he got on last night? With a very long face he told me that he had slept in the fields again, as he had most nights. I suppose the bits of leaf and grass clinging to his hair should have been a bit of a give-away. The trouble was that he couldn't bear to be parted from his dog. Plenty of people would have offered him shelter, but the dog had to stay outside. I could understand his feelings, but I could understand theirs as well - after all, they didn't know his dog did they? In fact that was one of the things I noticed about pilgrims who had brought dogs, the animals never were allowed in the dormitories. Either they stayed outside alone or their owners stayed outside with them, it was as simple as that - although perhaps an exception could have been made in the case of someone who was deaf and obviously unable to communicate all that well; but evidently not. I never saw him again so I never found out what he did about it in the long run. But I often wondered.

The street in which we were standing was lined with refuges. Up until then, when I had arrived in a town, finding somewhere to stay had merely been a matter of knocking on a door and asking to be let in - or calling at a tourist office for the key. But here the sheer volume of pilgrims, many arriving by train, resembled a mass migration from a war-torn country or a famine. It's only a wonder that some budget airline hasn't cashed-in on the craze, with cut-price parachutes. Before I could find a bed in this town therefore, it was necessary to go to Pilgrim Reception where, once they had taken down just about every detail bar my fingerprints, I was given a slip of paper with a number on it which matched that on a bunk somewhere in the town. I half expected the kindly man behind the desk to get out the louse powder, but instead he pulled out a sheet of paper with a wiggly line on it, representing the route to Roncesvalles, and very gently, rather like a doctor with one of his more nervous patients, he talked me through the climb which, the following day, would threaten to knock the life out of me.

Kilometre by kilometre he described the path, as if it were a particularly nasty disease for which there was a cure if I would be prepared to persevere. I asked him if the Camino was crowded, and in answer he pulled out a graph showing the population's rise and fall. The bad news was that I had picked the most crowded month, bar August, to do my 'lone walk'. The even worse news was that the population increases by roughly fifty percent each year. So much for the Age of the Couch Potato.

Finally I went off to locate my bunk, finding it the only one in its dormitory of ten without a sleeping bag unrolled to claim it; otherwise the room was deserted. Returning from dinner several hours later was a different story. I found every other bunk occupied by a man - the average age was probably around sixty. The noise of laughter and conversation, uproarious as I entered, was extinguished on the instant, rather like a prep school dormitory surprised by matron after lights out. Silence reigned. The floor creaked as I walked across it - in the silent, collective gaze of nine pairs of eyes - and climbed up to the sanctuary of my bunk. After a while sporadic murmurs began again, out of the sides of mouths and accompanied by the odd snigger. This was awful. If only I'd had banter-class French I could, perhaps, have joined in with a bit of repartee and it wouldn't have been so bad. Rummaging in my rucksack for nothing at all I could feel the self-consciousness radiating off me in waves. After about five minutes, which seemed like five months, the most raffish and disreputable-looking of them got off one of the lower bunks and came over holding out his hand.

"My name's Albert, What's yours? Have you just arrived? By train?"

On hearing that I had walked from home - and more to the point where home was - he turned to the assembled company with the air of a ring-master introducing his star turn.

"I know where she lives - and it's hundreds of kilometres away! This is a brave woman! Vital, where are your manners? Get up and say hello!" This was directed at a body on the bunk above his, and which rolled slowly over.

"Well, I thought you were doing alright by yourself..." But he held out his hand to shake mine across the gulf between our bunks, and then pointed out his friend Xavier who nodded shyly from across the room. One by one after that the others called out their names.

With the ice broken, the conversation returned to its former level, interspersed with gallantries. 'Need to mind our language...' 'flower in our midst...' that sort of thing. Their badinage was fun to listen to if sometimes too fast for me to understand - deliberately so I suspected, from the ribald laughter which often followed it. They were a group of friends, it appeared, who deserted their wives every now and then to make a pilgrimage for the camaraderie and the religious buzz. They reminded me of Just William and his gang - or rather of the way they might have turned out had Richmal Crompton ever allowed them to grow up. But they made me feel welcome, they made a fuss of me, they shared their Mars Bars and their Tiger Balm with me; and they kept me awake with their snores.

Never judge a walker by his age. I found this out years ago, in the Lake District. Puffing to the top of a particularly steep hill in the Langdales, and reflecting that if I had been any older I might not have managed it, I found a row of bronzed, sinewy pensioners basking in the sun. Could they possibly have been dropped by helicopter? My room-mates were of the same calibre. By a quarter to six the following morning every one of them was up. Tim Moore talks about the early risers noisily stuffing their rucksacks by torchlight. In our dormitory it was a much brisker story. Torchlight? Pah! Turn on all the lights! That's better. Sleep well Susie? Friendly hands shook my feet. By the time I was up and dressed, Just Albert and his gang were long gone.

Nor was there any sign, down by the gates, of the ruthless toll collectors who in Aymery Picaud's day demanded extortionate sums from pilgrims as they set out to climb the pass. In the twelfth century he had written that "The ferocity of their aspect and barbarousness of their language, strike terror into the hearts of those that encounter them." Perhaps his demand for their excommunication had had its intended effect; in any case they were a far cry from the kindly official who had advised me yesterday, and who waved as I passed today. Picaud's outrage was understandable though, because pilgrims were supposed to be exempt from tolls - a concession which other travellers often tried to abuse. There was one particularly delightful character recorded in the thirteenth century, a gypsy who, under the magnificent pseudonym of 'Count of Lesser Egypt', had attempted to get himself into Spain as a pilgrim with his entire tribe disguised as his entourage. The fact that it is recorded suggests that the subterfuge failed, which I think is a pity because he deserved full marks for audacity.

Leaving the town I bought my pain au raisin and began to climb. And climb. Dani had told me that the first ten kilometres would be the worst, but how far away was the ten kilometre mark? For hour after tortuous hour the path rose, pilgrims in front and behind. Now they were international. Passing the person in front, and gasping a "Bonjour!" I saw a beautiful, moonlike, oriental face turn towards me with a beaming smile.

Yesterday, my kindly pilgrim mentor had told me just to keep going, "very slow". He had reminded me of the sherpas in the Himalayas standing over me saying, "Slowly, slowly, take your time..." as I sat on a rock, doubled over with exhaustion, unable even to crawl. That had been the most taxing walk I had ever done until now - three weeks spent trailing behind twelve other people along the top of the world, with mules to carry our luggage. On more than one occasion I had been so slow that the mules had carried me. Here, I had no such support, but apart from that there wasn't a great deal of difference between the two mountain ranges - except that this one was green. But in the Pyrenees, being below the altitude level, there was no need to walk constantly in the throes of what felt like a violent asthma attack. More comforting still, the peaks here were enveloped ambiguously in cloud rather than etched against an unforgiving sky, forever out of reach.

Glancing back I saw a cowboy coming up behind me on a huge black horse. Complete with hat and poncho, he was comfortably ensconced in a long distance saddle, his baggage slung up behind him. That was the way to do it. A speed walker passed me, powering himself along on two sticks. There was something indefinably aggressive, I decided, about people who walked like that; perhaps it was the dual tapping sound of the sticks, a sort of Get.Out.Of.My.Way rhythm, or maybe it was the oblivion that concentration on speed evidently demanded. No time for pleasantries or greetings, no time to look to right or left as he motored along, though with fog to the right and fog to the left it could have been argued that there wasn't much point.

Eventually I came to the crown of the pass, at the exact time my Pilgrim Mentor had predicted - how accurately, and how quickly, he had summed up weight, build and fitness. Here was the cross marking the spot where Charlemagne is supposed to have knelt and vowed to rid Spain of the Moors with the help of Saint James. He had done this, according to the legend, because they had just ambushed and killed Roland, his favourite knight. In fact it wasn't the Moors at all, it was the Navarrese who were understandably upset because his soldiers had just sacked Pamplona. But then that is the sort of detail with which legends know better than to concern themselves.

I had promised the representatives of my TGWU, which now included my shoulders, that they would have a rest at that point, and so they did. The sun had broken through the clouds and shone warm on the grass, ants were flying, but so were a couple of what looked like eagles high overhead. To the sound of the larks was added the croak of the raven and the clonking of the bells which hung from the necks of shaggy ponies cropping the grass. Feet propped on my rucksack I reflected that this was possibly as idyllic as it got, and drifted into a doze. An hour later I rounded a bend onto another scene of pastoral serenity. The cowboy had run a makeshift fence round himself and his horse which was standing, head drooping, in an attitude of repose. He was lying back against his saddle, his hat over his eyes, his dog asleep at his side. He wasn't smoking a cheroot but he looked as if he ought to have been.

Now, at this height it was Spring again. In the valley below I had seen summer flowers in full bloom on the seventh of May. But here early violets lined the path, the short beech trees which clung to the hillside were covered with the young green of newly unfurled leaves, and in the distance the peaks were still capped with snow as I had seen them before St. Sever. I crossed a cattle grid on the path, and realised that I had 'crossed the border' that's all it was. After all that walking I was finally in Spain. I could hardly believe it, and was tempted to forget that there were still eight hundred kilometres left to walk. Now a lot of things would change. Refuges would become refugios, hospitaliers would become hospitalleros, café au lait would become café con leche, pain au raisin would become non-existent.

We had all been advised to follow the road down to Roncesvalles, in order to avoid getting lost in the woods. But one of the pilgrims at that convivial supper in Ostabat had described the path down through the beech trees as idyllic and well worth the risk. And so it was. It was one of the loveliest beech woods I have ever walked through; the silence, the dappled shade and the solitude (everyone else having apparently followed instructions) were a delicious, lingering recompense after the effort of the climb. In fact it meandered on so far that I began to wonder if it would go all the way to Pamplona and bypass everywhere in between. But emerging eventually, through a large party of Spanish picnickers on the fringe of the wood, I saw to my great delight the Cheerful French clustered round their car in the car park. Where was I staying? Oh no, not the refugio. The youth hostel was much nicer and quieter, and they had a spare bed in their room. If I would go with them they would show me the way.

The monastery at Roncesvalles is a forbidding looking place, rising to a towering height above the woodland path. It was extraordinary to think that less than half an hour had passed since I had gazed down through the trees at its grey, corrugated roofs far below. It is built round three courtyards, and we climbed a long, steep ramp to the outer of them, where the coaches and cars of day-trippers were parked and from which an enormous archway led through to the middle yard, which brought us to the magnificent door of the church. The most attractive of the three is the stone-paved inner courtyard, where the old infirmary has been refurbished to serve as a youth hostel. The refugio itself was certainly daunting. Located in the outer courtyard, the building turned out to be one enormous dormitory housing two hundred people, with just four showers between them. The youth hostel on the other hand was cleaner, newer and more private, having only ten people to each room. My sleeping problems were solved.

The arrival of the Cheerful French Car was a miracle I never really fathomed out. They explained it several times but still it didn't make sense. I did remember, though, that it had involved several phone calls from Ostabat to a professional third party, perhaps a mechanic in Burgette. At any rate, there it was out in the car park with mountains of smart luggage inside it. I felt a little like Cinderella, watching enviously as Fredi emptied her toiletry bag (a touch flamboyantly, all things considered) onto the bathroom worktop in search of a lipstick. Re-crossing the middle courtyard an hour later I heard my name shouted, and saw Just Albert and his gang waiting outside the church for the beginning of the Mass for the Blessing of Pilgrims. No, I wasn't sleeping in their dreadful dormitory, and yes, I was dining with the Cheerful French as it was their last evening. But we agreed that, in the unlikely event that I arrived in Larrosoaña before dark the following evening, we would have dinner together there.

I don't know what I expected of a Pilgrim Mass. Perhaps, had I not gone off to look around I would have arrived in time to hear the first crashing chords of the organ and I might have been more moved. It didn't help that it was in Spanish of course, but I found that the only really significant moment was the blessing itself, for which the pilgrims were called forward to stand before the altar. That of course was also in Spanish – well, after all we were in Spain. But returning from dinner an hour or so later, I heard the organist practising and slipped inside to listen. For about a quarter of an hour I sat silent, watching the daylight fading through the stained glass and listening to that glorious sound, feeling far more deeply moved.

The Cheerful French were ending that stage of their staggered Camino the next morning, and left early. I had been worried about the crowds of pilgrims going my way out of Roncesvalles - I'd seen them all in the church the night before - but I found that by leaving around eight o'clock I could drop into a pocket of solitude between the Dawn Treaders, who set out before it was even light, and the Easy Stagers who didn't intend to push themselves for anyone. In any case, breakfast was served at eight-thirty so anyone not on the path by then would be further delayed by a good half hour. Little did I know that it would be the last time, on the entire Camino, that I would wake up and set out so late.

Plumes of early mist drifted, chill and eerie, through the branches of the trees as the path dropped down through a wood, lined with the brambles that give Roncesvalles its name. They didn't seem to be very healthy specimens - I had far more prolific ones in my garden at home - but maybe an enthusiastic monk had been round with a strimmer. At any rate it was better this way than if they had been wrapping themselves round my legs. The first village you come to, after Roncesvalles, is Burgette. This is Hemingway Country; he set at least one of his novels here and I don't suppose it has changed much since he last saw it. A few newer houses off to one side perhaps but otherwise, at that hour of the morning, it was a perfect introduction to the shuttered dilapidation which characterises so many villages of the Camino.

For most of the morning I walked alone, only catching up with some of the slower Dawn Treaders around midday as they stopped to rest. Then of course I in turn was overtaken by the Easy Stagers when I gave my feet a break. It still seemed strange to encounter other nationalities after spending so long on my own. Half of Quebec, as well as most of France and Spain, seemed to be on the Camino that month. I caught up with a retired teacher from Montreal who was doing the pilgrimage with his two brothers. If it worked, he said, he was going to propose that next year they canoe down the Yukon together and camp on a glacier. It seemed somehow obtuse to query the connection. His pace was rather quicker than mine, so for a while I kept the conversation going in order to give myself the incentive to keep walking, until an ominous 'What On Earth Is Going On?' message from the TGWU forced me to let him go ahead. I would not see him again until I was two days away from Santiago.

As time went on I found that pilgrims in Spain normally greeted each other with a simple Buenas Dias, or Buen Camino. In the case of the French this was almost always Bon Camino - for why would anyone want to speak any language other than theirs? It was easy to identify the ones who might be in a chatty mood because they were the ones who threw in every language they could think of, to see which one drew a response. If they understood the responding language they stayed to talk, so if you weren't feeling like company this could be a tricky moment.

The change in company was not the only difference between France and Spain. In the Landes and the Bearne, the flow of pilgrim traffic is sufficient for the locals to know why it's there, but intermittent enough to keep their interest and their goodwill. Here in Spain they had a pilgrim-weary air about them and although, this early in the season, they would sometimes return your greeting there was little enthusiasm. One old lady, to whom I called out a "Buenas Dias" as she sat in her window, pointed dumbly in the direction I was already walking, and went back to gazing blankly across the street. Since when had "Buenas Dias" translated to "Which way am I going?" I wondered. There was one redeeming occasion, much later, when an elderly man whom I asked for water not only filled my bottle but insisted on giving me an armful of oranges and a can of coca cola as well – but he, it turned out, was Italian.

The path rose, dipped, and rose again. At Zubiri it passed a massive and hideous Magnesium plant which my mediaeval forebears wouldn't have seen. I had come to realise that the maintenance of adequate levels of Magnesium in the blood is essential to control the tendonitis which I had already found so crippling. So perhaps it was not inappropriate that this factory imposed a scorching detour of several kilometres, to test the stamina of the strongest pilgrim tendons. Along the path too I was beginning to see one of the downsides to the recent surge in the popularity of the Camino - the amount of stuff left lying around. In the far off days of Ignes' memory, when only a few dedicated people bothered to walk it, I imagine that they generally cared for the ecology and well being of the path, and that litter was a relatively unknown problem. It will probably be a long time before it reaches the level of rubbish on the notorious path to Mount Everest Base Camp, but it would be sad if it ever did. Of course there are bodily functions which have to be attended to, however remote the location. Weight alone would rule out carrying the sort of shovel Bill Bryson understandably refused to take with him on the Appalachian Trail 'for burying ones poop'. But I have often wondered why it should be so unusual to carry a small lighter to at least burn ones toilet paper rather than leaving it lining the path. Still, at least that can be expected to biodegrade, but tampons and sanitary towels? Oh please.

It didn't take long for them to dub themselves the Three Musketeers…

Chapter Twelve
Three Musketeers

Arriving, hot and exhausted in Larrosoaña at four o'clock in the afternoon, I was already too late to get a bed in the refugio, but the mayor's kindly wife directed me across the street to what appeared to be a disused garage containing the overflow. It was here that I heard English voices for the first time since that distant night in Sarah's hotel in Montferrand, (I didn't count the whingeing tourists of St. Jean) and almost the last for several weeks. It was also here that I first encountered the extraordinary trust and generosity between pilgrims which, I was to discover, is one of the hallmarks of the Camino. Lamenting the absence of a cash-machine in Larrosoaña's single tiny street, I found a 10 euro note pressed into my hand by an Englishwoman I had never seen before in my life.

"In case you don't have enough to pay for your dinner." She said. "We are bound to meet again sometime, so pay me back when you can." Fortunately I didn't need it and was able to give it back to her that evening, because I never did see her again. But the spontaneity of her gesture remained with me like a beacon for the rest of my journey, and has done ever since.

I found Just Albert sitting with Vital and Xavier at a table in the garden of a café at the end of the village.

"What kept you?" He asked. "The hairdresser?" The sarcasm was sharp - it had been twenty-four hours since I had seen a mirror. When I told him that I had found the day's walk even harder than the climb to Roncesvalles he was unsympathetic.

"You should set off earlier in the morning. You walk more quickly when it's cool. Look at us, we've been here since one o'clock." There were certainly enough empties on the table to support this claim.

"Walk with us for a few days," he challenged, "then you'll see."

"How many kilometres do you do in a day?" I asked.

"Oh, about thirty-five or thirty-six, I suppose."

"Thirty-six Kilometres?" I was aghast.

"Well do you want to reach Santiago before Christmas?"

All through this exchange I had been aware of the body language of a woman at an adjoining table, whose ears appeared to be positively trembling with outrage at Albert's attitude. Now she turned on him, her nostrils flaring in indignation; she could not remain silent, she said, and listen to them turning my pilgrimage into a race. This led to a furious argument as to what exactly was the definition of a pilgrim. They were all gabbling away so passionately that their French was far too fast for me to understand, but I gathered that amongst Madame's criteria was the lusty singing of hymns and marching songs. Of stout build and with a carrying voice, she could have been one of the zealots of the Inquisition out of a novel by Louis de Bernieres. I was embarrassed that this argument should be raging apparently on my behalf, especially since I didn't rate her ideas any more highly than I did theirs. Feeling that I should take some part in the discussion I asked her whether she believed in the legend of Saint James, but I wasn't sure whether the exasperated shrug with which she turned away from me was prompted by the naivety of my question, or the evidence of my scepticism. It was Vital, I noticed, who eventually restored the equilibrium by reminding everyone that it was up to each pilgrim to choose.

"To each his own Camino," was a phrase that I was to hear often in the weeks ahead.

My dormitory in the converted garage was full of young people mercifully tired enough to go to bed early, and who didn't snore. I woke from a blissfully deep and undisturbed sleep to register that it was still pitch dark, and that someone was shaking my shoulder. It was Just Albert.

"Susie? Is this you?" Well it would have been awkward if it hadn't been. "We are waiting for you in the café at the end of the street." He hissed, and disappeared down the stairs.

Oh lord. Of course, I had said I'd try walking with them today - and it still felt like yesterday. Everyone else in the building still seemed to be unconscious and I wondered fleetingly if I could just not go. But he had taken the trouble to come across the street and up the stairs to wake me, risking a bruised ear at best (and probably much worse) if he had picked the wrong bed. There were to be many times, in the days which followed, when I would wonder what it must have taken to do that.

For today however, I had become a Dawn Treader. Tim Moore's derision came to mind as I tried to stuff my bin-bag-lined rucksack without waking everyone else with its rustling. But no-one appeared to stir as I clomped furtively down the stairs and out into the dawn, where even the birds were sounding drowsy, and rummaged for my torch. I had bought one of those clever ones which strap onto your head like a miner without his helmet. I had thought that it would come in useful for reading books after lights-out, except that I had left all the books at home - and how I missed them. But now it would come into its own I thought, as I strapped it on and walked smack into the corner of a wall.

But how long was this sort of early rising going to have to continue? The last time I had got out of bed this early had been when the children were tiny, and home had been a self-sufficient smallholding. Getting up at five-thirty in the morning to milk the cow had always seemed impossibly like the middle of the night then, and it was no different now. But the half-light and the early air brought the memories flooding back; the compensating smell of hay in the cowshed as I led her into her stall, and the warm, buttery smell of her as I leant my head into her comforting flank and began to milk, and eventually the feeling of satisfaction as the creamy foam began to rise up the sides of the milking-pail. These, at least, were the idylls created by the books that lured one into the lifestyle, and sometimes it was all as they described it. But more often it was cold and I was grumpy, and just as the bucket was half full she would lift a muddy hoof and plonk it inside, so that what milk there was had to be given to the pigs. But memories are forgiving, and as I walked up the street nursing my nose I thought of the good days, and of carrying the bucket back through the garden as the sun was rising, sparkling on the dew.

Sunrise here was at least an hour away, but the café was warm and smelling of coffee. As I entered I was brought to a halt by a ferocious bark from the short, harassed man behind the bar.

"Senora! Pack outside! Please!"

Well, I suppose it was very small and incredibly crowded with Dawn Treaders, the sleeping dormitory I had left felt like a different pilgrimage entirely.

"Here, sit down," said Just Albert kindly, shuffling along the bench to make room. "What happened to your nose?"

His gang had shrunk to three by now, consisting of himself, Vital and Xavier, the others having wisely fallen behind. If his mates couldn't keep up, I wondered, what hope would I have? It didn't

101

take long for them to dub themselves The Three Musketeers - and what was my persona to be? Milady, the dangerously beautiful Siren?

Anne, fragile Queen of King Louis XIII of France whom the Musketeers had sworn to protect? Not a bit of it. All I got was a slap on the back and the role of d'Artagnan.

When Kipling famously wrote that 'He travels the fastest who travels alone' he evidently wasn't thinking of walking - or if he was he didn't know the first thing about it. Albert was right. It was much quicker in company, and my feet, which yesterday had been complaining from the first kilometre mark, didn't make a murmur until we were approaching Pamplona, an incredible seventeen kilometres away. Mind you, by then the complaint was less a murmur than a concerted yell. This trio evidently didn't believe in stopping merely to have a rest.

Hobbling up one of the tiny streets where, during the July festival, foolhardy men are chased by young bulls, I reflected gloomily that were a bullock to come tearing round the corner now it could take me with it feet and all. I simply wouldn't have had the energy even to step to one side. I was pinning my hopes on the cathedral where I could appreciate the stained glass from the comfort of a pew. But of course the cathedral was closed. A few streets further on, though, the door of the beautiful church of San Saturnin stood wonderfully open. Gratefully I sank into the first pew I came to.

"Rest your feet." Said Albert kindly, if superfluously, as they continued up to the front to say their prayers - which didn't take long. Not nearly long enough.

"Go back again." I said sourly when they returned, "you haven't prayed enough and my feet still hurt."

They took no notice, shouldering their packs and rather pointedly holding open the door. But perhaps their religious observance had caused a softening of heart. At any rate it was only another five minutes before I was installed in a chair outside a bar, my feet up on another, and allowed to remain there for forty-five blissful minutes whilst we ate lunch - at eleven-thirty in the morning. If this was bizarre for me, the late-dining Spaniards stared in frank amazement. But this is what happens when you are a Dawn Treader, the entire day is advanced by several hours; could people really keep this up for the whole of the Camino? And what on earth happened to their body clocks afterwards? I would find out soon enough.

Leaving Pamplona, I noticed something curious about Spaniards. Walking with a group of men, I was treated with far more friendliness and courtesy that when I walked alone. Or perhaps it was just the Pamplonans. As we crossed a park, a woman patted us each on the shoulder and wished us "Courage to arrive in Santiago!" As Xavier said, that sort of thing gives you heart. We needed it too because between Pamplona and Uterga is a long, long, *very* long hill which climbs to a ridge of heart-stopping height, crowned with a line of wind turbines - or Aeolians, as the French romantically call them. I thought that the climb would never come to an end.

For a time the effort was blunted by conversation as, thinking of Madame-Of-The-Indignant-Nostrils with whom he had crossed swords the evening before, I asked Albert whether he considered himself a pilgrim. Without hesitation he answered that he was. But did he believe in the legend of Saint James? No, of course he didn't, the whole thing was a fabrication, but he did look for the spirituality of the pilgrimage all the same. This was the second time he had walked to Santiago, and the third time that Vital had. They both believed that the spirituality was to be found in the people one met rather than in the places one visited. In this way, he believed, all pilgrims carried the Camino already in their hearts.

But now it was becoming difficult to talk and walk, and gradually I fell behind. From the start I had insisted that absolutely nobody waited for anybody on that hill, knowing that it would be me they'd be waiting for. Fine, Albert had agreed, but then everybody would wait for absolutely everybody at the top. It was well over an hour and a half later that, puffing and stumbling my way over the ridge, I found more than the Musketeers waiting for me. Parked beside the road behind the windmills was a camper van. The notice propped against a table outside it advised one to leave there ones rubbish, ones fatigue, ones regrets, ones anger, and a good many other emotions besides - obviously a New Age Therapy Unit or a Buddhist Soup Kitchen. On the contrary, a cheerful and decidedly rotund Englishman dispensed beer, Coca Cola and coffee with an assortment of cakes and encouraging compliments, as well as advice for the treatment of sore limbs and feet. Taking one look at mine as he poured my coffee, he popped a magnesium tablet into a glass of water and handed it over.

Shirley Maclaine, in her dreams of past lives on the Camino, claimed to have been protected by a monk called John, from the twelfth century. Pilgrims of the twenty-first century don't have to go back that far. John from London, as Tim Moore had discovered, spends the best part of his year driving up and down the Camino looking for people who need help, usually at the tops of hills. He told me he lived alone in his van, but I hoped it wasn't always a monk's life - he deserved someone to look after him from time to time. The Camino phenomenon has, perhaps inevitably, spawned a good deal of self-interest in various forms. You can't really blame the Spanish people for cashing in on the sheer volume of passing strangers. But here were kindness and self-sacrifice on a grand scale. The two euros I paid for my coffee and plate of chocolate biscuits can't have done more than cover the costs.

Originally a pilgrim, John had spent a couple of years running refugios before it occurred to him that he could do more good by providing care for pilgrims in the middle of the day. So he took his van, with its first aid chest and cupboards full of refreshments, to all the energy-sapping, blister-inducing places along the Way of St. James - as an Alternative Pilgrimage it was certainly impressive. But my companions, not understanding a word of a conversation in English, were become restive. So off we set to walk down into Uterga. It was only as I reached the bottom of another cruel hill that I remembered that I hadn't even offered to pay him for the magnesium.

The Uterga refugio was spacious and comfortable. It also had a separate bathroom for women, an unheard of luxury. At dinner three silent, swarthy men came and sat at the table next to ours in the café next door; they were powerfully built and taciturn, carrying an air of menace about with them. They were probably just builders, tired after a long day, but Xavier and I were convinced they were spies for ETA. I hadn't seen all that much evidence of Basque as a separate culture since the now distant cemetery before St. Palais, but a display of aggressive graffiti on the walls along the path seemed to combine with these chunky Che Guevaras to prove that the Independence Movement is alive and kicking.

During the night I woke barely able to breathe, and it wasn't hard to see why. In a dormitory crammed with twenty people, one window had a sign warning you not to open it or it would fall out, whilst the one on the other side, above the dog-kennel, had been firmly closed. It was Xavier who had done it, he claimed the next morning that the barking of the dog had kept him awake. This was a problem I didn't have to share, thanks to my ear-plugs. Why didn't Xavier try them? A pilgrim shouldn't need ear-plugs, he replied primly, but I couldn't help thinking that death by irritation or suffocation must be a sad choice for a pilgrim to have to make.

The bridge at Puenta la Reina, built in the twelfth century to save pilgrims, and no doubt better-heeled travellers as well, from being fleeced by the ferrymen of the Arga.

Chapter Thirteen
Estella

God, but men are grumpy when they're hungry; not for nothing has the way to their hearts traditionally been via their stomachs. Since we had bagged two pairs of adjoining bunks in the Uterga refugio, there was no need to wake anybody at five-thirty the next morning. Albert's snores at close range had done that already. But breakfast would not be served until the far more civilised hour of six-thirty. Whilst I could see the point of this, the discontent amongst the Musketeers was palpable. Unthinkable that departure could be delayed until such a late hour, but without food there were to be serious withdrawal symptoms. By the time we had stomped through two shuttered villages a grim silence had descended which was in stark contrast to the cheerful bonhomie of the day before.

Eventually we found some bread and coffee, but by then Albert was taking his revenge on the day with a furiously paced march which allowed no stops. Apart, that is, from the obligatory pause to admire and photograph the bridge at Puenta La Reina. This was built in the twelfth century to save pilgrims, and no doubt better-heeled travellers as well, from being fleeced by the ferrymen of the Arga. Aymery Picaud was graphic about the iniquities visited by the boatmen on unsuspecting pilgrims. Among the atrocities they perpetrated, apparently, was the practice of overloading their boats, having taken a fee from everyone on board - and considerably more for the horses, only to capsize them deliberately in mid-stream. They would then scuttle off down-stream to rob the corpses of those drowned passengers who, with any luck, had been washed up on the banks.

Opinions vary as to which Reina it was who built the bridge, though Edwin Mullins is pretty sure it was Queen Urraca. In fact there were two royal Urracas living around that time which makes it all the more confusing. One of them, the sister of the king of León, was known for her charitable acts and had much to do with the embellishments of that city's Basilica of St. Isidoro. She would be a promising contender for the gratitude of generations of pilgrims. The other was a close friend of Archbishop Gelmirez of Compostela and feisty ex-wife of Alphonso I of Aragon. Were it not for historical details like dates, my money would have been on her since she is known to have carried out a bitter and expensive war against her husband, which involved much pillaging of church wealth - hence her strategic friendship with the Archbishop I imagine. It would surely have been very much in her interests to have had a means of getting her loot safely across the river whilst, at the same time, earning extra credit for helping pilgrims along the way.

It was in Puenta La Reina that I came across a growth area on the Camino - the Packless Pilgrim. This must have been what Mr. and Mrs. Smart were up to outside Ostabat. I had found it really annoying, months ago, that whenever I told anyone that I was thinking about walking the Camino they almost invariably assumed that this would be the way I would choose to do it, as if nobody believed in self-sufficiency any more. With a van to carry the rucksacks and each day's distance planned in advance, it is more a tourist excursion than a pilgrimage, a mere stroll between refugios. And this is where the trouble arises. All the guidebooks will tell you that the refugios are strictly reserved for people who are 'without motor vehicle backup' but this isn't entirely true. Many tour operators seem able to obtain Credentiales for their clients - and somehow to get them stamped. This enables them not only to get their Compostela when they arrive in Santiago, but also to take up the beds which genuine pilgrims, arriving limping and heavily laden, are later denied. We nicknamed them the Camionettes, after the French word for van, and saw to it that they stayed out of ear-shot of Albert's derisive comments.

About half an hour out of Puenta la Reina we came to a massive motorway-under-construction. Already a great gash stretched across the once beautiful valley as far as the eye could see. Cutting across the original Camino, it had imposed a detour up a hill of a height and steepness to rival the Pyrenees. Vital slowed to my pace, counselling and encouraging all the way up the cruel climb until at last we came to the village of Cirauqui capping its hill in the sunshine, full of balconies hung with flowers, its walls carved with emblems of the House of Navarre. I remarked that, as far as I could remember, a

Henry of Navarre had been king of England in the Middle Ages, Henry IV.

"No, he couldn't have," said Xavier. "You didn't have a Henry IV, in England." Adding helpfully, "You had a Henry VIII, though, are you thinking of him?" This was mathematically so obtuse that I could only stare at him in silence until the penny dropped. He began to giggle and then to laugh, tears trickling down his cheeks, until it was impossible not to join in. The hilarity lasted far longer that the remark deserved, but then Xavier had a very infectious laugh.

After Cirauqui the path descended to the stone bridge over the river where Aymery Picaud's horse had died after drinking polluted water. Evidently this was not unusual at the time, since gangs of swarthy men used to wait by the river in order to flay and steal the equine skins. Several centuries later Edwin Mullins had enjoyed the walk from here to Estella, in the early 1970s, but in those days there would have been no sign of the massive roadworks. For us there was yet another paralysing climb and its companion descent, designed only to nurture a burning resentment towards the internal combustion engine - two tortuous detours, for no better reason than the destruction of both the landscape and the ozone layer in one go.

Here, sadly, I gave up trying to walk with the Musketeers and urged them to go ahead. It was no good. I couldn't continue to match their pace, and I was pretty sure I'd never make the distance anyway. I might meet them in Estella, I said doubtfully, if I got there − but privately I didn't think I would. My last sight of them was skirting the motorway, marching single file against the skyline; the advance guard of the Gascon army.

Left alone, I picked my way gingerly down the next hill until, rounding a bend at the bottom, I came upon a disgruntled Irishman. He looked up plaintively from examining his feet.

"I never committed all these sins - I'm paying for somebody else's! And who's bloddy idea was this whole thing anyway?"

Retying his boot-laces he walked on alongside me, and as we walked he shared a pear from his rucksack, at that moment the most delicious thing I had ever eaten, or shall - even if I live to be a hundred and fifty - and his opinion of Shirley Maclaine's book.

"What a load of robbish!"

He deeply resented paying good money for what he firmly believed to be a hoax at the expense of the reading public. Nor was he impressed by my suggestion that she might have believed it herself.

"Not even she could believe that!"

Eamonn's standard conversation opener, "Why are you doing this, where did you start and are you famous?" reflected a new preoccupation among some modern pilgrims which was perhaps inevitable. Shirley Maclaine having immortalised her pilgrimage in print, and Jenna Bush having attributed to hers her ability to predict that her father would be re-elected president of the United States the following year, celebrity spotting was bound to have become part of the pilgrim experience sooner or later. It probably isn't such a novel idea either - they probably had crowds lining the route in the fourteenth century when Ferdinand and Isabella passed by with their entourage, not to mention Hannibal and all his elephants. But if my negative answer to his third question caused Eamonn some disappointment, my reply to the first, that I had wanted to 'Walk Out One Midsummer Morning', brought a smile of recognition.

"Laurie Lee!" He breathed. "D'you know, I haven't thought of Laurie Lee for twenty-five years. But this is more or less what he was doing, isn't it?"

I pointed out that Mr. Lee's circumstances had been even less comfortable than ours when he made his journey. He really had slept on straw in cowsheds, and at one time had nearly died from dehydration. We walked together for a while until we passed a very pretty Russian girl who had stopped to take a photo.

"Hello! Where did you start from?" He asked her. "Why are you doing this and are you famous?" I left him to it. If I stopped now I'd never make it up the next hill, let alone to the next village, by the end of the day. Northern Spain, that early May, was either gushing with rain or blisteringly hot. There seemed to be nothing in between. No bright, gusty days of fresh, dry breezes to call 'ideal' walking weather. The conditions underfoot were correspondingly the consistency of sticky slime, or had hardened to baked furrows of tendon-bruising rigidity.

After another two hours of stumbling along in the searing heat, legs wobbly with fatigue, I could see a cluster of roofs in the distance. Oh please, please, let this be Estella! I could see a bridge ahead, and Vital had said something about passing a bridge just before the refugio; the path went over this one, it was true, but that was a mere detail. Now I could just see the outline of the town's name on the signboard. Straining my eyes hopefully, I saw with a plummeting heart that it began with a 'V'. This then was Villatuerta, not Estella.

Knees buckling with disappointment, I just managed to drop my rucksack before collapsing heavily onto a bench in the deserted square, everyone else being wisely in the shade. I consulted the Confraternity Guide with a last, flickering glimmer of hope; perhaps Estella was only just round the corner. The Guide told me that it was four crushing kilometres away - the outer reaches of the galaxy might have been nearer. It also told me that there was a refugio here in Villatuerta. I had no choice, I simply could not walk another mile - let alone getting on for three. It had been fun walking with the Musketeers, but the urge to hang on to their company was a wish too far. I had said goodbye and left them to their male-bonding exercise, so I might as well stop here.

A last despairing whimper from my famished stomach penetrated my misery. Feebly hoisting the pack again, I shuffled on in search of a bar where I could order a boccadillo, my share of Eamonn's pear having vanished over an hour ago. This was, therefore, the most delicious half baguette ever to have had a meagre sliver of dried ham inserted into it, and I was doing my best not to ram it whole down my throat in between swigs of Coca Cola, when a massively overweight German pilgrim wheezed in. His immense knees were squeezed into tight bandages and seemed hardly able to support his bulk. Whilst he waited for his sandwich he asked me how far I was intending to go that day. I replied that I had been thinking of Estella, but that it was another four kilometres so...

"Oh, but you are young and fit!" He interrupted. "For you Estella will be no problem!"

He looked no older than I was and certainly no less fit than I felt at that moment, but his confidence was a challenge. I never saw him again so I was never able to tell him how much he, an anonymous fellow walker, had done to determine the outcome of my entire pilgrimage. I finished the Coca Cola and got shakily to my feet.

The approach to Estella is flanked by a massive chemical plant and a sewage farm. Between them they make inhaling a hazardous business - I could only suppose the locals got used to it. Mind you, for the past two hours, all the way since Villatuerta, I had noticed that every breath I took brought with it a nostril-flinching stink of stale sweat that could only be mine - I really did smell awful. The concrete road leading down to the town seemed to go on forever. As I staggered down it, meandering from side to side and terminally oblivious of the oncoming traffic, I found my hand gravitating subconsciously to my mobile phone, like Frodo's to his ring. I had an almost irresistible urge to call for Bernard, or a taxi – anyone who might possibly come and get me out of there. I'd had enough of this game, and it wasn't as if I hadn't given it a good try. I would have to stop walking with the Musketeers in any case - if this was their idea of a short, easy day it wasn't mine. They would have forgotten me by now anyway, I reflected with more than a touch of self-pity, and even if I did turn up I didn't suppose they'd take much notice now that they knew how slowly I walked.

But then, hobbling miserably down towards the refugio, I saw three familiar backs in the distance, walking away from me up the opposite hill into the town. Cupping my hands I tried to shout, but my long-since-desiccated throat could only croak, and in any case they were far too far away to hear and kept on walking. A passing pilgrim cyclist took in the situation in an instant.

Stopping his bike, he stuck his fingers in his mouth and gave a piercing whistle that made all heads turn.

The effect was dramatic. Spinning round in unison they came running back down the road, cheering and waving. Pulling my rucksack off my shoulders they enveloped me in huge hugs. They smelt wonderfully of soap. At this point Anne of France (had she ever walked this far) would have fainted away and been carried supine into the refugio to be fanned back to life with smelling salts by her Musketeers. Instead, my androgynous persona was shoved inside, with pats on the back, and pushed into a chair in front of the reception desk.

"I never thought you'd make it." Albert kept saying. "I was certain you'd have stopped long ago."

The young hospitallero, looking through my Credentiale, gave a low whistle and mimed a 'hat's off' gesture when he saw the distance I'd walked since I'd begun.

"I know," said Albert proudly, for all the world as if it were his doing, "A courageous woman!" Another pat on the back.

Fortunately the refugio doorway was a wide one, so that my swollen head had no difficulty in getting back out into the street and round to the building next door, which housed the dormitory. There I was hugged stickily once again and directed, forthwith and firmly, to the showers. Later, lying on my bunk, I became drowsily aware of whispered voices and hands gently prodding my feet. They had crept back from their sightseeing and were inspecting them for blisters.

Small wonder, then, that all the demoralization and exhaustion evaporated - thirty kilometres suddenly seemed a perfectly reasonable day's walk.

The refugio at Estella is huge. One hundred and sixteen bunks and all of them taken by the end of the day. Ignes, I reflected, would have writhed at the thought of sleeping in such a crowded space. But I was so tired that I slept soundly – or I did until a tall cyclist, whose bunk was at a right angle to mine, stretched his legs and kicked me in the head.

The enchanting little octagonal church in the village. Built in the twelfth century, it is famous for the exquisite balance of its architecture...

Chapter Fourteen
Kiwi Taxis

In the morning, by six o'clock, the reception area of the refugio closely resembled the concourse of a major airport at the peak of the holiday season. People and rucksacks were everywhere. The first Dawn Treaders were already disappearing up the street into the dark whilst, in the huge kitchen, Bob Marley was playing at full volume over the speakers, and the young hospitallero was cheerfully replenishing bread baskets and jam pots. A delightfully vivacious Italian girl opposite us so entranced Vital that he dropped his toast into his coffee, much to his disgust. It served him right for flirting, I thought grumpily. For her, however, the Camino was finished; she had hurt her foot and was only waiting to find transport home. I thought she was remarkably lively given the circumstances; the injuries I had suffered seemed almost miniscule by comparison - at least I was still walking.

As we set out the rain began and didn't stop until the end of another very long, very hard day. It takes only moments to turn the dry earth which produces the marvellous Rioja into a paste with the consistency of half set glue. As it became harder and harder to lift each two kilo footfall I told my companions I'd catch them up and watched them disappear into the distance; stockily built, with legs like sinewy tree trunks, they seemed so much better able to cope. Eventually, as I was struggling along the sticky lane towards Torres del Rio, which never seemed to get any nearer no matter how many hours I walked, my legs simply came to a complete standstill. The TGWU had put up a Puffed Foot Picket at the beginning of the day and the discomfort had been constant, but this was an all out strike. For about five minutes I just stood there glued to the ground, unable to move. I was overtaken by a New Zealander striding smartly along without a pack. Eyeing her sourly I decided she must be a Camionette, on her way to steal the bunk I might have had, and very nearly ignored her.

In fact Bronnie and her sisters, who were walking some way behind, were to prove good company in the days ahead. On a tour of Europe they had decided to squeeze in a week on The Way of St. James before skiving off to Barcelona. Unorthodox perhaps, but by the time they stopped at Burgos I was as sorry to see them leave as they were to go. Chrissie, one of the sisters, had done the first leg - from St Jean Pied de Port to Puenta la Reina with her husband the year before and, though none of us knew it then, she was to finish the trek alone the following year. Apparently the reason they were walking light was that that morning they had furtively booked a taxi to carry their rucksacks, just for one day. They had hoped to be able to load them round the corner, out of the sight and derision of serious pilgrims, but to their acute embarrassment the taxi driver had helpfully drawn up right outside the refugio, and leapt out to load up their packs in full view of the Dawn Treaders. These of course included the Musketeers who, when I caught up with them an hour or two later, were dismissive.

"Yes, I saw them," said Albert, "They aren't real pilgrims." Well, no.

But blonde hair and Antipodean vivacity can work wonders as I was to find out. On the way out of Estella that morning we had passed the famous monastery at Irache, where there are two taps in the wall, one running water and the other, a silver one, running Rioja. On orders from my Musketeers I had left the smaller of my water bottles empty so that I could fill it with wine. It seemed that every other pilgrim had done the same, and that evening there was a convivial gathering on the stairs of the refugio as everyone shared their bounty in paper cups.

Xavier was late. He had been to visit the enchanting little octagonal church in the village. Built in the twelfth century, it is famous for the exquisite balance of its architecture which must have been learnt from the Moors.

I had noticed that the techniques which lend such grace and symmetry to Moorish architecture had been borrowed by more than a few Christian designers down the centuries. I was beginning to think they can't have been such a bad lot really, the Moors. Their culture encouraged religious tolerance, it promoted learning and the creation of beauty; it gave the world the Alhambra Palace. Not much wrong with that I'd say, especially when one compared it to the Mediaeval Christian culture of austerity and ignorance. A culture which burned Tindale at the stake for offering the Bible to the masses a culture which gave the world the Inquisition. It is chilling

114

to remember that it was the celebrated piety of Queen Isabella and King Ferdinand, committed pilgrims both, which plunged Spain into the terror of those purges which must rank among the most frightening examples of religious bigotry ever to have been perpetrated in Europe. Every time I came upon some gift they had bestowed, or monument they had endowed, I wondered at the connection between their narrow brand of religion and the spirit of tolerance and generosity with which the entire Camino seems to have been imbued.

Xavier though, had gone off to admire the Moorish influence and arrived now with shining eyes. He had found the Kiwi Taxis, as the New Zealanders were to be forever dubbed, and had persuaded them to join us. By the end of that evening it was game set and match to the New World - they had captured the hearts of all three of the Musketeers.

The refugio in Torres del Rio was small, with two-tier bunks packed tightly into a stuffy roof space at the top of the stairs. When we had arrived I had gone automatically to dump my rucksack on a bunk next to Vital and above Albert, but had been forestalled by an imperious cry from Carmen, the owner.

"No! Susie goes there!" It was good humoured, but firm. Women had their own corner and were not to sleep near the men. Since the overcrowding meant that my men were sleeping a mere three metres away, and since an hour later she allocated the bunk directly beneath mine to Jean-Michel from Tours who was unmistakeably a man, the whole idea of segregation seemed a bit pointless. Perhaps it was her Italian ancestry.

The final straw, though, came when I opened the door of the lavatory - a barely screened cubicle in a corner of that crowded room - and found a hole-in-the-ground arrangement. The Kiwi Taxis had been fortunate in arriving too late to get a bed and had ended up in a lovely new refugio, in the same town and for the same price, which offered not only modern lavatories and twice as many showers, but a washing machine and a tumble dryer as well. They were virtually the only pilgrims there, and it seemed a pity that Italian Carmen didn't redirect her overflow rather than putting latecomers on mattresses in reception, where everyone fell over them.

I could cheerfully have murdered Albert the next morning. Not content with dumping us in a grotty refugio (it had been his choice) he hauled everyone out into the rain at six-thirty in the morning, for breakfast in a bar which didn't open until seven o'clock. We stood in a gloomy huddle which even café con leche and toast couldn't brighten when eventually we were allowed in to dry off.

We had intended to stick to the road that morning, to preserve our boots, but eventually the traffic drove us miserably back into the mud. After an hour we stopped to visit the lovely church in Viana, closely associated with Cesar Borgia - not, one would have thought, an auspicious connection for an overtly Christian path. When they had prayed and my feet had recovered we set off again, but as usual I soon got left behind. Considering how crowded the refugios were, it was amazing that it was possible to be solitary on the walk. And yet I walked alone that day for three contented hours, accompanied only by the ubiquitous nightingales, until I dropped down the hill into Logroño. As usual the downhill into the town was followed by a steep uphill to the cathedral, past which the Camino always ran, and there I found Bronnie with an immensely tall Austrian called Josef. Who yodelled.

"You want cold? Is cold in there!" He said, shivering as he emerged from the building. The interior was Baroque, with a great deal of gold, and was rather splendid but I didn't think it was nearly as pretty as Viana; Cesar Borgia had chosen well.

There were still twelve kilometres to walk before we could rest in the refugio at Navarette, and they felt like the longest of my life. Singing helped. You really do pick up your feet when you sing, so that you are walking rather than shuffling along. I lost count of the times we worked our way through 'Lilli Marlene', Josef's rich baritone providing the harmony. We sang our national anthems. We sang nursery rhymes. We sang every song we could think of and still the village didn't get any nearer. Finally, with the sixteenth round of 'She'll Be Coming Round The Mountain', we found ourselves trudging wearily up the hill to the refugio. We were completely exhausted by the time we staggered to the door to be told by Cruella de Ville's nastier sister that the place was full.

Now, I had been reading my Confraternity Guide (in fact I practically knew it by heart since it was the only book I hadn't chucked out in that weight-reducing exercise, back home, in what seemed now to be another world) and this Guide stated very clearly that this refugio had a strict admissions policy. Priority was given to anyone who had walked from further off than Logroño, which was far enough, but it would have been impossible to have walked from further away than Torres del Rio, where we had started out that morning. Yet I saw several faces - beaming, complacent and above all showered faces - that I definitely didn't recognise from the refugio there. Perhaps she didn't understand how far we'd come, I thought, as I began to explain. I hadn't got very far before she pushed her face close to mine shouting "C.O.M.P.L.E.T.O! C.O.M.P.R.E.N.D.I?" I felt ridiculously close to tears. Bronnie saved the day by asking, more reasonably, where we might find another refugio. The Witch-of-the-West stuffed a card into her hand and slammed the door. Josef, however, had been admitted. She obviously had a male harem in there.

Disconsolately we trudged on up the hill, way beyond exhaustion. If this refugio was full I was going to lie down in the gutter, there was no way I could walk any further; at that moment my phone bleeped a message. Almost beyond caring, I took it out and looked at it with glazed eyes; I saw that it was from Peter:

'OH MY GOD IT'S FRIDAY 13TH! ROME AND GLFRD ALL PRAYIN 4 U MY DRLNG AN WISHIN U STRENGTH TO CARRY ON.'

I hadn't even stopped to wonder what day it was. When we found the building the door was locked. It was the first time we had come across a security system in a refugio, but if such a thing seemed slightly at odds with the principle of pilgrimage we were too tired to care. I pressed the buzzer, summoned just enough energy to croak "Pilgrims!" into the mouthpiece, and the doors of heaven swung slowly open. Rome and Guildford had delivered.

We climbed a pristine marble staircase to an apartment of sparkling cleanliness. The dormitory had comfortable new bunks, the kitchen was spacious and the drying area for laundry boasted unlimited supplies of clothes pegs. It really is amazing how little it takes to create a paradise for pilgrims, clothes pegs and clean mattresses. The first concern of the stunningly handsome hospitallero was to take our rucksacks off our backs and give us a cup of tea. Our first concern was to get under some hot water before he breathed in again. I rang Albert to tell him where we'd ended up.

"What's it like?" He demanded tersely, "This place is disgusting!" Relief and exhaustion combined to make this very funny but he didn't share the joke.

After an hour Bronnie's sisters arrived along with Jean-Michel who took the bunk next to mine. He had been walking beside Albert that morning but eventually, he told me, he had given up the pace. Lying back on our mattresses, showered and laundered, I mended his trousers while he gave me the benefit of his philosophy. A veteran of several solitary Caminos, he guarded his individuality fiercely. He was a small, wiry man whose gentle blue eyes always wore an expression of mild amusement, and he talked with the quiet air of someone who has discovered his own truth.

"Each one has to make his own Camino." He told me. "Walk with your Musketeers by all means, if that's what you want to do, but if you walk in a group there will always be restrictions. You won't find your own path unless you walk alone. Meet other people. Everyone on the Camino is interesting, that is why we are here." From the bunk beyond his Bronnie, who had nicknamed the Musketeers the FMBs ('Fast Moving Bastards' - with a ruder version for when I was fed up) put it more bluntly.

"Face it, Sus, those blokes are on a mission. They aren't going to let any woman slow them down. Best let them get ahead, aye."

I sensed the truth in what they said, but it made me sad all the same. I would miss my Musketeers. True, it was hard to keep up with them and sometimes I hadn't, but on the other hand I had rarely felt so happy or laughed so readily as I had with them. I bit off the cotton at the last stitch with an increasingly heavy heart. This, though, was true to the traditions of Ignes' Camino - everyone sharing what they had. I gave Jean-Michel back a sound pair of trousers, he had given me sound advice. I would miss him too. So that night we all met for a last supper, joined by the Kiwi Taxis with whom the Musketeers were by now helplessly infatuated. D'Artagnan observed all this with quiet amusement - Susie, acting as interpreter, felt a pang of envy. Still, tomorrow would be another day.

I lay awake a long time in the night, thinking about Jean-Michel's advice and wondering what it was that drove me to try to keep up with three men I barely knew, who gave no quarter when it came to my complaining limbs. Was it merely a craving for male company or approval? Dear God, that would be almost as bad as Technology

Dependence. But the joyous welcome I had received when I had arrived, against all expectation, in Estella had been a watershed. I had realised then that we were a family, a unit, and that perhaps I was as important to their pilgrimage as they were to mine. That in some way I filled a need for them almost as great as the one they obviously filled for me - even if I couldn't define it. The problem though lay in the principle of the pilgrimage, the tradition that it is all about giving up and leaving behind ones old life and personality including, if necessary, ones need for other people. It was all so difficult to understand. Eventually I decided that there was only one thing to do - leave all decisions to instinct. If I woke early enough I would go out and join them, if not I would continue my pilgrimage alone. With that I fell asleep.

At five-thirty it was pitch dark and I was completely awake. I had surfaced suddenly, and with intense relief, from a nightmare in which I had ticks buried in the skin all over my face. In fact, a few days before, I had found several ticks on my arms and even one on my stomach. Peeing in long grass had been a worry from the start - what about the less immediately visible parts of ones body to which they might choose to attach themselves? Evidently this had become something of a subconscious pre-occupation - but all the same, I was awake. Outside, I found myself alone with the sunrise on the Camino, and looking back I could see the church tower silhouetted against the reddening sky. I noticed that I was walking more easily, and wondered whether I had crossed some fitness threshold after which everything became easier, or maybe it was just that the ground was flat.

I had been walking for an hour and had not been overtaken by the Musketeers, or indeed by any Dawn Treaders at all, when I resigned myself to the evidence that they had left before me and would be far away by now; if they had had to get up even earlier than this to reach Santo Domingo de la Calzada that day, it would be far too far for me. I had been trying hard to be philosophical, but now I felt utterly desolate. For comfort I switched on my phone and found a message from Robin's girlfriend, Marie-Hélène. It must have been a quiet night in their restaurant last night because she had obviously spent the previous evening paraphrasing Max Bygraves:

SMILE WHEN YOUR FEET ARE HURTING, SMILE WHEN THE SUN AIN'T SHINING, SMILE WHEN THE BLISTERS ARE BURSTING, SMILE WHEN YOUR KNEES ARE GOING, SOON YOU'LL BE THERE AND THE REASON WILL BE SO CLEAR, AND ALL YOU'VE GOT TO DO IS S-M-I-L-E !

I had discovered that one of the most comforting things, when I was feeling lonely, was to find that people to whom I might not have spoken for ages were nonetheless thinking of me and wishing me well. At the end of her message my son had added his own, it was succinct and to the point and left me uncertain which to do first, laugh or cry; I did the latter.

'GO ON MUM JUST KEEP BLOODY WALKING! WE LOVE YOU. GO! GO! GO!'

After another long half-hour of climbing, up a narrow twisty path through thickets of scratchy gorse, I had acquired a blister to rival the discomfort in the swollen foot. Sitting on a rock at the top with the contents of my first aid kit scattered around me, I looked up at the sound of voices to see a familiar trio breasting the brow of the hill. The rush of joyful hugs and laughter clinched the deal - I would follow them to Santo Domingo if it took till midnight. They didn't tell me that it very nearly would. Their astonishment was not flattering.

"We could see a pilgrim half an hour ahead," said Albert, "But we didn't think for one moment that it could be you!"

I lost them again of course, an hour later, but my mind was free of dilemmas and for the moment the walking was easy. I was content. In Azofra, as I was resting beside a spectacular water fountain, I saw Josef stomping down the street evidently having been released from the harem.

"If ve heff vorter zen ve are fresh!" He announced stoutly, filling his bottle.

'Fresh' would have been a hopeful adjective to attach to any pilgrim in that heat, but in the case of Josef's nylon shirt it was more than ever a misnomer. I know he washed it - I saw it drying on more than one occasion, but it was still a good idea to stay up wind of him whenever there was any wind. Breathing carefully I walked on beside him.

Josef was very religious and very much into angels. His house was full of them, he told me, in fact his wife was an angel. But then I too was an angel, and so were all the women on the Camino come to that. Not the men? I quizzed. No, no, not the men. It was the women that he was particularly fond of. Ah. I think I preferred him when he was yodelling. To change the subject I asked him about last night's refugio. He snorted with disgust. It appeared that he had been given a mattress on the floor right next to the bunk where Albert had snored all night, with the result that he had hardly slept at all. But now he had a plan. Proudly, and not a little furtively, he showed me a map he had found with a short cut to Santo Domingo. This would get us there in record time, and we could choose the best and quietest beds. It might involve walking along the main trunk road for a few minutes, he admitted, but that wouldn't be too much of a problem. By the time I limped into the city, long after I had lost him, I had walked that terrifying highway for two hours.

The problem as usual was my bladder. Bronnie had warned me, from experience, that Josef had appeared to lack awareness of the difference between the sexes on this point. Men, of course, only had to turn away and pee on the nearest piece of grass, but women needed at least a modicum of privacy to perform the same function. Only a few days before I had found a perfect hiding place at the edge of a field, protected by a hedge from the eyes of pilgrims and passing motorists, only to look up over my knees and watch in horror as an immense crop-sprayer appeared over the hill in front, and advanced slowly down the field. Flight – or indeed any sort of movement - being impossible at that moment, I could only return the driver's outraged stare with as much aplomb as I could muster as he turned his vehicle only inches from the place where I was squatting. And here in this flat landscape there were no trees or bushes to provide privacy within a five kilometre radius, and the need was becoming pressing.

Eventually I found a deepish ditch at a fork in the path and let him walk on ahead round a bend. Glancing hastily over my shoulder

I came face to face with an Italian who introduced himself as Pedro. Did I know which was the path? He had been following us because he was lost. Could I advise him? I pointed out the direction Josef had taken but he wasn't sure that it was the right one. What did I think? This was really not a moment for idle conversation. Tightening my pelvic muscles, I forced a smile and announced brightly that I would be continuing, in that direction, but after I had had a pee, OK? He nodded, surveyed me curiously, and waited. Knees pinched together, so did I. This was ridiculous. Eventually nature dictated that only one course was open, and I began, self-consciously, to undo my zip. He continued to wait. It felt like some incongruous striptease - ill-clad as I was for lap-dancing. Finally, when my shorts were half way down my hips and I was in a semi squatting position, he continued calmly on his way apparently quite unfazed. Italians.

By this time, of course, I had completely lost Josef and all the yellow arrows. The only navigation mark was the main road - most of the way in the company of Italian Pedro, who had dodgy knees to match my swollen feet. I was reminded of the terrible trudge southwards from Monsegur, where the blast of air as each lorry passed had threatened to blow me into the ditch. Only, at Monsegur it had been raining stair-rods, whereas here we were walking under a broiling sun.

At last I stumbled into the vast municipal building which houses the newly restored refugio at Santo Domingo de la Calzada. On the third floor. Hauling myself up by the banisters I fell into a bright and cheerful common room lined with pictures of the Spanish royal family shaking hands with happy pilgrims at its inauguration, whose present counterparts looked up at me curiously from their books. An elegant woman with a Bostonian accent eyed me languidly over her spectacles. I tried - and failed - to imagine her carrying a rucksack.

"My dear, you appear to be suffering," she drawled in a voice of vague concern, "and, believe me, we are all suffering with you."

Having no answer for this, I asked her if she had seen three Frenchmen and got the impression I might have said Martians. However she did tell me that, the refugio having been full since eleven o'clock that morning on account of there being a festival of some sort, the refectory downstairs yes, down all three flights of stairs - had been cleared to take the overflow. Down I sidled, my knees by now refusing to bend as exhaustion had cut off their blood supply, and found the refectory heaving with people. From the doorway I gazed round, bewildered and lost.

"*SUSIE!*" From three voices in unison.

Hugs, laughter and congratulations. And an overwhelming feeling of relief. They told me that we had all walked forty kilometres that day and I tried not to think of what Jean-Michel might have said. Actually it was highly likely that I hadn't walked as far as they had, since the main road was supposed to have been a short cut. But they bought me my dinner that evening in any case, as a reward. Could I help being so fond of them?

Xavier proudly showed me the slab of foam he had been guarding for me and was appalled to hear, when we compared notes after my shower, that I had walked so far along a major trunk road.

"Susie that's illegal!" he gasped.

"Illegal or not, it was bloody stupid!" grunted a voice from inside Albert's sleeping bag. "All you have to do," he continued, surfacing, "Is to follow the yellow arrows. Yes, of course there were yellow arrows, there always are. You weren't looking."

Cleaned up and rested, we went to find the cathedral with the chickens. I have always been fascinated by this story. Apparently, sometime in the Middle Ages, so the legend goes, a pilgrim rejected the advances of an innkeeper's daughter who in retaliation accused him of theft. The townspeople of course believed her story in preference to his, and he was condemned by the mayor to be hanged. At this point the ghost of Saint James stepped in and held him up so that the rope round his neck didn't throttle him. The mayor had gone home for his dinner by then, and was in the middle of eating a chicken when he was told that the prisoner was still alive.

"Nonsense!" he is supposed to have said, "If he is alive so is this chicken!" At which point the chicken – presumably a cockerel - stood up and crowed. Believing that all legends have a basis in fact I have often wondered at this story, not only about the physical logistics of the chicken's resurrection, but also about the likely state of the mayor's table cloth. Ever since that time, in a tradition going back through the centuries, a cock and a hen have been kept in a cage near the altar. This is not a sentence for life, they take it in turns - with local families vying for the honour of providing the pair. Legend has it that they are fed only the bread provided by pilgrims, but they must get thin pickings, I reflected, if all pilgrims followed the advice I had been given by Pierre in Hagetmau. Domenico Laffi, however, claimed in 1670 that when genuine pilgrim bread was scarce the locals were allowed to dress up as pilgrims and beg for it - the products of this subterfuge, apparently, being every bit as spiritually nutritious as the real thing.

As we prepared for bed that night, on our rows of foam mats, a Geordie pilgrim from the posh dormitories upstairs wandered in. In silence he surveyed the rows of sleeping-bagged bodies.

"It's like a morgue." He remarked eventually.

"That's very rude." Drawled a female voice, with a Canadian accent, from somewhere over the other side. "This is my bedroom." Sometimes the Camino could be quite surreal.

In a lonely lovely clearing overlooking a wooded valley the simple cairn had stood, decorated with the scarves and shells of passing pilgrims...

Chapter Fifteen
Déjà Vu

On the way out of the town next morning there was the usual post mortem.

"Albert, you snored last night."

"No I didn't. I never snore."

"Yes you did. I hardly slept."

"Actually, Susie, you snored as well."

"Omigod, Vital! I didn't did I? I'm so sorry!"

"Not at all, Little One, it was only a little snore."

"There's no such thing as a little snore..." And so on, until they moved ahead and into the distance, joking, laughing, telling stories, while solitude and birdsong wrapped me round once more.

And this was the pattern which began to emerge. Every morning we walked together for an hour, or maybe two if the TGWU weren't mounting too strong a protest. Then I would drop behind to watch them become miniscule cereal packet figures in the distance, and the Camino would be mine for the rest of the day to walk alone or with other people as the opportunity arose. And every time I let them go I kicked myself for not saying a proper goodbye in case I didn't make it to the designated refugio. And every time I remembered to say goodbye I didn't, because somewhere deep down I knew that if I grew tired and allowed myself to stop at an earlier village I would never catch them up, and if that happened I might never make it to Santiago at all.

I'd worked out long ago in France that, given the eighteen kilometres I was doing each day, it was unlikely I'd finish the pilgrimage in the time available but I'd refused to think about it. Something would come up - and something had. The Camino is not a comfortable place, at times it is impossibly hard; if I had thought about it at all I had expected only the spiritual challenge and growth. That the physical challenge might be far greater, and its growth every bit as important, I had never even considered. If my daily goal - to catch up with the Musketeers - was helping me to meet this challenge why interfere with the system?

It was extraordinary to have gone from utter solitude to the familiarity and affection of a family in only a few days. I suppose I felt closest to Vital, the gentle wood carver with the dry sense of humour so like my Dad's had been. Vital whose mental barometer always exactly measured everyone else's moods and balanced them; who seemed constantly to be thinking about other people and how they were getting on. With his good-humour and his preoccupation with food, the original Musketeer he most closely resembled – except for his girth - was Porthos.

And no pilgrim, man or woman, could resist Albert's charm. He could swing from practical joker to thoughtful philosopher in a moment, and he was a true romantic. I have a deeply rooted loathing of sea travel born of chronic seasickness. But Albert's shiny-eyed description of approaching land after a month alone on the ocean, in a catamaran, was enough to make me want to give it a try, just for the sheer romance of it. Like all charming men, gentle flirting was part of his nature, but he had his own rigid demarcation lines. One night I drew the short straw (short, because he really did snore) and slept next to him. For all the good-natured banter and innuendo, exchanged as we were getting ready for bed, he nearly leapt off the mattress with embarrassment when he inadvertently touched my arm as he was dropping off to sleep. After all the nights of being cheerfully biffed by Vital, in and out of sleep, I found that amusing and rather charming. He was our Aramis.

Then there was tall, professorial Xavier who always made me think of Athos. With his ready smile and his devastatingly infectious laugh he could have us clutching our stomachs long after we'd forgotten why. But his life had been marked by tragedy; his elder daughter had been killed in a car accident a few years before. She was only twenty. And sometimes, behind his laughing face his eyes betrayed a deep sadness. Xavier, who never failed to offer the traditional kiss-on-both-cheeks when he got up in the morning, was always the last to turn and wave as they dropped out of sight along the path.

Since meeting Bernard I had noticed something about the French. As a general rule they don't hug each other much, but they kiss. They kiss every passing acquaintance - women kiss women, women kiss men, men kiss women (naturally) and men kiss men. But the secret is not to touch. You keep your hands firmly by your sides and you elegantly present first one side of your face and then the

126

other - it's as simple as that. But it's a vital part of polite social intercourse. Not to kiss a friend in greeting, however fleeting the moment, is almost as bad as cutting them dead. Xavier was meticulous. He would rise from his bunk in the morning (almost always below mine) and proffer his face to my semi-recumbent one. Albert, if I bumped into him on my way back from the bathroom, (by which time he would invariably be heaving on his rucksack) would usually get the ritual out of the way then. Vital was always pre-occupied in the morning, worrying about the route and everybody else's feet, and he usually forgot. It was often only as they were about to walk on ahead that I would say, "Au revoir, and by the way, Bonjour!" And this would send him into agonies of embarrassment over the rudeness of his oversight.

All this I considered as I trudged alone along the dusty gravel path to Tosantos. It made a huge difference when the ground was reasonably firm, even to feet shod with all the benefits of modern technology. To ancient pilgrims, walking without any shoes at all, the hermit Domingo's paved roads (Calzadas) and bridges must have seemed sent by heaven. It is small wonder that at the end of a life devoted to improving conditions, and caring for pilgrims, he was made a saint. Arriving at last at the Tosantos refuge - a tiny period cottage - I found a genial reception committee waiting, made up of three Spaniards whom I had never seen before in my life.

"Ah! The Englishwoman!" No need to explain myself then. They sat me down and explained in perfect English that a place had been saved for me by three Frenchmen who had then gone out.

"Out to pray?" I asked, remembering that it was Sunday.

"Well, I think they are doing their praying in the bar..."

The hospitallero however, being a lay monk, had gone to pray in the church. Juan, who spoke such excellent English, was only his stand-in. He proudly showed me his battered Volvo with its J registered English number-plate which he had bought during the two years he had spent working in London. Two years had been quite enough apparently. Chattering away, he led me up a delightfully uneven staircase to a low, beamed room full of vinyl mats of the gymnasium variety. These were our beds. Regarding them with a sinking heart, I was nevertheless touched to see that the space the Musketeers had left for my sleeping bag was now in the middle, rather than out on the edge as it had been before.

"You see, they have saved you a place between them," said Juan, evidently reading my thoughts. "They are your bodyguard, yes?" Queen Anne herself could not have felt more royally protected.

I found my bodyguard reverently downing a bottle of Rioja in the bar across the road. The village was empty, this being a Sunday, and very, very quiet. Returning to the refugio for our siesta, however, we were joined by a German cyclist who declined to return our greetings, launching himself instead into a flamboyant and gruntingly noisy exercise routine - as if thirty five kilometres had not been enough. We watched him from our mattresses, open-mouthed. Albert of course was incorrigible, and by the time he had run out of asides to mutter we were helpless.

I thought the refugio at Tosantos was one of the loveliest on the Camino. Small and pretty with low windows beneath a steeply pitched roof. True, it was basic, there were no beds and you had to hold the lavatory door closed with your foot, but it had a charm that was lacking in the forbidding monasteries with their large dormitories and rows of double bunks. Perhaps I loved it because it was so small - there can't have been more than ten people there at the most. When the gentle hospitallero sang a lilting Galician love song as he cooked our evening meal I was enchanted. Albert was less impressed.

"It was dreadful." He said uncompromisingly the next morning. But I think that was because breakfast was late and the hospitallero had locked the front door to stop everyone leaving before it was served. Well, he had warned us of that the night before. The Camino, he had said, should not be a race from one refugio to the next, it was a contemplative walk and should be treated as such.

From the birthmark below his eye I recognised him as Jose-Luis, whom Ignes had described as one of the last true guardians of the refugio system. He had rescued Ignes in León one winter when, starving, cold and on the point of giving up, he had arrived at the convent there. The monk had found him outside the door, and instantly comprehending his need had taken him in, fed him, cared for him and talked to him for several hours. It was entirely due to his gentle solicitude that Ignes had continued to Santiago. They had met again at Tosantos a couple of years later, where Ignes had been impressed by the lengths to which Jose-Luis had gone in order to accommodate a New Age Pilgrim who had not wanted to be separated from his dog – someone like the pilgrim I had met in

Ostabat. How different this was from the attitude of the municipal hospitalier there. I hoped that, if they were still walking, he and his dog would pass by Tosantos and rest there.

Supper was a communal affair round a huge table. Sitting next to us were a young Flemish couple who were doing the pilgrimage in reverse, from Finisterre to Flanders. One of the surprises of the Camino was its variety; from Ignes, merely crossing paths en route for Assisi, to the Returnees with their far-away eyes, and now this couple going backwards just for the hell of it, each one cast a completely different perspective onto the ancient Way of St. James.

If I had been Shirley Maclaine I would have been convinced that the Musketeers and I had visited Tosantos together in another life. Certainly, as I snuggled into my sleeping bag between Vital and Xavier, with Albert beginning to snore just beyond, I felt the most extraordinary sense of homecoming. I'm not claiming anything for this life or any other, I can only say that I have rarely felt so contented or so secure since I was a child and all was well with my world. Had I woken with my thumb in my mouth I should not have been in the least surprised. Much later, in Ponferrada, I met an American woman who told me about her motives for making the pilgrimage. She said that the idea had kept coming back, as it had done to me, no matter how many times she pushed it away. A Buddhist friend of hers had suggested that it might be that she had begun the walk in a former life but had not completed it. I told her about the feeling I'd had in Tosantos.

"Oh my!" She exclaimed, "I've got goose bumps all over me just hearing about it!"

The walk to Tosantos had been largely a boring path running parallel to the main road. This must have been the bit Frank-of-the-Log-Cabin had been talking about when he had described the Camino as a dull trek. But the following day was an enchanting walk through a wood along the top of a ridge. And here it was spring again. The trees were in bud, primroses lined the path and the cuckoo had replaced the nightingale. If Shirley Maclaine's pilgrimage had been a journey back and forth through the centuries, mine was turning out to be a journey back and forth through the seasons.

In the middle of the wood I found Juan dispensing coffee and advice in return for a donation to charity, a primus stove hissing invitingly on the bonnet of his Volvo. Like his English counterpart and namesake, he drove up and down the Camino looking for places where people might need something to cheer them up; the first pilgrims had passed him about seven o'clock that morning, he said. It must have been barely light. I asked him about the crowding on the Camino and he told me he had walked it three times, and always in winter. In winter, he felt, you could still find the old spirit, whereas nowadays it was ridiculous with everybody getting up in the middle of the night and racing madly for a bed in a refugio; that wasn't how it should be. But we both agreed that the popularity of the Camino, which I found difficult to understand given the stress of it, made it unlikely that the situation would change. He wondered aloud how I could match the pace of the Musketeers, and why I bothered to. I said I should have been glad to know, myself.

I left him and continued at my pace past a massive and moving monument to partisans killed during the civil war, reflecting that it couldn't have been put up all that long ago - it wouldn't have been there in Franco's day, would it? And why here, on the Camino? If only I could have understood the Spanish I could have read the inscription. Earlier I had passed another memorial, this time to a Japanese pilgrim who had died of a heart attack only a few years ago. In a lonely, lovely clearing overlooking a wooded valley the simple cairn had stood, decorated with the scarves and shells of passing pilgrims, some carrying touching little messages.

Eventually, the path dropped down through cool pine woods to San Juan d'Ortega, where the saint's tomb is housed in a crypt below the church. It's a weird experience, going down the stone stairs into the dark. You grope your way in and, as your eyes become accustomed to the gloom, a huge cross slowly shimmers into view on the wall in front, almost glimmering in a faint halo of light. That's all you see, but the effect is strangely haunting.

I was not alone down there; another pilgrim was also transfixed by the magic. Roberto had been a journalist covering arts programmes for Swiss television - and he certainly had the handsome, perfectly proportioned looks of a classic television presenter. Although he lived in Zurich he often visited London, and for him one of its continuing delights was the existence of the Tate Modern Gallery. Modern Art was his passion, and the effect of this cross, he thought, reminded him strongly of the light installations of James Turrell. We walked on together. He had been on the path thirty-five days, and one of the treasures of his pilgrimage which had begun in Le Puy had been meeting people, liking them and getting to know them in a matter of hours, but then (and here was the point) letting them go and moving on. Jean-Michel would have approved. I had first seen Roberto in St. Jean Pied de Port and been immediately struck by his charm and his fluency in several languages. Aged forty, he fell into an unusual age group for the Camino; most pilgrims seemed to be post-retirement or pre-career. Ignes had had strong views on this, blaming the decline in the spiritual power of the path on the average senior citizen's need for comfort.

"They are too frightened to give up their incomes." He had declared in disgust. "And so they wait until they have retired and have lost their sense of adventure. And so the spirit of the pilgrimage is being lost!" Perhaps he had a case, certainly those few in Roberto's group seemed to be the true seekers, searching for a new direction or motivation in their lives. Perhaps it was because I too felt that I was searching that I had been so immediately drawn to him. Being Swiss, it was no surprise to learn that his parents were from different nationalities. From his German mother, he said, he had inherited his love of art. It must have been from his Italian father that he had inherited his thick dark hair and luminous eyes.

Arriving at last at the refugio in Atapuerca - well it wasn't that late, only two o'clock in the afternoon - I found the air around my Musketeers crackling with irritation. Vital, usually so gentle and accommodating, tapped his watch and called out "At last!" Albert merely glared. Xavier, who had been posted out in the road to wait for me, told me they had had to put up with a lot of 'aggression' in order to save my bunk next to Vital. The place had been full since midday and a lot of people had been turned away. In fact it wasn't the last bunk, Roberto got the one on the other side of mine, but I suppose various couples might have wondered why they couldn't have taken both. Poor, long suffering Musketeers - I caused them such problems.

The refugio was what might be called 'atmospheric'. The roof hung low over the top bunks like the interior of a cowshed, rough and rustic. Well I suppose it could have been worse - it could have been thatch, it could have housed a million spiders - but it still felt claustrophobic. Albert found it charming, but then he was on a bottom bunk. All the walls ended at least a metre below the roof so that absolutely everything that went on in showers, lavatories or the reception area could be heard in the dormitory. I found the ambiance far from relaxing.

When the light was put out it became immediately apparent, from the noise, that Albert was already asleep. Sighs of exasperation could be heard around the room, and when somebody snapped it on again every other occupant was sitting up in bed glaring at his bunk. Waking him didn't help much either, the respite only lasted until he drifted off again. Poor Roberto was becoming desperate. He had told me as we walked that he hadn't slept properly for over a week, due to the snoring problem, and was wondering how he could carry on. Kiwi Chrissie had her own way of dealing with it.

She spent entire nights visiting each snorer in turn, waking them and politely asking them to stop - heaven knows when she actually slept. And that didn't work either because they only started up again as soon as they fell asleep. The only remedy, as I had told Roberto, was ear-plugs - and the right sort. Roberto's were foam - ah no, it's essential to have the waxy ones. The trick is to hold them in the palm of your hand until they are really soft then roll them into long, thin spikes which you feed into your ear canals as far as they will comfortably go, squishing the rest round the outer part of the ears. I had found that this method effectively blocked out about three quarters of the noise. I passed two nicely softened spikes across to his bunk in the dark, and in the morning his gratitude was overwhelming. I had also offered my spares to Xavier, who still professed not to need them even though he grumbled about Albert. As I pointed out, I hadn't been bothered by the canine disturbance at Uterga. But perhaps it was a macho thing.

It was unexpectedly cold in Atapuerca. I was amazed to find that over a million years ago prehistoric man should have wanted to settle there, but maybe everywhere was cold then. That evening the Kiwi Taxis had to trudge through snow to meet us for dinner after a spectacular thunderstorm had turned to hail and ice. They had only got to the village at all by living up to their name, ducking guiltily out of sight every time their car whizzed past anyone with a rucksack; they must have done the entire journey with their chins on the floor. But once having arrived in Atapuerca they had found a covetable room in a hotel. With a bath. Not for them anymore the privations of a refugio; this last supper was to be our final evening together and the Musketeers were desolate. So was I, come to that; on a napkin, Bronnie wrote the words of 'She'll Be Coming Round The Mountain' lest I forget.

Climbing the hill out of the village before dawn it was impossible to see how much of the snow was left. But it was cold, with an icy drizzle driving in our faces. I remembered Clive, my solicitor, ringing me before I left, to discuss my will; a comforting thought.

"It's cold in Northern Spain." He had pointed out before ringing off. "Take a vest." How very English, I had thought at the time. How very helpful, I thought now.

"Don't lose sight of us, now!" commanded Vital. "Stay close, at least until it gets light, or you'll get lost." Yes, well, it would be nice to be able to; that by slowing down they might actually help me to stay near them didn't seem to enter their heads.

As the drizzle cleared and the sun rose, the smell of the gorse was like wine. From the top of the hill, by a tall cross marking the Pilgrims' Way, I gazed at the path to Burgos descending and looping, like pale ribbon, over the intervening hills; far in the distance I could see the lights of the city twinkling in the dawn. But when we reached the suburbs, the sheer dreariness of another hour plodding through an industrial wasteland was enough to drain the energy from the most resilient of feet - and that morning the Puffed Foot Picket had summoned reinforcements. Now I was walking on two swollen feet.

Besides, I needed to pee. It was alright for Xavier up ahead nipping behind that lorry, but there were two brick-layers behind it as well and they might feel differently about a middle-aged woman relieving herself by their barrow. I caught up with Roberto just beside a handy bar, and together we dived inside. We'd have a coffee, we decided, and then we'd hop on a bus and be waiting outside the cathedral by the time the Musketeers arrived on foot. Just about every other pilgrim seemed to have had the same idea. Inside the bus it was standing room only and I really felt for the hapless commuters of this town, squeezed between rucksacks on their way to work. But what I had not bargained for was that the Musketeers might wonder where I was; by the time they found me, admiring the filigreed spires of Burgos cathedral, they reacted with all the irritation of anxious parents towards a wayward child. Chastened, I followed them into the tourist office, paid my euro for a pilgrim pass into the cathedral and wandered out to stand in the sun again.

"I suppose you really do want to go in?" Snapped Vital, stuffing into my hand the ticket I had left lying on the counter. "Really!" He scolded, "I don't know why we're all so fond of you. You cause us nothing but trouble!"

Villasirga with its multiple layers of stunning carvings over the church porch which is now a National Monument.

Chapter Sixteen
The Meseta

Burgos has an incredibly violent history. It was overrun by the Moors in the tenth century, and fought over throughout most of the eleventh, chiefly by the members of one Royal Family. That squabble led to the rise of El Cid, whose tombstone lies in the centre of the cathedral. The power struggle continued off and on for another three centuries until, in the fifteenth, Queen Isabella took over. By then the city was the commercial capital of Spain, and it was here that Isabella and Ferdinand received Columbus on his triumphant return from America in 1497. Napoleon occupied it, and Franco made it his headquarters during the Civil War. Despite the violence, however, it took them only a couple of hundred years to build the cathedral, which would become a magnet for the finest in Gothic, Renaissance, Baroque and Rococo art. The result is a veritable glut of wonder which is almost overwhelming. Richard Ford, who visited it in 1845, described it evocatively as a 'superb pile of florid Gothic'.

Certainly I found it too much to take in at one go. Some people recommend as many as six hours for a visit - though this would definitely interfere with a pilgrim's preoccupation with lunch - but even the fast-moving Musketeers reckoned to spend at least an hour and a half there. It is just an incredible display of beauty and skill which is all around you from the moment you enter. Everywhere you look there is something to take your breath away.

I ended up exhausted, and with a crick in my neck from standing so long beneath the extraordinary filigree of the Lantern Vault (built, incredibly, in 1568) staring upwards, open-mouthed. Indeed, as King Felipe II said, it is the work of angels not of men. Chapel after chapel is filled with marvellous carving, gilding and painting until one is quite simply sated with richness.

Standing outside again, gazing up at the thirteenth century sculpture of the Day of Judgement above the north door, I was reminded of Edwin Mullins' analysis of the sculptor's role. In a secular age grown accustomed to viewing religious sculpture as an historic art form, appreciated in that measure alone, it is easy to overlook its essential purpose which was to educate not only the illiterate local population but also the itinerant pilgrim population, also largely illiterate. Not only to educate them moreover, but to strengthen them in their purpose as they continued an increasingly arduous journey. Who wouldn't make an extra effort, I wondered, if they thought it would save them from the terrors of Hell so graphically illustrated there?

Burgos is still a landmark on the Camino, but once it was supremely important. Boasting more hospices than any other town, it even catered for pilgrims with special needs. In the fourteenth century there was a hospice dedicated to blind pilgrims, as well as three for lepers. Leper hospices were not unusual, pilgrimage being considered one of the few possible cures, but what was significant about Burgos was that one of them was situated actually inside the city walls. This seems to suggest either a sophisticated quarantine system, or a particularly enlightened attitude towards contagion on the part of the population.

After Burgos we began the climb up to the Meseta. Tim Moore hadn't liked the Meseta much, "miles and miles of nothing". Shirley Maclaine hadn't been keen either. The confraternity Guide had warned that it would be flat and boring. What absolutely nobody tells you is that the Meseta isn't flat at all. It's a plateau, certainly, but none of the villages (and there are more than a few) is built on it. They are tucked into hollows. This means that each time you come to one, and the Camino seems to pass through most of them, you have to drop down to it - which isn't too difficult - and then climb back out again which is a real pain. It's only amazing that no enterprising Spaniard has thought to set up a giant abseil system to bypass this problem, but then, all the enterprising Spaniards have probably set up bars in the villages themselves, to cash in on all the exhausted pilgrims tramping through.

We came to the village of Rabe de las Calzadas just at the beginning of the Meseta. Albert adored the refugio there because he got on so well with the friendly hospitallero - and breakfast was early. There was certainly a very warm atmosphere to it, with soothing music floating up the stairs, though from the Senora's looks in my direction I was sure she thought I was sleeping with all my Musketeers at once. There was just one problem with this refugio, and it was huge. There was only one bathroom for all three

136

dormitories, each of which housed at least eight or ten people, and that one room contained the single lavatory, shower and wash-basin for us all. Inevitably, this meant that the following morning the landing outside it closely resembled the central aisle of a jumbo jet, an hour after lunch on a long haul flight.

One of the characteristics of the Camino is that, although you may walk alone, you will be moving at the same pace as several other people with whom you will meet up every evening. It becomes rather like an extended family; having covered the same distance, everyone has that part of the journey in common. Certainly we four were a family, and an increasingly close one, but we were like Time Travellers. The speed at which we travelled meant that we were continually entering new pilgrim zones and every evening seemed to bring a complement of faces I had never seen before. Occasionally people like Roberto might catch us up, but usually we found ourselves on our own in a continually changing human landscape; and in Rabe this was more noticeable than ever, since we found ourselves among a group who hardly seemed to want to communicate at all - least of all in that interminable queue on the landing.

Following our shadows across the Meseta in the morning, the sun rising behind us, we discussed as we often did the reasons for making the pilgrimage. All three Musketeers were serious Catholics – Xavier had even been groomed for the priesthood when he was a child - so I was alone in not having a religious motive. Vital, who had done this twice already and had also walked alone over the Alps to Rome, had the simplest reason. He felt that to make the effort deepened ones faith, and that the gain was in the journey rather than the destination. It had been his idea to start out from Lourdes this time, with Albert, and before setting off they had spent a week helping invalids seeking a cure at the shrine there. In their rucksacks they both carried sheaves of requests for special prayers to be said at Santiago.

Xavier was a little like me. He had considered the pilgrimage from time to time, but for him the catalyst had been a labourer who had come to help him in the vast market garden where, before beginning his retirement a mere eighteen days ago, he had grown Lilies of the Valley to be sold all over France on the first of May. This man had mentioned casually one day that he was working to earn the money to buy a donkey which would accompany him on his pilgrimage to Santiago and this had so inspired Xavier that, the

137

moment he had retired, he had caught the train to St. Jean Pied de Port and joined his friends. It was strange - he had never before struck me as an impulsive person.

Predictably it was Albert who had the most complicated, philosophical reason. He had set out on his first pilgrimage, the previous year, partly out of curiosity and partly out of faith. He believed that what made the Camino a journey apart was the spiritual imprint left by thousands upon thousands of pilgrims over the centuries, and he felt that he had returned a better person. But the feeling evidently hadn't lasted because now he was off in search of that spirituality again; in fact, as he told me over and over again as we walked, that feeling was like the Holy Grail. But Albert had an Achilles heel in his obsession with time; he wanted to feel the influence of the path on his life, but he also wanted to get to Santiago, get it over, get his spiritual credits and go home – very like those superstitious pilgrims of the Middle Ages. He missed his wife and hated having to leave her in order to make the pilgrimage - so why hadn't he just brought her along? He claimed that she couldn't have kept up, which didn't come entirely as a surprise. I suspected privately that Albert's attitude to speed had a lot to do with the culture of masochism which lies at the root of the catholic attitude to pilgrimage. He claimed that the pace at which he insisted on walking was all part of the effort which brought the reward on arrival, and that it enabled him to free his mind; but that reason was clearly secondary to this need for his home and his family.

It was a pity, because the speed at which he walked reduced his chances of experiencing the interesting conversations which, for him as much as anyone, were a large part of the magic of the Camino. Jean-Michel, a veteran of several pilgrimages, had only managed to keep up with him for half a day and Albert had loved his conversations with Jean-Michel - he would have liked nothing better than for him to walk with us; but not enough to slow down, which I found rather exasperating. One evening, when Albert told me he was having a problem with the tendons in one of his feet, I wanted to cheer - perhaps now he'd slow down. But in an act of what could have been called Divine Retribution, it was my tendons which gave me grief the next day, his were fine. And to make matters worse my Puffed-Foot picket had been joined by a knee and an ankle. Although they allowed me through in the morning, they spent the day chanting aggressive slogans outside the cranial office where my will-power was continually involved in negotiations with the TGWU over whether or not to keep on walking.

But how could I stop when, reaching each refugio hours before me, the Musketeers would invariably save me a bed in their corner even if it meant paying for it, and would take it in turns to wait out on the road to make sure I didn't miss the entrance. Each time I arrived they would congratulate me hugely, no matter how pathetic my performance had been, and however hungry they might be they never went to eat until I had arrived. How, I asked my rebellious body, could I betray such camaraderie? And on one particular day they excelled themselves in thoughtfulness. I had made a tentative request for a stop - just the one - at a refugio with a washing machine; it had been the Confraternity Guide and the Kiwis that had alerted me to their existence. In Castrojerez Albert met me at the crossroads beaming with delight.

"You're going to love this one. It's got a washing machine and a tumble dryer!" After only two days Vital had managed to build it into the schedule as a surprise. It might have been Christmas.

But it was after climbing out of Castrojerez that my feet called in really heavy union support; my right knee threatened serious industrial action. The cereal packet Musketeers had faded to specks on the horizon, and the designated refugio at Poblacion was an impossible twenty-five kilometres away, when it finally brought all movement to a halt. There is also virtually no pee camouflage on the Meseta and my stomach had given notice, almost the moment the refugio door had slammed irrevocably behind us, that this was not going to be a straightforward day; in fact it was utter misery. But even through all the discomfort it was impossible to ignore the beauty of the Meseta; with its perfect emptiness stretching out to either side, it was like an infinitely calm sea whose green undulations met the blue of the sky on the distant horizon – though the path, it had to be said, was always stony and very, very hard on feet and legs. In a wonderful Camino moment I saw a woman in the distance walking towards me. A Returnee? But she had no rucksack. As she drew nearer I recognised her has a Parisienne with whom we had all had a long conversation in a bar in Castrojerez the previous evening. Drawing closer to me she flung her arms wide.

"Isn't this wonderful? Aren't we lucky to be walking on such a beautiful morning?" She called out in English, evidently remembering my nationality. Lucky indeed. As Xavier would have said, she gave me new heart - and a new determination to complete the distance that day. So, binding up my knee, I shuffled on over the stones and gravel; it was difficult but it was possible. Pilgrims passed me whom I didn't know, but evidently at least one of them knew me because by the time I saw my Musketeers again they had heard all about my knee, and the Camino Telegraph had warned them of my slow progress.

It was, indeed, many hours later that I hobbled into Poblacion and the care of Vital who was the nearest person we had to a physiotherapist. A retired baker, he now divided his time between wood-carving and organising long distance treks for vast groups of walkers; there weren't many walking-induced injuries he hadn't dealt with. He had a particularly nifty way with blisters; in his rucksack he carried a tin box inside which were a lighter, a stub of candle, a needle, some strong thread and a very sharp penknife. Having threaded the needle, and sterilised it in the candle flame, he would pass it through the dead skin of the blister. Then he would cut the thread, leaving the whiskery ends sticking out on either side. This was the trick because these whiskers would drip like melting icicles for about five minutes until they had completely drained the blister. Finally he would slap on a plaster, and that would be that until the next day when you could painlessly pull out the thread. That bit was crucial though - once I forgot about it for several days, by which time the skin had started to grow again and pulling the thread was anything but painless. But my knee was obviously going to be more complicated than a blister. Now he looked at it, his face grave.

"Sleep first," he advised, sleep being always Vital's panacea. "We'll make a judgement later." And collapsing forthwith onto his bunk, he began to snore.

But no sooner had I showered and climbed up to my bunk than a minor commotion in the doorway heralded the arrival of Hansi, a curly haired, exuberant German who was walking with Roberto. Hansi and I had a special bond since he claimed that my spare ear - plugs, passed on by Roberto, had transformed his pilgrimage. Now he was ecstatic.

"I told Roberto zat ve vill see somebody today, and zat it vill be Sussi. So ve heff been to shopping, end ve heff brought food and good vine to cook for you a huge meal tonight!" Waving his arms above his head. "Oh I em so heppy zet ve are here!" Behind him, Roberto leaned against the doorpost, looking quietly bemused.

140

"Amazing." He murmured. "It's as if he's clairvoyant."

Hansi's pilgrimage had been his fortieth birthday present to himself. As far as I could see it had been his present from his family and almost his entire hometown as well. The greatest financial outlay, for any pilgrim, was in buying basic equipment. So for his birthday Hansi had organised a huge party on a Spanish theme, for everyone he knew - which was pretty much everyone in the town – and instead of giving him presents, his guests had contributed to the cost of his rucksack and all its contents. Not only would this have saved him a huge amount of money, as I knew from my own empty bank account, but it gave everything he carried an extra significance.

The refugio was in an old school on the edge of the village. It stood in a delightfully unkempt patch of garden where washing and pilgrims were, respectively, hung out to dry and laid out to recuperate. Whilst Roberto chopped the ingredients for a vast risotto, Hansi a little unwisely showed off the prize of all his many treasures, his Ipod system - he didn't see it again for several days. As Roberto succinctly put it, after a month without music it had the soothing power of a joint. I had been offered an Ipod by the children, but had refused it because I had felt that it would intrude on the meditative aspect of the Camino. Much of the time it would have done, but there were times when, willing though the spirit might have been, it was all but impossible to keep the body walking. At those times, and the times when the feet, or legs, or shoulders were shouting with pain, at those times, as Hansi said,

"In zoze times I put on my music end pouf! I em zere, end I hev not notice!"

Before supper Vital took another look at my knee. He was not encouraging.

"This is not a slight injury. I've seen it before, and it could easily turn into something serious. You will have to stop."

"What, altogether?"

"No, not altogether perhaps, but for at least three days."

"Oh." I might have been back with Ignes, in St. Sever. Whatever would I do in this tiny village for three days?

"Give me your address before we sleep tonight." He said. "Then I can send you my photos when I get home. Because I don't suppose we will meet again."

The thought was suddenly unbearable. Evidently the time had come to broach the taboo subject of The Bus. When I had

141

mentioned, during that discussion way back in Larrosoaña, that if one were tired one could always cheat a little and take a bus for a day Albert had been uncompromising.

"That would ruin your pilgrimage. In fact, you would no longer have a pilgrimage." Nobody, I noticed, had disagreed, not even Our-Lady-of-the-Indignant-Nostrils, and the subject had never been mentioned again.

But the idea was not entirely without support. To console myself during that painful day I had sent a text to Peter telling him about my knee, and his reply had gone straight to the point:

'SO SORI ABOUT URE NEE. CLEARLY U MUST TAKE IT EZI 4 WHILE. BUT DON'T LOSE MEN! USE BUS 2 KEEP UP WIV MEN TIL NEE BETR. GOOD LUCK!

But would they feel the same way? Well, it was worth a try.

"I could... well... I suppose I could take the bus for a bit?" I ventured. To my astonished relief Vital hugged me.

"That's what I hoped you'd say!" He laughed, "We are a family now and it would be a pity not to finish our pilgrimage together." And immediately he began to work out my itinerary. To my even greater astonishment, Albert agreed to the plan as meekly as a lamb, and it was decided that I should leapfrog not only the length of one day's hike, but at least three - that I should, in fact, go directly to León and rest there for three days until they arrived. And get a haircut, they added. And so it was that I ended that painful day full of Roberto's risotto, and relief that there were to be no more goodbyes - for the time being at any rate.

~

It was very strange to see my Musketeers disappearing the next morning before I'd even got my boots on. I didn't set off to hobble the sixteen kilometres to the nearest bus stop, at Carrion de los Condes, until an hour later. By nine o'clock I had reached Villasirga, with its multiple layers of stunning carvings over the church porch

142

which is now a national monument. It seemed to me that the side wall was leaning out at rather an alarming angle, but no doubt the National Monument Authorities have this under control.

The knee was hardly protesting at all as I walked, and the feet no more than usual. I had to fight a sudden desire to carry on after Carrion, do the rest of the day and surprise the Musketeers at Calzadilla, their goal for that evening. But it was probably good for them to have some space. After all, they hadn't set out with the idea of dragging this slow moving limpet all the way from Larrosoaña, and it would no doubt be a relief not to have to guard my bed against all rival contenders, not to have to take turns watching for me at village crossroads or treat my injuries when I finally arrived. They could spend a few evenings talking freely too, without the constraints of my language difficulties. Not that they often bothered about that - sometimes I used to wonder whether I was there at all. One evening Albert had stood, his hands in his pockets, thoughtfully surveying the debris from my rucksack which littered the mattress on which I sat writing my diary. I looked at him, waiting patiently to hear what was on his mind, but eventually he had turned to the other two.

"Where does she sleep?" He asked in a voice of wonder. "Her bed's a tip."

"I know," agreed Vital. "But it's a funny thing, you know, however much of a mess it is, she's meticulous about putting her water bottle in exactly the same place when she goes to sleep. I've never quite worked out why." They never did ask my opinion. Anyway, they had given this scheme their blessing, so why not spend the weekend doing justice to the sights and tapas bars of León? The single day they had allocated the city wouldn't allow for very much at all.

After three hours I arrived at Carrion de los Condes. Finding the bus station, or somewhere to buy a ticket, was not a straightforward matter but then the Camino doesn't expect one to need this sort of knowledge. Walking had become painful again which made it more than usually difficult to find a safe place to cross the road. Considering that in Franco's day jay-walking was a criminal offence, the lack of pedestrian provision in the towns through which the Camino passed was always a puzzle. Though I noticed that this was never something which worried Albert.

"I am a pilgrim." He would announce, stepping blithely across the lanes of racing vehicles. "I am protected." By whom was never

143

entirely clear, but protected he apparently was. Traffic would screech to an exasperated and loud-mouthed stand-still, but nothing worse than verbal abuse ever followed.

Such audacity wasn't even an option for me though; it required a major effort, by then, just to step on or off the kerb, and if I inadvertently put the weight on the wrong knee at the time, the operation was likely to end in collapse. The few seconds allocated for crossing the road at traffic lights hardly allowed me to get past the first lane of the modern ring-road which circles the tiny town centre. In the comparative calm of the narrow alleys in the old town the pace was quieter, and here it wasn't difficult to appreciate how important the town had been in the Middle Ages since quite a lot of the architecture of that time survives. Strategically situated and agriculturally successful, it became one of the wealthiest in that part of Spain. It was a popular resting place on the Camino in those days, and boasted no fewer than fourteen pilgrim hospices.

Aymery Picaud was impressed for once, describing it as "industrious and prosperous, rich in all wine and meats and fruitfulness." It was also famous as being the home of the Counts (after whom it is named) who earned the wrath of El Cid by their mistreatment of his daughters, though I was never able to find out exactly what it was they did. Perhaps, had I been able to get as far as the hotel which used to be the monastery where their tombs were kept in the cloisters, I might have. But the TGWU's members had decreed otherwise. They did however let me poke my nose into the little church of Santa Maria del Camino, where the porch is carved with a mass of female figures arching over the door. These represent the hundred virgins which, according to legend, the province of Asturia was forced to send annually as tribute – or protection money – to the Moors, otherwise they'd come and beat the place up again. By 834 King Ramiro I had understandably had enough of this and took on the Muslim army at Clavijo just outside Logroño, and the legend of Santiago Matamoros was born. With the battle not going at all the Christians' way, the cause would have been lost had not Saint James apparently arrived at the last minute, on a white charger, and decimated the Muslim army single-handed.

It was in Carrion too, that I encountered one of the idiosyncrasies of the Spanish transport system. When at last I found the tourist office it was closed. I had come to expect this by now, and was not at all surprised to find a notice on the window directing all passengers to buy their tickets at the Bar Espagnol across the road, where I was told that the bus was full and that I would have to wait until the next day to travel the hundred or so kilometres to León. There appeared to be nothing for it but to buy a ticket for tomorrow and find somewhere to stay in Carrion that night. But when the bartender brought the ticket, although it said it was for tomorrow he told me in a conspiratorial whisper that it might be for today if I were to leave it to him - tapping the side of his nose for good measure. When the bus arrived (half an hour late) he bustled out importantly and crossed the road to speak to the driver. As I lugged my rucksack out to join him, he announced triumphantly that I had a seat and could leave immediately. Since the bus was only half full, and remained so for the rest of the journey, this pantomime seemed rather superfluous. I began to regret the tip I had given him for his trouble.

Crossing the Meseta was surprisingly frustrating. I really wanted to be there on the path. At one point I was sure I recognised the tee shirts of my Musketeers in the distance. Involuntarily, I found myself holding up a hand to the window in a silent salute which I knew they would never see, but which made them feel closer somehow. I would miss them over the next three days.

The maze of tiny streets which are today a mass of tapas bars and the haunt of scruffy pilgrims.

Chapter Seventeen
León

Arriving in León was as confusing as in any major city. Where was the city, anyway, in relation to the bus station on its outskirts? The directions in my Confraternity Guide didn't match any of the street names that I could see, but then the directions didn't expect you to arrive by bus. The hotels were either grotty or pricey, and I was temporarily barred from the refugio system by the length of time I planned to stay - the rules are strict, only one night allowed. Sometimes a second one might be granted, in cases of injury or illness, but unless you are lucky enough to find an empty one, as I had done in St. Sever, any more than that is out of the question. Eventually I found a hostel that was slightly less grim than the others in which to install myself for the pilgrim friendly price of fifteen euros a night. If I didn't have my own shower or lavatory, at least I had my own bedroom which was a luxury in itself.

Feeling cheated of the Meseta experience, I set out to compensate with a haircut and a search for some better looking clothes. Sartorial elegance never having been a pilgrim priority, it had worked its way even further down the agenda after a month of heat and grime. The pilgrims I saw all around me, having looked perfectly at home in the villages of the Meseta, appeared incongruously lumpen beside the self-conscious stylisti of León - and so, without a doubt, did I. One of the stranger phenomena of the Camino was the way one could go for days without seeing people who then just popped up out of the blue. Across the Plaza San Domingo I saw the cyclist who had unapologetically kicked me in the head in Estella - weeks ago, or so it seemed. I thought (and then thought better) of spitting in his tapas as I passed.

I chose the hairdresser for the cropped and razored styles in his window - I didn't want a blow-dry which I couldn't keep up. Extrovert and energetic, he was obviously used to talking throughout the styling process, but this was difficult without a common language. Clearly unable to work in silence, he compensated with expressive grunts of appreciation which rose to an orgasmic crescendo as the creation was completed. I emerged with a fluffy crew-cut which David Beckham might have coveted - it might have suited him better too, David Beckham hasn't got wrinkles on his neck. Vital had told me to go and get a doctor's opinion of my knee as well, but I soon gave up that idea. The hospitals were all so far out of the centre that an hour's walk or a taxi ride were the only options; I had already experienced taxi fares at Hagetmau and wasn't keen to do so again. Besides, a doctor might tell me to give up the walk altogether and I didn't want to hear that.

So I went to see the cathedral instead. León cathedral is breathtaking. You wander in and you stop. You stop because you are overwhelmed by the sheer impact of colour - well I was at any rate. Never in my life have I seen such spectacular stained glass; I thought of my mother passing through here years ago and wondered why she had never mentioned this. Perhaps she had forgotten, or perhaps she just didn't want to spoil the surprise. I knew that Albert preferred Burgos to León, judging it to be more splendid and more elaborately carved. Not that León is without its splendid sculpture - the porches alone are a superb feat of harmony and balance. But splendid and awe-inspiring though Burgos might be, I was far more deeply moved by this glorious, all enveloping rainbow.

The crypt beneath the beautiful Basilica of St. Isidoro, on the other hand, was a bit of a disappointment. It wouldn't have been if the tourist blurb hadn't gone a bit over the top by comparing it to the Sistine Chapel, albeit the Romanesque version. The impact of all those painted archways and ceilings (presumably endowed by Queen Urracca The Good) ought to be considerable, and it is. As an example of twelfth century art it's probably hard to beat - it's certainly elaborate. But in common with most painting of that period the characters all have that vacantly bemused, frozen stare and the movement is all in the clothes, never in the limbs. Actually there was one exception; one archway showed an agricultural activity for each month of the year which was worth seeing for the historical information alone.

Among the delights of the Camino are the people who travel always alone and resolutely do their own thing. Wandering back to the hostel I bumped into Pierre, who reminded me of Ignes in his solitude and rejection of contemporary comforts, and who kept popping up in unexpected places. I had last seen him outside Burgos

Cathedral, where he had refused to pay even the special fee of one euro for Pilgrim Entry, preferring to pass straight on to the Meseta leaving its treasures unvisited.

"A pilgrim of Saint James should not have to pay to enter God's house." He had insisted. He had a point of course, but how many modern pilgrims were truly 'of' Saint James? Now he told me that he had walked fifty-four kilometres in a day, in order to get to León, starting the last stage of the journey at nine o'clock the evening before. He had walked until three o'clock in the morning, wrapped himself in a blanket and slept beside the path until seven o'clock, and then carried on. Here was Laurie Lee's true descendant. Apparently he had slept rough all through the Meseta and the stars had been wonderful some nights; we passed tactfully over the nights when I knew he must have got very wet and concentrated on the romance of the others. And here was one of the paradoxes of the whole walk; there we were, my Musketeers and I, going faster than the speed of light - well the Musketeers were anyway, my speed more closely resembled the flickering of a dying torch, I was just walking longer days than they were. Anyway, there we were, leaving earlier and travelling further each day than most other pilgrims, and yet people we had left behind long ago kept popping up ahead of us, already in places as we arrived. Only the day before, in Carrion, I had all but fallen over Pedro-of-the-Dodgy-Knees, last seen way behind me as we struggled into San Domingo de la Calzada. And he'd been taking rest days.

Albert, when I taxed him with this, maintained stoutly that they'd been taking the bus but they just as stoutly maintained that they hadn't. I couldn't understand it, but when I questioned other pilgrims they merely nodded sagely as if it were one of the well known mysteries of the Camino. It did make me wonder, though, at Albert's obsession with speed. If it really didn't get us anywhere all that faster than anyone else, why bother? Though I could never argue with Albert's trump card, the Refugio Problem. For there was no denying that Ignes had been right; the Camino is becoming overcrowded though heaven alone knows why since it's no picnic whichever way you look at it. But by midday the refugios were often full, and had I arrived alone in the early evening, as I had done so often in France, I would have had the uncomfortable choice between sleeping outside, on whatever rough patch of thistle passed for a garden, or walking on (sometimes ten kilometres or so) to the next

149

shelter with no guarantee of a bed there. I was in no position to argue with Albert since it was thanks to the Musketeers keeping me a bed that I could arrive, often hours later, confident that I would be able to rest.

But Atapuerca had changed things for all of us; the experience had been salutary. Even though I hadn't been much more than an hour and a half behind them, the Musketeers had had to mount a tough rear-guard action to defend my bed. The time had come to change the system. In fact the Camino itself has changed; until very recently the refugios were free, or very cheap, and beds were allocated on a strictly first-come-first-served basis. But in response to the overcrowding dilemma, private refugios have opened; usually more expensive, and rarely much better equipped, they offer one priceless service in accepting bookings. So now in the evenings it was not only Vital who sat hunched over his map, muttering the names of possible destinations, these days Albert sat beside him, mobile phone in hand, ready to make our reservations – for all the world as if we were Camionettes. It didn't always work, either, and sometimes they had to change the length of the marches in order to fit in with the location of these places. I was not unaware of the reason. Left to themselves they could have worked the original system; it was to accommodate my pace that they had had to change, and I was well aware of how much I owed them.

I had been in León a day and a half when Roberto and Hansi arrived, having walked over seventy-four kilometres in two days. I was tempted - as I had been when I saw Pierre - to ask them what illegal substance they were using, and whether they had found it hidden among the tomato plants I had seen growing in giant greenhouses just before the Meseta. On at least one occasion, they told me, they had walked all night shoulder to shoulder, sharing Hansi's Ipod - one ear-piece each - to keep themselves going through the dark. It was good to take time with them, to eat tapas, to stroll through the quiet Sunday streets, to sit in silent contemplation in the Basilica of San Isidoro.

"The Camino doesn't give us many weekends." Observed Roberto dryly.

Roberto was interesting. He and Hansi had walked nine days together, but now he was ready to walk alone again. He had the same inner solitude as Jean-Michel. Both of them drew on the lessons and stories of other pilgrims, and of The Way itself, but kept the core of their inner resolution apart. In that way they always had the emotional independence to move on when they felt they had outgrown a situation. But Roberto was an unusual pilgrim; not only was he in the early forties age bracket, less common on the path, but he had the gift of being able to see, with an aesthetic eye, situations and personalities to which he responded simultaneously with his reason and his soul. This enabled him to take a more objective view, and to remain always a little apart.

I respected him for moving on, as I had Jean-Michel for dropping behind. But I hoped he wouldn't go too far out of reach. On the whole I had found that Jean-Michel had been right - most pilgrims were interesting, and of course we all had the Camino in common. But occasionally, if you were lucky, one would come along with whom you could share every wavelength. One of those was Roberto, with whom I had instantly felt the deeper bond that Ignes had anticipated weeks ago: "You will recognise the pilgrims who are on your particular journey - as I recognised you." We talked endlessly - and not only about spirituality or mysticism. The rich diversity of León invited discussions on every subject, right down to ordinary things like hair and clothes.

"What are you going to wear for your daughter's wedding?" He asked one afternoon, as we sat in the sun in the cathedral square.

"Dunno, really. I had something in Dusky Pink...?" (Remembering the saleslady.)

Roberto stared for a several minutes at the gargoyles before returning his gaze to the square.

"Perhaps it's just the way you describe it." He said kindly. He recommended Silver Grey; in the end we compromised on Aquamarine.

We shared the buzz and bustle of everyday León, pressing our noses like starving children to the windows of expensive shops. The Gallery of Contemporary Art was closed the day we went to look for it, which was frustrating because its courageous exterior raised intriguing questions about its contents. Built out of huge panels of primary coloured glass, it resembles nothing more closely than a giant children's play area - but its position, half an hour's walk from the historic centre, brings a splash of style to an otherwise drab urban landscape. And in the centre we feasted on the beauty and tranquillity of the city's ancient treasures. Roberto loved the cathedral; in fact he adored all of León, its cleanliness, its orderliness, the feeling you got that every part had been carefully planned. Well perhaps not every part - the cathedral square, for instance, wasn't opened up until the sixteenth century. Before then you wouldn't have had the feeling of spacious elegance that you get now. According to an inscription on the front of the cathedral it was opened up to provide an area for the 'judicial settling of public disputes'. Until then it had probably resembled the maze of tiny streets to one side, which are today a mass of tapas bars and the haunt of scruffy pilgrims. The atmosphere in these narrow alleys, and the little cobbled squares they lead into, positively hums with life; they are so much more vibrant than General Franco's main street with its smarter, relatively sterile, cafes and bars.

Roberto particularly loved the precision of the cathedral architecture and decoration - what he described as "the feeling you get that the very best and most secret techniques of the time were used." Even I could appreciate the clever way the flying buttresses were designed to take the weight of the roof, leaving the interior open and free of pillars; and it is precisely this clear, open space which creates the impact of all that stained glass. León Cathedral has more glass, in proportion to its stone, than any other in Spain; and in a practice unusual in the early Middle Ages, so they say, much of it is actually signed. Roberto had grown up in Lausanne, which also has a very beautiful cathedral.

"But Lausanne cathedral is dead." He shrugged. "I feel that this one still has much to say to me."

What it had to say to me was that there must have been one almighty fundraising campaign going on when it was built - and over a great many years. Take all that glass for instance, the Gothic methods for making stained glass made it an incredibly long and complicated business which must have been expensive - the blue glass alone having to be brought from Venice. And it was probably for that reason that mediaeval fundraisers used windows for tempting rich donors - the reward for their generosity being their portraits worked into the design. It must have been rather splendid to be able to point yourself out to your grandchildren, halo and all, as you struggled to keep them quiet during Mass.

In the Middle Ages a pilgrim's estate was protected by law for a year and a day. After that it was free for all - or for his successors, since it was assumed that he would have either died on the way or settled down somewhere and decided not to come back. I was fascinated to learn from Roberto that when he had contacted Les Amis de St Jacques in Switzerland, the discerning secretary of the association had warned him along the same lines.

"Be careful." She had said. "You may not want to come back. This may change the whole course of your life." Somehow I couldn't imagine anyone from the Confraternity of St. James being so mystical, but in Roberto's case the warning seemed well-founded. For him, León was like Odysseus' Lotus Island, the longer he stayed the less he felt like leaving.

In the evening I visited the cathedral again and this time a Mass was taking place. What is it about stained glass and statuary, mixed with organ music, which so catches the emotions and sweeps you up into the enchantment of the ritual? If you choose the right moment to view the rose window at León, the sun in the west beams the pattern down onto the floor in all its glowing colours. I didn't catch it, but a smug Dutchman was on hand to tell me what I'd missed. Emerging into the square I found Roberto hopping with impatience.

"Quick! Quick! We have just time to get to the convent in time for their service."

Oh lord, another? But after the richness of the cathedral, the bare cream-washed chapel and the soft singing of the nuns was like clear water after a heavy wine. Looking at them all, in the choir stalls they had occupied several times a day for goodness knows how many years, their gentle serene faces invariably crowned with a little quiff of grey hair peeping from under the veil, you couldn't fail to be struck by the timelessness of the ritual, whose participants wore the same clothes as the statues of those mediaeval forebears who stared down at them from their niches in the wall. The congregation of pilgrims was less well ordered. Not knowing quite when to stand and when not to we tended to follow the nuns' lead, some with more alacrity than others. The result was a sort of perpetual Mexican Wave, which rippled ridiculously back and forth along the pews for more or less the whole service.

After the service I said goodbye to Hansi who was moving on the next morning. Except that, as Ignes had told me, you didn't say goodbye on the Camino because, though you never knew when you would meet again, you knew that you probably would. Left behind, Roberto and I applied ourselves to re-testing all the tapas bars, in readiness for the arrival of the Musketeers. One aspect of Spanish life that I felt I could definitely get used to was their habit of throwing everything on the floor. Cocktail sticks, napkins, bits of food, everything. Down it went. And every so often they would kick everyone out of the bar, sweep the floor and let everyone back in again. The fastidious French recoiled in horror ('Dégueulasse!') but I thought it was rather mediaeval - our ancient pilgrim forebears would have felt at home; and at least we weren't having to sleep on straw. But even so, it tended to go against the grain of one's upbringing at first.

"Chuck it on the floor," advised Roberto, seeing me fingering my redundant napkin uncertainly. "They all do." And feeling rather like a rebellious teenager, I did.

The following day the Musketeers were due to arrive early, having walked the last stage from Mansillas de las Mulas nineteen kilometres away. This time it was I who intended to save their beds for them, and the problem that morning had been to decide how early I could decently turn up at the door of the convent, without inviting questions as to how far I hadn't walked? I had decided to wait until nearly ten-thirty, by which time the doors would be opening and, according to my reckoning, I would still be a couple of hours ahead of everybody else. So off I went to buy strawberries for Xavier, who had been gazing wistfully into shop windows in every village through which we had passed, ever since he had seen a Dutch couple working their way through a bagful at Castrojerez. A little before ten-thirty I lugged my stuff across the road to the convent steps and was a bit disconcerted to find a lengthy queue already formed; and at its head, marking the pitches of their absent owners, were three familiar rucksacks. I might have known it. I couldn't get ahead of them even when I only had to travel a hundred yards. However early had they got up that morning?

Already the competition for a bed was making itself felt amongst the early arrivals who had not, like the Musketeers, gone off in search of breakfast. I was interested to see that the most aggressive element was an English one. In Tim Moore's experience, the disagreeable voices were invariably foreign, but this one belonged to the only really unpleasant person I met on the entire pilgrimage. A dead-ringer for Magwitch, the convict in Great Expectations, his reply to a polite remark in some broken, Aryan accent: "I sink zere vill be enough bets for effryone here?" was so disagreeable as to invite a double take, if not a doubled fist.

"I've got a brain." He snarled, though quite where was not evident, "I don't need you to do my thinking for me." This exchange, taking place as it did on the steps of a convent where, traditionally, kindness was extended to all pilgrims, seemed to embody the altered atmosphere of the modern Camino. No wonder that veterans like Vital said that this would be their last pilgrimage.

Magwitch prowled through and around the otherwise patient little crowd with a sneer in which there was neither charity nor joy. His presence cast a malevolent shadow over what was largely a good natured reunion of passing acquaintances, not passed for several days. All the same, it was only ten-thirty in the morning and already so many people.

I knew exactly what Vital's first question would be when the hugs of welcome were over.

"Well, what did he say, the doctor? Can you continue?" I looked at him in silence as his expression changed from one of eager enquiry to resigned exasperation.

"You didn't go, did you?" Aiming a swipe at the top of my head.

"Well..." I could hear the whine creeping into my voice. "There didn't seem to be much point really. If he said I couldn't go on I wasn't going to listen anyway..."

"Women!" He exploded. "You are all so stubborn!"

Finally we were admitted to the refugio and allocated our beds. I wouldn't have been able to save theirs for them in any case since men and women were segregated, much to the annoyance of the Musketeers. How could they be sure now that I would get up in the morning? But had we considered history we wouldn't have expected anything else of a convent in this city. When San Marco's was the principal hospice in León the rules stated clearly that "It is a dishonest thing to have women and men in a single dormitory." The nuns were only obeying orders - though one wonders what the original Knights Of Santiago would have made of the dormitories in most modern refugios. Still, perhaps pilgrims were more partial to orgies in those days - the rules of San Marco's also limited the occupants of each bed to two. But in the event, the Musketeers needn't have worried about waking me up; in the convent the lights went out at ten o'clock in the evening, extinguished by some apocalyptic hand, and at six in the morning they just as mysteriously came on again.

It was in that dormitory that I found myself caught once more between the two poles of the Camino of today. On one side of my bunk was an idealistic German girl who shared her biscuits and raved, starry-eyed, about the joy of being among pilgrims. The one on the other side was occupied by an Italian woman who was lamenting all the belongings she claimed to have had stolen since leaving St Jean Pied de Port - even her knickers. "And they were such pretty, lacy ones."

Returning to the convent after a lingering lunch swapping our various experiences, I found trouble brewing. I had tucked a folded blanket under my mattress to raise my feet, as Dani had taught me. This did not at all please Sister Sarah, who seemed to be in charge of the pilgrims, when she did her round of inspection that afternoon. Pausing by my bunk she rapped out a few sentences to the knickerless Italian who appeared to have been conscripted as her interpreter. Apparently the blankets were for covering cold bodies, not for supporting parts of them, and if I didn't want mine for that purpose there were plenty of people who did. Protesting my predisposition to hypothermia I found myself hugging it as if it were the last lifejacket on the Titanic. After a steely-eyed stand-off she swept on out of the door, her entourage in tow, to harass someone else.

Two hours later I shuffled off to meet the Musketeers at the chapel for the blessing of the pilgrims; Roberto, who by then had de-camped to an hotel, had told me not to miss this but rather to my dismay it appeared that, before we were to be blessed, we were to be given a lesson in psalm singing by Sister Sarah herself. The result was rather like an ineffectual supply teacher trying to control a class of unruly fourteen year olds; everyone insisted on talking amongst themselves and frustration began to glimmer through the mask of professional serenity. Why on earth, I wondered, had Roberto recommended this? Eventually, satisfied or resigned to defeat, she opened the door to the chapel and we were admitted. Grabbing my wrist Vital marched us all to the front pew, which was well and good until the indomitable Sister Sarah started conducting the congregation. Since I had only intended to be there in an observational capacity I hadn't bothered much with the rehearsal, and now I hadn't a clue as to what we were supposed to be singing.

Standing as I was in such an obvious place, she was unable to ignore this subversive behaviour and her initial nods of

156

encouragement became severe stares in my direction. I had the unnerving feeling that at any moment she would rap on the pew for silence and make me continue on my own, to prove that I had been listening and I did my best to avoid eye contact. Far more touching was the little speech given by another of the nuns at the end of the service. Having said a prayer for our guidance and protection - comforting, even if one was inclined to scepticism - she went on to say that she had never been able to make the pilgrimage herself because she had devoted her life to God and to this Order. But a pilgrimage, she reminded us, was not made with feet, it was made with the head and with the heart; and in that sense she had made it many times. Roberto had not been wrong after all.

~

It had perhaps been a mistake to point out the window of his hotel room to the Musketeers as we crossed the Plaza San Isidoro at six-thirty the following morning. I should have known that it would invite a deafening chorus of "Au revoir, Roberto!" which resounded round the sleeping square. How we didn't get a torrent of abuse from every window I shall never understand.

The Camino descended through the old city towards the river, finally passing the imposing façade of the immense Parador San Marco, which nowadays is an extremely smart hotel. Long ago it was the headquarters of the Knights of Santiago and the principal of León's hospices, where many pilgrims would have sought shelter - not any more, though, not at the prices it now charges. The hotel stands beside the ancient bridge over the river where, since the twelfth century, countless pilgrims had passed before us. In the old days it would have led across the ravine into dense forests. Nowadays it leads into dense suburbs.

I stayed to watch the tiny figure of Pedro Mato come out with his female counterpart to strike the hour on the bell at the top of the Town Hall...

Chapter Eighteen
Survival

It took two interminable hours to climb out of Greater León, and after that there followed an everlasting stretch of flat heathland - presumably the tail end of the Meseta. Walking in that landscape was rather like those nightmares where, no matter how much effort you put in, you scarcely seem to move at all. The sun beat down mercilessly and the sandy track stretched endlessly ahead; it was like being on a perpetually turning treadmill. How on earth could I keep on pushing one foot in front of the other, knowing that there was still so far to go? How could I continue to withstand the temptation just to lie down by the track and die? Not that I would have been unique (except perhaps in the choice of location) I had seen enough monuments to twentieth and twenty-first century pilgrims to know that. The cemeteries for the dead lepers of the Middle Ages, those whose pilgrimages failed to cure them but got them on to a fast track to heaven all the same, might have been consigned to history, but the modern Camino is by no means reliably safe.

At regular intervals I had passed plaques and cairns erected to pilgrims killed on bicycles, or whilst crossing the road, or who had died of heat exhaustion or heart failure. One evening, the usual discussion concerning our arrival date in Santiago was interrupted by a Frenchman, well into his nineties.

"You talk about when you will get to Santiago." He said quietly.

"For me it will be enough *if* I get there." This was the thirteenth time he had walked the path. Why so many times?

"Because each time I do it," he replied, "I feel that I have cheated death for one more year."

I very nearly failed to cheat death for one more day that afternoon. I was plodding along, oblivious of everything except the track two metres ahead, when I arrived at an unprotected railway line apparently in the middle of nowhere; it seemed rather a dangerous thing to have crossing the Camino, I thought, picking my way over it - perhaps it was disused. I had barely cleared the rails when an express train thundered round the bend, knocking me onto my knees with the whoosh of passing air. Well it certainly served to wake me up, I positively pounded along for the next two kilometres on an overdose of adrenalin. Wondering shakily why there was not a forest of monuments to dead pilgrims at this point, I noticed a path coming in from the side further along; in my soporific state I must have completely bypassed a village on the Camino and taken an unwitting short cut down an unmarked track.

It was some considerable compensation though, after nine hours, to walk into Hospital d'Orbigo over the ancient bridge - a staggering two hundred yards and twenty arches long - by which pilgrims have entered the town since it was built along with so many others in the twelfth century. Of the many legends which surround it, perhaps the most delightful is the romantic story of Suero de Quinones, a knight of the fifteenth century. He was hopelessly in love with a lady, so the story goes, whose indifference to his suit prompted him to declare a tournament in which he proposed to fight off all comers on that very bridge. Presumably he hoped that she would be impressed.

The event was not only blessed but promoted by the king, and attracted knights from all over Europe; as it was coming up to St. James' Day, and a Holy Year into the bargain, one can imagine that there must have been a fair few pilgrims trying to get across the bridge as well. Among them was a nobleman called Gutierre de Quijada, who decided to take on Suero and was soundly beaten.
After all that, the victorious Suero decided that he had got over his passion for the lady, setting off immediately on a pilgrimage to Santiago to prove it. There he left a fabulous gold bracelet in the Cathedral, as a token of his gratitude. Gutierre, though, had a long memory, which was just as well since he had to wait twenty-four years to get his revenge; apparently the two men met, completely by chance, in a field where they promptly charged each other and Suero was killed. They seem to have taken their defeats very much to heart in those days.

Standing on the bridge today, it is not difficult to imagine a sort of Knight's-Tale-Meets-Camino, with pennants fluttering above colourful pavilions, knights practising for the lists, horses with their splendid harness, feisty female blacksmiths swinging their hammers, Heath Ledger on the bridge with his lance. Though I'd find it difficult to imagine someone as seductively wicked as Rufus Sewell making a pilgrimage, as Gutierre was, but there you go. The vast riverbed has long since dried up, but in every other way the town from that angle seems to have changed very little, which may be partly because motor vehicles are barred from that side. The more modern part is found further in.

The refugio, to my relief after the austerity of the convent, was brand new and modern, with lots of warm pine and brightly checked upholstery - Ignes would have been scathing. Clean and light, with lovely hot showers, it was owned and run by a charming artist who also offered short painting courses to anyone who was interested. At eleven euros with breakfast it was not bad value for a private refuge, though it was near the top end of the price scale. Not that private refugios were a modern concept in Hospital d'Orbigo, in Domenico Laffi's day there was no alternative. He wrote that the townspeople were so poor that he and his companions had to pay just to take shelter in their hovels. From his tone, it would seem to have been a practice with which he was less than familiar.

But after only a few nights on my own in León it was difficult to get used sleeping within the restrictions of a shared dormitory again, even in our usual formation, curled up on one of a pair of top bunks next to lovely, kind Vital, the other two snoring below. One lesson I had learned from the Camino was to regard solitude not as a deprivation, but as a luxury.

~

Walking down the hill towards Astorga the following morning, it seemed an incongruous looking town. As you approach it from the east, the only obvious characteristics are modern houses and building sites. High in the centre stands the old cathedral like an old fashioned toy fort in a nursery full of Lego. Just before climbing the hill into the city (they all seem to be on hills) the Camino crosses an ancient stone bridge over a stream, its original flagstones worn into dips by centuries of pilgrim feet. It was here that I got a third - and by far the strongest - sense of being accompanied.

It seemed to me that this pilgrim would have been a woman travelling alone, though in her time she would have had to have been considerably braver that I was to have done so. Together with my shadowy counterpart I climbed the winding hill towards the town where in past centuries pilgrims would have been given rest and care in as many as twenty-one hospices. Now there are only three. However overcrowded the modern Camino might feel, it evidently doesn't begin to compare with the mediaeval one in that respect. With all those barefoot penitents, not to mention the sizeable households who would have accompanied the wealthier pilgrims and the vast entourages of royalty - Hannibal is supposed to have done it with his entire army as well as his elephants - it must have been in perpetual pedestrian rush hour.

Toiling up the hill I heard clapping above me and looked up to see a lone woman sitting on the grassy bank outside a monastery, applauding. It was another example of the wonderful quirkiness of the Camino that someone, who perhaps knew how it felt to be walking alone and tired and hot, should devote a whole day to waiting to cheer on each pilgrim as they climbed that punishing hill. Whenever I compared notes at the end of that day, I found that she had been there to encourage each one of us.

In the eleventh century, Astorga was the site of one of the fiercest battles between Queen Uracca The Militant and her estranged husband Alfonso of Aragon. Apparently he got the worst of it, the fiercely passionate Asturians routing the Aragonese and sending them packing back to Carrion on the other side of the Meseta. The cathedral in which the Asturians would presumably have given thanks for their victory, however, isn't there any more. It was rebuilt in the fifteenth century and most of the decorative work was done between the sixteenth and eighteenth centuries. Albert thought it was beautiful, he told me later, but I found it all a bit ornate - perhaps I was tired or hot, or just cathedralled-out.

Had it not been midday when the place was closed, I should have preferred to visit the chocolate museum. The Spanish have been chocaholics ever since Cortez brought the first beans back from South America. Actually they weren't the first, Christopher Columbus had brought some back a couple of centuries earlier but nobody had taken much notice then. In the eighteenth century Astorga was particularly famous for it - perhaps it was chocolate that had kept the cathedral's sculptors and painters going - and even today the window displays of the Patisseries are particularly mouth-watering. I stayed to watch the tiny model of Pedro Mato, who is supposed to have fought in the battle of Clavijo alongside the ghost of Saint James, come out with his female counterpart to strike the hour on the bell on top of the Town Hall. Then I set off again to rejoin the path.

Beyond Astorga it stretched, white and blinding under the limitless blue sky. I wondered if Shakespeare had ever been to Spain.

If he had, one didn't need to look far to find the inspiration for King Lear's 'blasted heath' and it wasn't Bagshot[2] . The day and the way stretched ahead interminably in the heat. A pilgrim from Brittany caught up with me and insisted on walking with me the rest of the way to Rabanal. Useless to express a desire for solitude.

"It's much too hot to walk alone." He protested.

"What if you fainted or had an accident? How do you think I'd feel if I'd left you behind?" I hadn't realised that d'Artagnan had grown to look so frail, had the Musketeers shared his view we'd never have reached Santiago. The endless path stretched on and on; always another hill, always leading out of the shade. Only today filled with endless, inane chatter in a foreign language.

As I thought again of my pilgrim forebears I felt nothing but profound admiration - indeed, the cynicism with which I had originally viewed their motives began to feel a little misplaced. Who after all was the bigger fool - the one who believed devoutly in a heavenly afterlife and the pilgrimage which would ensure a place there, or the one who was finding out the hard way that curiosity was not a good enough reason for all the pain? The last hour of any day was always the worst.

You clung to anything that would help to keep your mind going, like a sign saying 'Wherever you are, keep walking!' which I found myself repeating like a mantra, or graffiti on a wall urging you to 'Smile!' or the breeze in the pine trees lining the path on the wrong side for the shade, so that you had to be content with just the sound; or the sight of a tumbling river, even though you couldn't stop to dabble your feet lest you arrived too late for a bed and had to walk still further. You would find yourself gasping out the words of a single verse of the naffest song you ever heard:

"And I will walk five hundred miles / And I will walk five hundred more / To be the one who's walked five hundred / Miles to fall down at your door / And I will walk five hun..." And so on. Just because you couldn't summon the energy even to try to remember the rest of the words.

This was not what I had envisaged. Before I set out on this pilgrimage I had seen myself in my mind's eye, sitting in restaurants through the midday hours, eating wonderful meals like Paella, which

2 Bagshot Heath in Surrey, notorious in past centuries as a haunt of thieves and highwaymen.

never ever materialised, or cooling off in babbling brooks of sparkling clarity.

Perhaps it was just because I was trying so hard to keep up with the Musketeers - but no, I rarely saw anyone doing these things. It was as if, by now, we all had only one thought with regard to Santiago: Just. To. Get. There. One morning as I trudged uphill out of a village, exhausted almost before the day had begun, I picked up a text from a friend of Peter's:

"RUMOUR HAS IT THAT YOU ARE PROGRESSING ACROSS SPAIN IN A SEDAN CHAIR CARRIED BY 3 HUNKY MEN. NOW THAT'S WHAT I CALL STYLE!"

If only...

Day after day I would stumble along through the afternoons, blind and soaking in the heat, rehearsing the conversation I would have when finally I caught up with the Musketeers at the refugio.

"I can't go on walking these long days." I intended to tell them.

"You can all go on ahead, and maybe I'll see you in Santiago and maybe I won't." Of course I wouldn't. I'd never catch them up. But invariably when I got there the welcome and congratulations would put it all out of my mind, and after a shower and a rest well... tomorrow would be another day. Wait and see. Today though, I was almost too exhausted to smile when I found Albert waiting at the crossroads - and how ever long had he been waiting? Hoisting my sweaty rucksack onto his freshly laundered shoulder, as he always did, he led me inside.

"Elle est morte! La pauvre petite!" He announced loudly to a dormitory full of semi-somnolent Spaniards who, it had to be said, didn't react with unqualified expressions of concern. We had walked seventy-five kilometres in two days, he told me, which in his book made me a 'Super Courageuse' woman - giving my shoulder a congratulatory shake. No wonder I only ever had that conversation in my head.

The ritual at the day's end never varied:
1 Take off boots and socks.
2 Wince
3 Sigh
4 Try not to inhale.
5 Empty pockets onto bed.
6 Lay out sleeping bag to allow down to puff up.
7 Ditto Pillow.
8 Take sponge bag, towel and shampoo off to showers, usually empty by this time.
9 After shower take all clothes worn that day to a sink and wash. (Very important this bit but even so they still smelled dreadful)
10 Hang out to dry in remaining sunshine.

Since losing that precious sock, drying my only pair in time for the following day had become a major problem. Actually, one day I had walked right over an abandoned sock in the pouring rain, too tired and demoralised to bend down and pick it up. I never saw one again. The Camino does not offer its gifts a second time.

By the time all this was done the Musketeers would be sound asleep and snoring well. I used to clear a space among the debris of my rucksack in which to sit, write or just stare into space, thankful to have arrived. Then just as I became relaxed enough to doze off, they'd wake up energised and ready to find a restaurant for dinner; they were brilliant at finding interesting restaurants, even in the unlikeliest of villages. In Rabanal, where the refugio resembled a caravanserai - built round a courtyard, milling with pilgrims, festooned with laundry and lacking only camels - they found a delightful terraced cafe, unexpected in a village until so recently abandoned. Xavier's French guide to the Camino gave full credit for the restoration of the village to the English Confraternity of St. James. It was since they had established a refugio there, apparently, that the village had come back to life and now boasted four restaurants and as many hostels. With typical modesty the Confraternity's own guide merely stated that they ran a refuge there.

It was in Rabanal, too, that the knicker snitcher struck again. Weight having been always the prime concern in packing a rucksack, I had chosen three pairs of the lightest knickers I possessed. Two were sensible, Marks and Spencer stretchy ones and the third, lighter still, was filmily transparent with touches of lace here and there. It

165

was this pair that I had rinsed out at the end of that day and which, when I went to retrieve them, were conspicuous by their absence leaving only an empty peg dangling in the gap between my camping towel and teeshirt. In shocked disbelief I went inside to tell the Musketeers of this outrage which seemed so out of character with the pilgrims I had met. Vital's reaction was to go outside to check the line for himself, his belief in my powers of observation never strong. Flamboyant Albert, on the other hand, marched majestically into the dormitory and ordered all the men to drop their trousers. I stared at him in astonishment. Why the men?

"Well I could hardly ask the women to, could I, Little One?" He replied. "I'd get arrested!"

Thankfully nobody seemed to understand the order anyway and I dragged him from the room; the knickers were never found. Albert insisted on regarding the incident as proof of the presence of perverts among modern pilgrims – most likely, he suspected, among the Camionettes. I suspected a more mundane motive, and for days I regarded with suspicion a particularly hefty German woman who looked as though she might well have coveted a pair of filmy briefs. Whoever took them, I never saw them again but it wasn't worth worrying over. All the same, I felt more kindly then towards the sad Italian woman who had complained of the same thing in León.

~

The full moon still shone in the sky as we stepped out into the dawn chorus the following morning. The heat of the previous day rising from the ground made the walking warm, even though the sun still lingered over the Kiwi Taxis now back home in New Zealand, and would do for at least another hour. The Race For A Space had been superseded by Beat The Heat which, like its predecessor, dictated a rising time well before it was light. After only half an hour I fell back, leaving the Musketeers to motor ahead on their amazing turbo-powered legs. But then, with the possible exception of Xavier, they never started the day with feet that screamed at them to stop; and even Xavier's usually got better after an hour. I once tried to explain to them the story of Hans Christian Anderson's Little Mermaid condemned to a lifetime of pain as if she walked perpetually on sharp knives, all for the love of a prince. The point being, of course, that for the love of three princes I was suffering three times the pain.

They thought it was a charming story but I'm not sure they understood its significance. At any rate it didn't slow them down.

That day I was rarely alone on the path for longer than a minute and a half. It climbed up and up between bushes of broom and heather, pilgrims behind and in front as if we were walking in some vast organised party. Coming round a bend in the hills I could see up ahead the village of Foncebadon, made notorious for its enormous, savage dogs, by Paulo Cuelho and Shirley Maclaine. Ignes, too, had said he had been attacked there, but the only dog I saw could barely be bothered to lift its head. In fact, on the whole of the Spanish Camino, I didn't see a single large dog roaming free who was the slightest bit interested in any passing pilgrim. Tethered or behind wire it was a different story, but then restrained dogs weren't a problem anyway. Today, Foncebadon seems to be largely a village of holiday houses. One or two ruins had For Sale signs on them, possibly hoping to cash in on wellheeled pilgrims who might be enchanted enough to come back on a regular basis. The place did have a certain dilapidated charm, but passing through is one thing; I wasn't sure I'd necessarily want to stay. Climbing up and beyond Foncebadon, the path crossed a wide heath. On all sides were hills and deep valleys, not unlike the Scottish Lowlands or the Lake District. And there, not far above, was the Cruz del Ferro - the Iron Cross - immensely tall, and standing on a wide cairn made out of all the stones brought from home by generations of pilgrims.

Originally, so it is said, the cathedral of Santiago de Compostela was built with the stones carried by pilgrims from this point. In time the tradition had metamorphosed into a penance (perhaps in order to replenish the stock) the stones coming to represent the sins which each pilgrim brought from his or her past life and laid at the foot of the cross before continuing, presumably with lighter consciences - certainly with lighter packs, to Santiago. Still more recently the stones have come to represent loved ones left behind or in need of help, similar to the letters from Lourdes that Vital and Albert carried in their rucksacks. A small path runs up the front of the cairn to the pillar at the centre, and here groups of pilgrims were standing to have themselves photographed.

I took out the stone I had marked with the names of my children, and was immediately submerged beneath a wave of homesickness; this had to be a private moment. I took it round the back, away from the cameras and the people, and buried it in a small hollow. Along

167

with it went two smaller pebbles from a Flemish couple at home. Originally, Regine had been going to walk with me - though given her pace and stamina it was more likely that she'd have been walking with the Musketeers - but Frits was dangerously ill and she hadn't wanted to leave him.

"There's no point in asking for prayers for him." She had said, her face tense with anxiety. "Because he doesn't believe in that. But perhaps, if you were to put these stones on that cairn on the hilltop - well, you never know, do you?"

So, trusting to whatever spirit might be watching over the place I placed a tiny stone for each of them alongside mine, and turned once more to the West.

The town is dominated by the ruins of what was once a magnificent castle, built by the Knights Templar on the foundations of what had been a Roman fortress.

Chapter Nineteen
Galicia

It was only because I set off immediately down the other side of the hill that I had my single solitary quarter of an hour on the path that day. Just below the top I passed the refugio of Manjarin; I got the impression that it is a place which has remained true to the hippie era of the Camino, certainly more to Ignes' taste than the Five Star Hotels which, he claimed, passed for refugios now. I had long since decided that Ignes' and my ideas of what constituted 'Five Star' were somewhat disparate. I had heard that sanitation was minimal in Manjarin, and that it was 'mediaeval' in ambience, though this would probably be less important were one to be making the pilgrimage in the winter. Juan had told me that it was one of the very few refugios to remain open all the year round and I could imagine how welcome it would be to arrive there after struggling over the hilltop in a snowstorm. A bell hanging in the porch was rung at frequent intervals by a wild haired woman, though it was not clear whether this was to give encouragement to passing pilgrims or to invite them to stop. I was tempted, but I passed it by - anxious to out pace the camera-happy hordes about to descend behind me. I was not about to trade solitude for curiosity that day.

The path which goes down from Foncebadon to Molinaseca, just before Pontferrada, passes through one of the prettiest valleys of the Camino. It is lush and green, full of tinkling streams inviting you to cool your feet, and broad, ancient chestnut trees offering you their shade. I wondered whether it was here that Shirley Maclaine had been woken by journalists and, ignoring them with singular self-control, had rolled over and gone back to sleep; it certainly could have been. It was a place that gently beckoned you, beguiling you to stop and doze, and I might have done just that had it not been under constant attack from pilgrims on mountain bikes, hurtling down the narrow path at breakneck speed.

Now serious signs of Camino Fatigue were beginning to show in various ways, like a complete mental blackout on all the places in which we had stayed. I would forget that I had paid the hospitalleros for my bed and try to force them to take a second fee - the Musketeers kept an eye out for that one.

"Of course you paid, you idiot, I passed you the change."

One morning, soon after León, I couldn't find my boots. It was salutary to notice the speed with which mistrust can take hold; before the incident of the knickers I would simply have assumed that I had mislaid them but now I immediately began to suspect that someone had stolen them. The Musketeers were calmly eating breakfast, oblivious of my rising panic.

"Albert, have you seen my boots?"

"No, Little One, I don't think I'd know them if I did."

"But you put them on the shelf for me! You know you did!"

"Did I? Well I can't remember." Another piece of toast. (Oh God! Oh God! Whoever had stolen them was walking further away with every minute, probably also wearing a pair of filmy knickers.) Vital got up slowly from the table.

"Let's go and have a look. Are these the ones? There you are."

As he passed me, sheepishly tying my laces, Xavier patted my shoulder.

"Bravo, Susie."

It was only later that I realised how perfectly this little exchange had encapsulated the character of each.

I wasn't so wrong to worry about my boots though - a few days later I met a pilgrim who really had had his stolen, albeit inadvertently. Eric was a diminutive Canadian who was walking alone, and one day he had gone to look for his boots after breakfast only to find that they had disappeared. Concerned, he approached the hospitallero who had immediately bundled him into his car (this had evidently happened before) and driven off at furious speed along the Camino. After bumping along for about two kilometres they had passed what Eric had described in wonder as a "simply enormous" woman tramping along in his tiny boots - one could only wonder that she hadn't noticed. They had both had to return to the refugio, sort out the confusion and start all over again, which must have taken a chunk out of the day.

Actually boots weren't the only things that Eric lost. Originally he had set out with two friends, but he had taken the wrong path on the second day and had never caught up with them again. He had a rough idea where they were though, thanks to a complicated telegraph system which involved them all diving in and out of phone booths to phone a mutual friend in Canada whose job it was to relay progress reports back and forth. By the time I met him he was becoming philosophical and had decided that maybe walking alone was the Camino's gift to him - he was certainly meeting more people. And this was perhaps one of the things that set the pilgrimage apart from an everyday hike - especially if you were walking alone – that you took all the people you met at face value. None of us knew, or cared to know, what sort of houses we lived in, where we worked or what our families or friends might be like. We were just who we were on the pilgrimage, and our thoughts on that subject were far more likely to be of interest to each other. I had noticed that people who started out in couples or groups never seemed to have quite the same openness and acceptance as those who walked alone - presumably because they brought their backgrounds with them.

Walking mostly alone, and knowing no more about the Musketeers than I had gleaned since our meeting, I counted myself among the lucky ones and my solitude was often rewarded by interesting encounters. In a convent-run refuge one night, as we were filing in to dinner beneath the reproving gaze of the saints in their niches, we were joined by a tramp who slid silently, and a little sheepishly, into a seat at the other end of the table. Though clearly the recipient of the nuns' charity, he was served by them as attentively as were we who had paid for our dinner, bed and breakfast.

The next day I was walking alone when I saw him again, his small mangy dog dawdling companionably along on the end of a bit of string, and learned that he claimed for himself the unlikely name of Bilbo Baggins. He told me that he had walked all over Europe and some of Africa too; he had followed the pilgrimage routes through Morocco and Ethiopia several years ago. I asked him about the fighting and bandits he must have seen, but he claimed to have encountered only kindness and hospitality. Well, with his matty hair and ragged clothes - quite apart from his distinctive odour - I didn't suppose that bandits would have found him worth attacking.

Small and wiry, with a wizened weather beaten face and a well-worn rhythmic stride, he gave the impression of timeless antiquity and absolute self-containment. Most of the time he seemed content to bumble along, conversing amiably with his dog, but every now and then he would come out with a sudden rush of information. He told me that he had given up walking, and had settled permanently in the Alps, until his brother had died in Limoges and he had gone to help sort out the family's affairs. Intrigued by all the cockleshell emblems he had seen in the town, which is on the Voie de Vezelay, he had decided to follow them and had arrived after a fashion on the Spanish Camino, by way of Rocamadour, Cahors and numerous other detours, all of which had taken him several months. But time didn't matter; he slept where he needed to, accepted charity whenever it was offered and, he claimed, only ever begged on behalf of his dog. And after Santiago, what then? I asked. He had no idea, he replied, he would simply keep on walking until the weather changed. I was reminded again of Ignes.

My encounter with Bilbo Baggins was interesting not only for its glimpse into his liberated world, but also because it revealed the prejudice I have found so often lurking in the French psyche. The musketeers were far ahead by then so they weren't involved, but another French pilgrim, who had been kind and friendly to me and had cared for me most solicitously one afternoon when I had been suffering from dehydration, took me on one side and warned me against talking to 'Clochards', adding for good measure that "His dog will undoubtedly be carrying rabies." I watched the animal snuffling happily amongst the undergrowth. He didn't look rabid to me.

Another phenomenon of this stage of the Camino was that I was becoming decidedly parti-coloured. Albert had warned me about this with the nonchalance of an old hand. Walking always west, your left side becomes far more tanned than your right. I had first noticed it several days earlier when I had stretched out both hands and been struck by how different they looked; they might have come from different bodies. The backs of your legs, too, get far browner than the fronts since you are walking with the sun behind you for most of the time. And it was indeed a long, hot, dry trudge through a flat, largely urban valley from Molinaseca to Ponferrada.

The town is dominated by the ruins of what was once a magnificent castle, built by the Knights Templar on the foundations of what had been a Roman fortress. Twenty years later they had abandoned it in the wake of the accusations of treachery, real or invented, which brought down the Order in 1312. Some stories say that secret information was hidden in the immensely thick walls before they fled, and that it remains there to this day. Wandering round the ruins, and reconstructing that time in my imagination, I was struck by the possibility that the Knights of Santiago had not, in fact, been an off-shoot of the Knights Hospitaller at all. It seemed just as likely that the Spanish Templars had adopted the name of Saint James, and the role of pilgrim protection, to save themselves from persecution after their Grand Master had been burned at the stake by the French in 1314. After all, the Scottish Templars had covered their tracks by becoming the 'Knights of St. Andrew', and the Portuguese had turned themselves into the 'Knights of Christ' to save their skins, why shouldn't the Spaniards have taken the same way out? The castle seems to have changed hands, usually by force, hundreds of times over the next half dozen centuries before coming under the rule of the Marques de Villafranca. More recently, much of its stone was carted away for building work in the town during the nineteenth century. It's just a ruin now, but a very romantic one all the same.

At the newly built refugio there was an influx of American voices. Well not an influx exactly, since they had been around all along, ever since they had left St Jean Pied de Port nine days before we had done; we had simply caught them up. It was good to talk easily again in my own language. Winston Churchill famously quipped that the English and American nations were divided by their common language, but here those disparities were offset by our common interest in the Camino. In a gesture which typified the generosity of the American pilgrims, a man I had known for ten minutes, as we talked in a café, dived into his rucksack and presented me with a pair of insoles designed to lessen the strain on my tendons; the TGWU was instantly mollified and reduced their demands for an immediate cessation of all movement. It was a surprise to find my approach to the pilgrimage being treated as something special. Hearing my story, his wife called over some friends who had installed themselves at a nearby table.

"Do you know," she asked in a hushed tone, "That Susie just set out from her house one day, and began Her Camino? Now, isn't that something?"

Remembering the benignly reproving gaze of Marion Marples at the Confraternity of St. James, I wondered whether I should explain that I didn't actually begin any 'Camino' until I got to the Spanish border. But it didn't seem to matter all that much by then.

Leaving Ponferrada I was hoping to visit the ancient gold mines of Las Medulas. According to Ignes, the Roman civilization had depended on the existence of these mines and others like them - the gold they had produced with slave labour being used to pay the armies which made and maintained the conquests. But mines have a way of becoming exhausted, and it was when that happened that the Empire had begun to collapse; the citizens of Rome had had no option but to take to the countryside and become farmers in order to survive. Thus it was that when the Visigoth armies arrived, so much smaller in number and far less disciplined, they were able nevertheless to conquer the once invincible Romans without any trouble at all. Ignes had told me all about this in St. Sever and warned me that the path to the mines would be a stiff climb, but in the end the climb was immaterial because I couldn't find the signpost.

But the Camino itself had taken on a new significance since I had seen the ruins of the castle at Ponferrada. Now I was not only walking in the steps of my mediaeval pilgrim forebears, but possibly following the trail the fugitive Templars had taken, fleeing towards the sanctuary of the Cathedral at Santiago de Compostela. How completely and how successfully, I wondered, had they had to reinvent their entire history and purpose in order to survive. And if, as Ignes had insisted, the history of the Templars went back far beyond the Druids, originating perhaps in Ancient Egypt, that would account for an influence on the path even greater than that of the Celts - it would enhance more than ever the importance of the stars above the route.

~

The following day my walk was enlivened and my solitude shattered by the presence, for the entire day, of the pilgrim from Brittany. He was kind; he massaged my knee, he filled up my water bottle, he sang me charming little Breton songs - he was never silent for a moment. After four hours it began to be irksome, over the next four I consoled myself by contemplating various ways of cutting out his tongue. He gave me warnings against eating cherries before they were ripe (because they'll be hard), instructions on how to identify unripe ones (because they'll be green) as well as observations on just about every passing blade of grass. He appeared to be of a rather nervous disposition because, with every car that passed - and there

174

were many - he jumped out of his skin, leaping to save mine by all but flinging me into the ditch. I felt guilty about weighing up the possibilities of avoiding him tomorrow, because at heart he had all the generosity and tenacity of a real pilgrim; it was not necessarily his fault that he was completely lacking in intuition. I had often seen him before but always in the company of Bertrand, a retired Legionnaire I had assumed to be his companion. He had only joined me that morning because Bertrand had left without him much earlier, apparently before he even woke up; airing this grievance had taken up most of the first hour. I wondered how desperate Bertrand must have been, but it wasn't until I caught up with him just before Santiago that I found out.

Not only had the poor man had to creep away in the middle of the night, but he had kept on walking for three days, virtually without stopping, terrified that the Breton might catch him up.

The problem was that if anyone were to make up their mind to walk with me, at my pace it was difficult to shake them off. Most of the time the conversation was welcome. If it flagged, or they got bored with the pace, they simply walked on ahead of their own accord. But the Breton didn't. Was Death-By-Conversation to be my punishment for past sins? The prospect of a second day was unthinkable and as far as I could see the possible solution lay in numbers, but could I persuade the Musketeers to stay with me as cover? That evening I cornered Vital by the washing lines and begged him to slow Albert down the following morning.

"Of course, Ma Petite Puce, but can you tell me why it's so important that you walk with us? Just so that I understand? Ah, I think I know. It is the Little Breton? He fatigues you? Yes?"

And there I had been, searching my mind for a translation for "gets up my nose". In their language, as with their clothes, the French can't help but display a natural elegance; it even made up for being addressed as "Little Flea". In the end, though, it was the Breton's own plans which came to our rescue. Like many people he had timed his pilgrimage to end in Santiago on a certain day - in his case the day of his Silver Wedding Anniversary. Eventually the penny dropped that this would fall nine days after we were due to arrive. So, after only two more tongue-biting days whilst he weighed up the pros and cons of sticking to his schedule, he decided to slow down and leave us to go ahead. No-one was more relieved than

Albert whose rapid-fire wit had found the turgid conversation frustrating in the extreme.

There really was no better feeling than the relief of arriving at a refugio at the end of a long, hot day. In this we were in complete accord with the ghosts of those ancestors whom every modern pilgrim - whether or not they recognised it - sought to emulate. We might be better shod and better fed, but their hardship was more than matched by the longer distances we walked each day. The sheer joy of a hot shower, clean hair and a halfway comfortable mattress was beyond price. And the refuge in Pereje even had clean sheets.

But now as we approached Galicia, I was divided inside. With less than a week to go before our proposed arrival in Santiago my feet were longing for the end of the walk, but my heart dreaded the end of the adventure. Always, as I had walked west, there had loomed in front of me the high mountain range, the Cantabrians, which in past centuries would have protected the region from the east. It had formed a sort of mystical watershed after which all the lessons of the journey might be expected to come together for the final stage. I always knew that it was impossible to reach Santiago without climbing up and over the other side but now the time had come to do just that, and we were woken by Albert at the terrible hour of five o'clock in order to get halfway before the sun grew hot.

It is a hard climb to O Cebreiro, twenty-two kilometres and always upwards, but it is also very beautiful. From the moment we left the refugio at Pereje we were accompanied by the sound of water. Everywhere. From the rushing and gurgling of rivers, with their tumbling waterfalls, to tiny cascades trickling over moss and stones beside the path. As you climb higher and higher the views are superb; dense, plunging valleys rise up to fertile hillsides folding one into the other. My heart loved it, my feet hated it. The path wound through villages where time and agriculture seemed to have stopped a century or more ago; ploughs were pulled by cattle and hay was piled in ricks. It wasn't entirely without modern methods though, in a paradox reminiscent of the modern solar systems installed on the roofs of ancient houses in the Himalayas, I came upon a heap of plastic-wrapped silage bales piled up beside a traditional haystack.

The Musketeers had long since moved ahead and I had been walking alone for quite some time. The steepness of the climb meant that there were long distances between pilgrims. But it's never a good idea to relax too much on these occasions since relaxation, especially combined with extreme fatigue, can make you careless. One such moment of blushing embarrassment was so dreadful it warranted the consolation of a text message to Peter.

JST DIED OF MORTIFICATN. WAS WKNG ALONE AN THORT WAS SAFE 2 RLEAS HUGE FRT AFTR WICH LOOKD BHND 2 C GORGUS SPANIRD NT 10 YDS AWAY. O GOD.

But where on earth had he sprung from, this man? He certainly hadn't been there when I had last looked over my shoulder, about five or ten minutes before. Scarlet-faced, I returned his smiling nod of greeting as he passed. And I sighed. There was nothing I could do about it now.

Trudging up at last to the village itself, I found the houses wreathed in a chilly mist. The refugio would not open for another hour and already a queue was snaking its way right round the building; O Cebriero is tradionally the place where Spaniards flock to join the Camino for the last hundred or so kilometres, the minimum distance needed to obtain one's certificate in Santiago. It is also the starting place for large numbers of energetic schoolchildren; presumably the ones whose exuberance contrasted so sharply with our weariness had arrived in the coaches which could be seen from the path as we had heaved ourselves up the final hill. Diplomatic relations between Spain and Rest of the World, or at any rate Spain and France, fell to a new low in the refugio at O Cebreiro. In fact it had all begun in Pereje, in the middle of the night when we had been woken by loud laughter and storytelling in the dormitory above us, which was occupied by a party of nocturnal Spaniards. At five o'clock the next morning Vital had gone to get his revenge by stomping upstairs to heat the water for his breakfast coffee, in the little kitchen thoughtfully installed in a corner of their dormitory. I could hear their protests from the bathroom in the basement, and would probably have been able to hear them from the other end of the village had I been there. Soon afterwards he had found himself propelled roughly out of the door and down the stairs. He wasn't happy about that, and he was even less happy about being deprived of his breakfast, but the full extent of his frustration did not become apparent until we were in the dormitory at O Cebreiro.

The queue for entry to the refugio had been a more or less orderly affair. In fact I never encountered any evidence of the shoving and elbow stabbing at the door, which Tim Moore's book had led me to expect. Inside though, it was a different matter. Two showers for a dormitory of twenty-four people does not perhaps seem a disproportionately meagre provision in the normal way; but when all twenty-four arrive at the same time, and when all twenty-four have spent an hour cooling to shivering point in a mountain mist after a long and sweaty climb, anything less than one shower each is going to seem sparse. It was clear from the moment I dropped my rucksack beside my bunk, that there was to be no careful unpacking of its contents if I wanted to get under some hot water before hypothermia set in, the queue was already forming at the bathroom door.

Albert and Vital, always near the front of any line, emerged, spruced and damp, to fling themselves on their respective mattresses. Xavier was still waiting his turn, and as I joined him the two people in front of him disappeared into the cubicles. Just before they emerged however, a Spanish woman calmly walked up and placed herself in front of me. Now, being British, I would probably have let it go quietly - after all, she was only one more person to wait for. But I had reckoned without the usually mild and gentle mannered Xavier who was having none of it, and who, when the first of the occupants of the showers emerged, immediately jumped in front of the cubicle and barred its entrance. In the ensuing and mutually incomprehensible exchange of views, it evidently occurred to Vital, watching from the vantage point of his bunk, that his friends were in danger of being deprived of their showers by the very same nation that had deprived him of his breakfast. Leaping down with a shout that said as much, he pushed his way through the queue and lifted her bodily out of the way as he planted himself solidly beside Xavier. Shoulder to shoulder they stood, these two normally gentle men, like a pair of particularly belligerent night-club bouncers, splendidly indifferent to the Iberian vitriol spitting up at them. Their adversary was small and determined, with a down-turned, malevolent mouth; her little gimlet eyes glared up at them with intense dislike; clearly this was set to turn into a battle of monumental proportions.

Almost the entire dormitory had gathered by now, and it began to be clear that they were fairly evenly divided between French and Spanish. Partisan opinions were beginning to be aired with ever increasing heat, and voices were becoming raised; any minute now someone was going to mention Napoleon and then all hell would be let loose. The only person not affected was Albert whose rest, once we had all safely arrived, nothing was ever allowed to disturb. He contented himself with calling out the odd translation over the din.

"She says take your hands off her. What on earth are you doing to her?"

Eventually the situation was saved by a charming and reasonable Spaniard, who emerged at that moment from the other cubicle. Omigod. The very same Spaniard who had been behind me on the road - was there to be no end to the mortification? Giving me a wry smile of recognition, he escorted the Senora firmly to the back of the queue replying to her protestations in her own language. Thus ended the bloodless battle for the showers of O Cebreiro, but it was a salutary reminder that in Galicia, especially among the new Spanish arrivals, a less dedicated type of pilgrim starts to appear.

O Cebreiro is a pretty village. Trading on its Celtic origins it's bound to be a bit of a tourist haven and there is plenty of incense and New Age music drifting from quaint souvenir shops; but there are also several superb specimens of the Palloza, the traditional roundhouse, tidily thatched and carefully kept. The best part of it is the tiny church which dates from the eleventh century. On this site, for over a millennium, every single pilgrim who has climbed that mountain - and there's no other way into Galicia on the Camino Frances - has stopped to pray and to give thanks, or simply as I did, to think. Although the original building was destroyed, and only rebuilt forty or so years ago the imprint on the area of all those lives, their hopes and their aspirations, is tangible.

It is almost inevitable that such a significant place should have a legend attached to it. The story goes that the chalice in the church was actually the Holy Grail. In the fourteenth century a peasant who had braved a terrible snowstorm, to climb up to the village for Mass, was ridiculed by the incumbent priest for putting his life in danger "just for a bit of bread and wine"'. Whereupon not only did the bread turn instantly to flesh, and the contents of the chalice to blood, but the statue of the virgin nodded her head in approval. The story spread wide, and earned the church the gift of a golden reliquary from Queen Isabella herself. Today the chalice is kept over to one side of the nave, but that is not where the extraordinary atmosphere, the spiritual energy, of O Cebreiro can be felt. I was conscious of it the moment I entered, though this could have been because Vital had tipped me off that it was a special place. If you pass that way, do go and see it. Ignore the people near the entrance who will stamp your Credentiale, you can get that done on the way out; keep your eyes on the windows at the end, walk slowly to the front and see if it hits you, as I felt it did me.

Galicia is perhaps the prettiest stretch of the entire Camino. Or maybe it appeared that way to me because it reminded me of home. Hardship apart, I loved all the Way of St James, the wooded hillsides of the Basque Country, the vineyards of Rioja, the emptiness of the Meseta. But Galicia is an enchanted land, a sort of microcosm of all those other places rolled into one. In miniature. The path that winds down through green valleys bright with yellow broom - in some places the height of trees - and through ancient woodlands, has sunk beneath the feet of centuries of pilgrims between banks bursting with life; it wasn't hard for me to imagine that I felt the spiritual imprint of all that faith. I walked through hamlets that time had barely touched, little more than clusters of farms where cowsheds opened onto the main streets, their occupants being driven out through tiny alleys between the houses as I passed. I can only say of Galicia, go and see it. And if time is limited, why not do what so many people seem to do and start out at León, just doing the last third of the walk. The oak and chestnut trees are joined eventually by the scent of Eucalyptus, and everywhere there are gurgling streams. Thatched and terraced bars with gentle celtic music tempt one off the path, especially in the heat of midday.

But if there was one problem with the pilgrimage through Galicia it was the enormous increase in the number of Camionettes. They were able to treat their few kilometres of the Camino as a picnic (which it most certainly is not) strolling along dangling the odd carrier bag, and of course out pacing everyone except the Musketeers. They infuriated Albert who could never resist making loud comparisons between their loads and ours as he passed. One of the requirements of any applicant for a Credentiale is to state their motive for making the pilgrimage, the usual suggestions being 'Religious', 'Spiritual' or 'Cultural'. On one of our morning discussions, before we parted company, we decided that for the Camionettes both 'Religious' and

'Spiritual' must be out of the question since they were effectively making the pilgrimage under false pretences. This was particularly true if they were staying in refugios which technically forbid any form of motorised backup. This left only 'Cultural' which I suppose is what they all put, though Vital swore blind that he knew of at least one man who had put down 'Gastronomic' and got away with it. None of us believed him though.

Just before Triacastela we caught up with a bubbly French Canadian called Carmen. I was always amazed by the number of people from Quebec who spoke no English, considering its proximity to the rest of Canada, though the Musketeers didn't notice because they didn't speak any either. Walking in front of Carmen and Vital, I overhead them discussing his proposal that we all continue the pilgrimage to Finisterre after reaching Santiago. She was asking his reasons for going.

"We are going to burn our little Englishwoman on the beach, in retaliation for what they did to Joan of Arc." He replied. The French really did take their defeats terribly seriously - Albert had never forgiven the English for locking up Napoleon - but forewarned is forearmed, and by the time we reached Finisterre I had negotiated the substitution of my sunhat and my remaining socks. Carmen didn't walk with us very far because the path divides for a time at Triacastela, and she wanted to take the route to Samos where the monastery was famous for its Gregorian chant. Roberto, up ahead, had sent a text message to say that the path itself was much prettier on the other route. The Confraternity Guide also said that it was eight kilometres shorter, so there was no contest really.

The next time I saw her was in Santiago, on her way to catch her flight home.

The hill is so named — Mount of Joy — because it is the place where, a thousand years ago at any rate, pilgrims to Santiago could see the spires of the cathedral a mere four kilometres away.

Chapter Twenty
The Mount of Joy

The refugio at Calvor stands out in my mind for having only one lavatory, which didn't lock, and cold showers. It was impossible to get warm there since we appeared to have left the sun behind on the other side of O Cebreiro, and it was also the place where one of Xavier's knees gave trouble, though being more stoical than I was he didn't think much of the bus idea. I lent him my stick for a couple of days and finally understood the instinct which had prompted me to take that particular one; Xavier's injury needed the support of a short walking stick rather than a staff, and all it took was a quick telescopic adjustment to solve the problem. As we climbed the hill out of Sarria after stopping for breakfast the next morning, we found compensation for all these ills; treading over a carpet of leylandii leaves and rose petals, left lying in the streets after a festival the day before, a delicious perfume rose through the cool air to refresh us.

If you are walking the Camino, and don't intend to stop at the refugio at Portomarin, it's perhaps worth knowing (well you might wish you had done, after you've climbed the steep flight of steps into the town, towards the end of a hot day) that the town itself, unlike almost all the others, is not part of the route - or not any more. Having crossed the Rio Mino you simply turn left and continue along the road until you cross a smaller river by the first bridge you come to. If you are feeling peckish however, you almost certainly will want to know that there is a rather good, if very scruffy, café just up the hill before you get right into the town, run by a wizened couple evidently well past retirement age. It's worth a visit for the entertainment value alone, quite apart from the food; you will not be treated with welcoming civility by the cook who will emerge from her kitchen as if you had just interrupted some important task which you probably have - but she will cook you an excellent meal from the vegetables which her husband brings, in constant supply, from the garden behind. One can't blame him for disappearing perpetually to dig up something else, since whenever he does come in she launches into what appears to be an exhaustive list of his shortcomings at full volume, whilst at the same time supplying an apparently endless stream of friends and relations, who turn up and take their places at the immense kitchen table to be fed. Their spit-and-sawdust bar, alongside the restaurant, doubles as a general grocery store, selling a limited supply of food as well as other bits and pieces - though you might have to wait until the end of a lengthy tirade to be served.

I had the Musketeers to thank for the introduction. They emerged just as I was struggling uphill into the town to tell me gleefully that I was going in quite the wrong direction, but that if I wanted to stop and eat they were off to bag me a bed in El Gonzo, so not to hurry. The rest was almost as delicious as the tortilla which overflowed my plate.

Once upon a time - well, until the 1960s to be exact - the Camino did run through the town of Portomarin, as it did through every other town. But when they decided to make a reservoir and hydroelectric dam to serve the region, the town was painstakingly dismantled and taken, stone by itemised stone, from its site beside the river to be rebuilt further up the hill. History doesn't relate where the inhabitants lived whilst all this was being done. It must have been done very carefully too, because the evidence doesn't hit you between the eyes as you walk across the enormous bridge; and it feels like a very long walk across, too, when you have already trudged all the way from O Cebreiro. This bridge has been destroyed and rebuilt countless times since it was first erected in the tenth century. A lot of the time this was due to the interminable wars between Urraca and Alfonso. When she was winning, though, Urraca did donate a pilgrim hospice to the town as well as rebuilding the bridge, though I don't suppose her version is the one I took so long to cross. Domenico Laffi thought Portomarin was 'a fine town', though of course he was looking at the one down by the river.

I had expected to feel fitter and stronger as I neared Santiago, and was more than a little disappointed to find that I felt increasingly weary and that getting up early was growing harder and harder. Mind you, some details had changed. Where in the beginning Albert would have woken me with a kindly kiss, and a whispered,

"Are you awake Little One? Did you sleep well?" Now all I got was a backhanded whack on the foot and a curt "It's time!" I confided this to Xavier one morning as we walked. Xavier habitually slept next to Albert.

"You're lucky," he replied, "All I get is a kick on the shin."

Well, familiarity has to breed contempt somewhere. In the end, though, it was not energy which got me into Santiago, nor was it ambition or even a spiritual uplift. In the end, as it was for most pilgrims, it was sheer bloody-minded stubbornness. And in Melide, where the showers were without privacy and the boiler threatened to shake the building to smithereens in the early hours, the spectre of the fifty kilometre day was raised. It was as well that Albert broached the subject at dinner because it was also in Melide that we first encountered Pulpo, a regional dish of Squid fried fast and served, sizzling and utterly delicious, on a cast iron platter; the idea is to pick at it communally, with little sticks, rather like a form of tapas. The area is also famous for its cloudy white wine which has a foaming head like Belgian beer and is surprisingly light and fruity, and between the two of them they did much to mitigate the general dismay which greeted the very idea.

The restaurant was an immense, barn like room where communal trestle tables shared floor space with sacks of raw ingredients, which from time to time were dragged off into the kitchens; I don't think there can be any jobs for hygiene inspectors in Spain. Between all these distractions Albert outlined his case for the hike to Monte del Gozo. The hill is so named - Mount of Joy because it was the place where, a thousand years ago at any rate, pilgrims to Santiago could see the spires of the cathedral a mere four kilometres away. It must have been pretty impressive to people who had braved untold dangers and privations for six months. It was also, argued Albert, a traditional and auspicious place for us to spend our last night together on the Camino.

The day got off to a bad start - five in the morning suddenly seemed impossibly like the middle of the night. We weren't the earliest risers, though, one tiny old man who looked so frail that a puff of wind might easily have blown him all the way to Finisterre and on out to sea, had left at four o'clock in the morning. As it was I nearly mutinied, and the only thing which stopped me was that I knew exactly what Albert would say.

"Fine." He would say. "You stay here then. We may see you later." And off they would go. Today as always, the decision and the responsibility for the pain which followed it were entirely mine. Even so it was extremely groggily that I staggered out into the dark, and despite their protests that we should walk together on our last day I dropped behind almost immediately. Behind, by miles.

Well, it might all feel better after some breakfast. Only, the bars in Spain don't open at five-thirty in the morning any more than they generally do anywhere else. Through village after village the path wound without hope of anything to boost the blood-sugar level. After four hours I shuffled into Azuar and almost past an unprepossessing transport café; but it was open, so what the hell... Inside were not only a warm, welcoming senora and a breakfast to sustain a trucker, but three surprised and familiar faces. They pulled up a chair. They cleared a space. They gave my order. They gave me a hug. And they decreed that from now on I would walk beside them. Actually, they had only been a quarter of an hour ahead of me; evidently I was not the only one getting tired. And so, for the rest of that long, scorching, draining day I marched in step with Albert the ex commando, and finally heard his story.

Parachuted into Algeria during the War of Independence to support the ailing government at the end of the fifties, he had been the subject of a feature in Paris Match after a journalist covering the campaign had been assigned to him. I could see why they had chosen Albert. Good-looking at sixty-five, he must have been stunning at twenty-one; extrovert, charming and with a formidable energy, I could only marvel that the journalist managed to keep up with him. After he had left the Commandos, he had gone into the motor trade and evidently done extremely well. He had kept a catamaran in the Caribbean and spent the best part of a decade knocking around that part of the world, until he lost it in a storm which culminated in a dramatic rescue by the American airforce. He reminded me a little of a modern version of Daphne du Maurier's buccaneer in 'Frenchman's Creek'. Returning from the Caribbean he had gone into the four-by-four car business, evidently with considerable success. True, he had experienced some of the downsides of success, such as divorce (a long time ago), depression and so on. But he had been married for thirty years to a woman he adored, and I couldn't help thinking that you'd go a long way before you could honestly claim that sort of success.

But why the pilgrimage? We had discussed the imprint of pilgrims past, and the vibes one picked up from the Camino, but why come back year after year when there were so many other places to see, and he had the money to see them? For Albert the pilgrimage was very

186

much a physical thing; in some dim, deep part of his Catholic psyche he felt that old compulsion to work one's passage to eternal life through suffering. Physical hardship was good for the soul - and for the body, he was as gleeful as the rest of us at the sight of his shrinking midriff. But he also felt that hard physical work freed his mind from dwelling on trivial problems. Hence the relentless marching, I supposed. By the time we were down to the last two hours of that interminable eleven-hour day, my reserves of energy had dropped to zero. We stopped at a drinks machine and bought Coca Cola.

"If you could just give me ten minutes to get going again, Albert..."

"You don't need time to get going. Just do it." Once a Commando, always a Commando. He was right, of course; if you did 'just do it', it 'just happened' and the muscles did get going again, but not that quickly. Inch by painful inch I crawled up the penultimate hill. Had I been aware that there was still one more to go, I seriously doubt that I would have.

Then something happened. Xavier reckoned it was the Coke kicking in, Albert was convinced it was the Virgin Mary. Perhaps it was the singularly telepathic text from New Zealand, which I picked up at that moment:

'SHE'LL BE COMING ROUND THAT FUCKING MOUNTAIN...'

Whatever it was, somewhere I heard myself saying, "Oh, sod it! Just go!" And from nowhere came the energy to march. And march. And march far outpacing my strapping Musketeers. I could hear them shouting to me from way back down the road, but to be honest I couldn't have slowed down had I wanted to; I was absolutely terrified that if I stopped now I would never get going again. Ever.

I shall never know where that spurt came from, but it carried me uphill through the last two kilometres to Monte del Gozo. It wasn't the first time I'd downed a Coke to get me through the last hour of walking, that was almost routine by then, nor was it a spurt of mere energy alone - it was energy mixed with more than a shot of exhilaration. There was a joy about the walking which I had not felt (certainly not at that stage of the day) in all the Camino. That's the bit I can't explain. But Monte del Gozo is, historically, a special place and one associated with euphoria; as I marched alone up the last hill it was not difficult to imagine the ghosts of past pilgrims cheering me in.

Once at the refugio, a giant complex built to accommodate the thousands who had thronged to share Santiago with Pope John Paul II in 1989, and strongly reminiscent of a Butlins holiday camp without the amusements, it took the Musketeers precisely one hour to break their sacrosanct promise of a lie-in till eight-thirty on the last day. Down by the washing lines, where all life-changing conversations seemed to take place, Albert had run into Bertrand who we had last seen in Hospital d'Orbigo, just after León. Predictably, Bertrand ran his pilgrimage with military precision and had been more than a little frustrated by having to queue for an hour and a half, the day before, to get his Compostela - the certificate which confirms the completion of the pilgrimage. That was too much for Albert who immediately began to re-sell tomorrow's plans.

"You'll still get a lie-in. It's just that we'll all get up at six-thirty, that's all."

Xavier and I looked at each other and promptly fell off our chairs; as usual, once Xavier started to laugh the hilarity went way beyond the joke. Albert was baffled.

"What's so funny?" He asked huffily. "You don't have to come. To each his own Camino. You stay here if that's what you want."
Oh well. Why change the habits of a lifetime – which was the length of time it seemed I'd been walking.

And so, hand in hand with my musketeers, I walked to the centre of the cathedral square and stood on the spot where so many of our pilgrim forebears must have stood down the centuries...

Chapter Twenty One
Santiago

We set off as usual with the sun rising behind us. It was impossible not to reflect back on all the mornings we had followed our diminishing shadows since that distant day in Larrosoaña; Gethsemane could not have been more poignant. This time there was to be no dual-speed Camino, the distance would be short so we would walk together. All the same, by the time we were marching through the suburbs of Santiago and into the city itself, Albert and Vital were well ahead, Xavier and I behind. Eventually they reached the entrance to a square where they turned and waited, holding out their hands.

"We began together," said Albert, "We finish together."

Oh heavens, then this was it! We had arrived. After all the sweating and the exhaustion, the loneliness and the exhilaration, I had finally walked to Santiago; all the way from home.

And so, hand in hand with my Musketeers, I walked to the centre of the Cathedral Square and stood on the spot where so many of our pilgrim forebears must have stood down the centuries, looking up at that vast portico flanked by its magnificent twin spires. And there, at the centre of their hugs of affection and congratulation, I dissolved into tears. They took this in their stride assuming it to be the result of an overwhelming sense of relief; actually, it was the result of an overwhelming sense of loss.

Of course no pilgrimage is complete until the statue of St. James has been visited and reverently kissed - best not to think about hygiene, and a hand placed on the pillar where so many hands have been placed, down the centuries, that the imprints of palm and fingertips have worn into the stone. It was irksome to have to shuffle in to do this behind a line of coach borne day-trippers, but modern Santiago is no longer the province of pilgrims alone.

We visited the reliquary in the crypt next, and here a final paradox dried my tears with incredulous laughter. All along the Camino we had discussed over and over again the religious motives for making the pilgrimage. Whatever our differences over degrees of spirituality there was one point on which we all agreed - that the legend of Saint

James was almost certainly a fabrication, a public relations myth concocted in the eighth century for entirely political reasons; the bones under the cathedral could have been anybody's. Yet there we were, gazing at an ornate gold box which, Albert informed me in an awed whisper, "contains the remains of the saint." I stared at him in astonishment, amazed at the way credibility shifts when the ritual kicks in.

But ritual can be a powerful emotional driver all the same. During the thanksgiving Mass for the safe arrival of the pilgrims, the organ music thundering through the cathedral, the timeless vestments of the priests, the long gold cross formed from a sword echoing the ancient connection with the knights of Santiago, and the immense silver censer, all combined to cause a painful lump in my throat. At a nudge from Vital I looked up to see the vast container being slowly lowered on the pulley by which it hung suspended from the arching stone roof far, far above us. Once lit, it took the combined and synchronised strength of eight burly men, uniformly caped in maroon, to haul it into motion. Gently at first they pulled, as a thin plume of smoke curled out and up into the space above, then suddenly and in perfect unison they hauled hard and fast lying flat on the floor; the weight pulled them upright and down they hauled again. And again. It was breathtaking to watch.

The giant, filigreed thurible, on it's immensely long rope, swung high into the distant arches of the vaulted roof along the length of the transept, and back low over our heads - impossible to resist the urge to duck - and on up, up, up to the roof on the other side, the incense now a dense cloud billowing all through the body of the cathedral. And through it all the organ thundered Bach, above which soared the clear, pure voice of a single nun. Eventually, as the music and the container together slowed and sank, one of the team pulling on the supporting rope broke away, strode swiftly into its path and caught it with an action that swung him full circle to a burst of spontaneous applause.

Then it was out into the sunshine and time for the Fruit de Mer for which Santiago is famous, and souvenir hunting. Even Domenico Laffi noted that, having knelt and given thanks to Saint James, he and his companions had made the inevitable shift from pilgrims to tourists. It was time for friends, too; like Bunyan's Celestial City, Santiago seemed to be full of all the people I had met and lost along the road and all with stories to tell. Roberto was there and Hansi falling over his broken English in his eagerness to share his experiences. Two very reserved and genteel English ladies stopped me in the street and asked what the pilgrimage had been like. Was there any privacy? They wanted to know. What were the sanitary arrangements like? I could appreciate their concern, but there was a sort of grim amusement to be gleaned from watching their faces slowly blanch at the list of privations which by now were part of everyday life. After all, I had lived them - it was just astonishing to think that they were nearly over. Nearly, but not quite.

Parting from Albert, early the next morning, was saved from turning maudlin by the knowledge that Vital and Xavier were stamping impatient hollows into the steps in front of the refugio. All our combined powers of persuasion had been insufficient to entice Albert into continuing with us to Finisterre; but what felt really weird, after all this time, was leaving him of all people having a lie-in before going off to catch his plane. He had bequeathed me his water pouch, since we had no idea how many water fountains we would find after Santiago, and I always felt that I slowed them down by forever needing to refill my little bottles. With much tutting and huffing he stuffed the thing into a pocket of my rucksack; it took several litres and felt awfully heavy, but I was touched by the gesture. Gulping hard - there were to be no tears this morning - I bent to kiss him and walked away down the dormitory. When I turned back to wave from the doorway his eyes were closed, and a sound suspiciously like a snore was already coming from his bed.

The rest of us set out rather like Tolkien's diminished band of ring-bearers, off to seek our spiritual fortunes at the end of the world. In a sense the religious aspects of the Camino end at Santiago. The journey on to Finisterre has an older, more pagan significance; it was, after all, literally the end of the known world in the days when the earth was thought to be flat. It was a sacred place to the Celts, and the Romans apparently used to make special journeys to the rocks on the clifftop, just to watch the sun sink off the edge of the earth into the sea; and now we, too, were setting out to walk the remaining hundred or so kilometres, just to stand on that north-westernmost tip of land.

I think I had imagined that the land between Santiago and the coast, over which the marble sarcophagus of Saint James is improbably supposed to have been dragged, would appear from the air to undulate gently to the sea; I had certainly expected that it would be roughly downhill all the way. In fact it descends in a series of ridges covered with eucalyptus forest, each of which imposes a cruel climb, even after forty-five days on foot. The TGWU, alarmed by the news of my continuing pilgrimage to Finisterre, had called up a major reinforcement during the night; I had woken to find, installed and ranting on the picket line, the Arthur Scargill[3] of the anatomy The Sciatic Nerve. All day it had continued its tirade, whipping the other members of the Union into a frenzy of chanting, "Can't Go! Won't Go!" orchestrated in precise unison. It was taking more and more reserves of will-power to resist them; fortunately this was a short day.

At Negreira the new refuge was modern, light and pleasantly furnished with plenty of honey-coloured pine. It would have been even nicer if someone had got round to installing the boiler. Xavier, in the shower room next door, claimed to know the exact moment I was hit by the freezing water. So, he maintained, did the whole of Galicia. It was at Negreira that we caught up with Bertrand also on his way to Finisterre. He had survived a notoriously tough career in the Foreign Legion, but with scars. He might have presented himself as a battle hardened soldier who concealed his emotions, but walking back to the refugio from the town after dinner I came upon him standing under a tree listening to music floating from a window. A woman's voice was singing; a low, sobbing, passionate gypsy sound.

"This is my kind of music." He said, and in the lamplight his eyes were wet. But the next minute he was gone, striding ahead, and the incident was never mentioned again. Much later Roberto told me that, having retired from the Legion which had been his family and his life since he had joined up as a teenager, Bertrand had made a disastrous marriage to an extremely beautiful woman; the subsequent divorce had left him penniless and homeless, sleeping rough on the streets, until he had decided to do the pilgrimage in order to make some sense out of what had happened. I think that by the end he had found again the camaraderie which must have disappeared along with his career - he certainly looked a lot happier by the time we reached Finisterre.

3 The leader of the British Mineworkers whose barnstorming rhetoric precipitated the Mineworkers Strike in 1974 which brought down the Conservative government. He tried – and failed – to use the same tactics to bring down the government of Margaret Thatcher in 1984.

Looking up from an involuntary fit of coughing at bedtime that night, I found Vital watching me narrowly.

"You're getting tired," he said, (No. Really? Well, what a surprise!)

"Take the bus tomorrow. It's fifty-two kilometres in any case, and if we walk at your speed we'll never arrive." And I thought that sort of pressure had disappeared with Albert - well, there you go. But it was somewhat comforting to find that Xavier too was 'getting tired' and quite fancied the idea of a rest. So it was decided; Bertrand and Vital would walk, and we would take the bus, get there early and bag the beds. All so simple.

I'd always been impressed, when I'd had the leisure to observe it, by the quiet efficiency with which Vital and Albert got themselves packed and ready to leave in the morning. Whilst I, cringing, woke the whole dormitory with polythene rustlings and cracklings, diving under strangers' bunks to retrieve escaping objects, they silently rolled and pressed and in five or ten minutes all was done. Bertrand was in another league - all those stealthy marches behind enemy lines had left their mark; I swear I saw only three quick movements from the time he sat up in bed to the moment when, staff in hand, he was leaving the room with his rucksack on his back.

The next time I awoke the sky was streaked with the grey of dawn and a fleet of tiny fishing boats was chugging past the rocks below the lighthouse.

Chapter Twenty Two
The End Of The Path

I have just two pieces of advice for anyone contemplating the trip to Finisterre. The first is, if you are in any doubt about doing it on foot don't do it; the journey is far from straightforward and after Negreira it's hardly waymarked at all.

The second is, if you are in any way inclined towards travel sickness don't even think about it unless you are prepared to walk there and back; the journey on the bus is grim beyond belief. After an hour of careering queasily round bends and up and over the tops of switchback hills I could take no more and had to get off, dragging bewildered Xavier after me. True, it can't have helped that Roberto had a hang-over and was being copiously sick into a transparent polythene bag just across the aisle, but the driver's erratic style had a lot to do with it. It was no comfort at all to note that the only multilingual information offered to passengers was a notice on one window announcing the existence of a book of complaints. There and then I made up my mind to walk back to Santiago if it took the rest of my life; I had my own counter-argument to Arthur Scargill now, in the ensuing negotiations with the TGWU my heaving stomach was more than a match for the Sciatic Nerve which caved in and agreed to the plan without question.

If however you do make the journey, on the third or fourth day you will come upon a lonely refugio hidden in the woods high above the coastal village of Corcubion. With only ten kilometres to go to journey's end you may be tempted to pass it by. This would be a mistake. It will be worth putting your head round the door to see if there is a young, dark haired and velvet eyed hospitallero inside, called Antonio.

He welcomed Xavier and me in what had obviously been a schoolroom in a previous life, but which he had made welcoming with huge bunches of wild flowers. As the place filled up with a mix of pilgrims that would have done credit to the UN peacekeeping force but which, to our concern, did not include Vital and Bertrand, he cooked us what was possibly the filthiest meal on the entire Camino. But his personality more than made up for his culinary shortcomings. The first half of the evening ran rather like one of those games you see at the Comedy Store where one participant, the Foreign Expert, talks incomprehensible gibberish with huge passion, whilst another, the Translator, makes what he wants out of it. Thus we had Antonio musing and enthusing with tremendous vivacity, smacking his lips, rolling his eyes and kissing his fingertips in ecstasy, whilst a lugubrious Swiss who spoke everyone's languages translated.

"He's talking about a sandwich."

An unlikely accountant from Burgos, Antonio had lived all his life close to the path. Listening to him, I began to understand how it must feel to grow up with the Camino in ones blood. It was a surprise to learn that he had never walked it himself, though he regularly gave up two precious weeks of holiday to run this refugio.

"I could do the Camino and meet some peoples, but here the Camino brings all peoples to me, and all are interesting." He explained in a rare attempt at English. Was this because the people who made the decision to walk on to Finisterre were more interesting? Yes, he thought so because, while Santiago marked the end of the religious pilgrimage, anyone continuing on to Finisterre was searching for something deeper than religion; something more primitive, further inside themselves.

"And in going to Finisterre," he continued, "You are following the sun. And when the sun sets into the sea, that is like a death. You die there. But, when the sun rises again, it brings with it a New Life."

Was this what made me want to sleep out on the Cape? Perhaps. Originally I had intended to bivouac all along the path, but it had never happened. At first, when I had suggested the idea to the Musketeers it had been met with blank stares of incomprehension. Why would you?

Later, when beds became harder to find and to hold, I had suggested it again to Xavier who had been unequivocal.

"Non!"

So I had appealed to Vital, always the most reasonable of the three.

"What, like a little pig you mean? You want us to find you a pigsty is that it? Hmm?"

So I had dropped the subject, only grateful that Albert had been walking too far ahead to offer his opinion. Now, I could have said that this pilgrimage had cost me an arm and a leg (I don't know about the budgets of people who regard it as a cheap holiday but I hadn't found it to be) and a great deal of the money had been spent on a bivouac bag that I had carried all the way and never used. But whenever the subject of bivouacking at Finisterre had been mentioned they had been uncharacteristically silent. I suppose they didn't think I would be their responsibility by then.

So Xavier and I chewed our way on through a barely edible meal, still wondering what had become of Vital and Bertrand. It was a surprise to learn when they found us again the following morning that Vital, that ace navigator, had got lost. In the end they had checked in to a smart Five Star (really Five Star) hotel on the seafront down the hill, whilst Xavier and I, who will never forgive them, passed the second half of the evening in an agony of mortification, after a party of jolly German pilgrims had insisted on a postprandial sing-song.

The idea, which appalled both of us, was that everyone should entertain the group with the songs of their respective countries. Fortunately they were so delighted with their own voices that we got away with only a quick burst of 'Alouette', which we sang out of tune and were forthwith excused.

Breakfast in the refugios had usually been a fairly muted affair. Vital was always quietly cheerful, Albert chafing to be off, Xavier and I moaning about our feet. The memorable exception had been Bob Marley's voice belting out in the immense kitchen at Estella. Here in Corcubion it was gentle celtic music. The celtic connection is strong in Galicia. They play the bagpipes; a lot and loudly. And the first glimpse of the Bay of Finisterre, as the Camino descends towards it, is reminiscent of the sort of small fishing village one might expect to find on the west coast of Scotland, only with sunshine.

The path that morning dropped gently through the pinewoods towards the sea giving us, as we descended, tantalizing glimpses of secluded little coves far below, where the waves whispered over the deserted sands. Nearing our journey's end we walked at a comfortable pace which had lulled even my TGWU into soporific silence. Roberto had told me that, of all the lessons the Camino had taught him, the most important had been to do with his walking pace.

"You find your rhythm in the first few days," He had said, "But the trick is to hold on to it. If you want to cover longer distances you need to walk longer days rather than step up the pace."

It was a lesson I didn't need to be told, as it happened, having begun to learn it even before he had left Le Puy en Velay, where his pilgrimage had begun. From the anger-fuelled march to La Reole, so long ago, to the morning on which I had attempted to match Albert's pace as we had climbed back up to the Meseta after leaving Castrojerez, both my injuries had been the result of trying to walk too fast. The exception had been the unprecedented spurt of speed which had come from nowhere on the last climb to Monte del Gozo - but Monte del Gozo is a special place, and the one where I had had the keenest sense of encouragement from pilgrims past, and evidence of their spiritual footprint, so perhaps that was the reason I had got away with it then.

Having compared notes on our experiences of the previous evening, nobody seemed inclined to talk as we walked that morning, in marked contrast to the jokes and stories of all the other days. It made a difference walking without Albert's irrepressible wit, of course, but perhaps we were all preoccupied with our own reflections on the journey we had made – I know I was thinking over all the days we had walked together, and trying not to think of the moment soon to come when it would all be over as we arrived in Finisterre.

But the village of Finisterre was not the final leg of our journey. Rather spoilt by tourism it resembled a minor coastal resort at any point in the British Isles, it streets dotted with ice cream vans and souvenir shops. The beach, however, was deserted and strewn, as it has been from time immemorial, with cockle shells – the symbols of Saint James and the Camino. Tradition dictates that each pilgrim takes one home as a memento of their journey. I picked up as many as I could hold – and then put them back when I discovered how heavy they were. They were all small ones though, not a patch on the magnificent specimens, four or five inches across and ready-strung on leather thongs, which I had seen other pilgrims buying in souvenir shops. The beach must have been plundered for centuries, to judge by the number of churches and refugios which have rows of shells cemented into the walls of their porches.

This was a huge disappointment, especially having looked forward so long to the traditional moment when, like all those pilgrims from ancient times, I could wade into the sea and pick out my own shell – my true credentiale – to hang round my neck. I had seen a video in one refugio which showed the waves gently lapping on the shore, washing in loads of lovely large shells; but they, of course, would have been planted by the props department. I was turning to go when a gentle little wave rippled past, washing up a small shell to nudge against my bare foot dabbling in the shallows. Bending down and putting my hand in the water, I felt around to pick it up and found that beneath the sand it was in fact a beautiful shell, a good five inches across and perfectly shaped. Here it was – the proof that I had finished the journey, just waiting quietly for me to notice it. I put it carefully in my rucksack and turned with a singing heart, to follow the Musketeers – who had, as usual, completely disappeared.

Hurrying down the cobbled village street to catch them up - they wanted to get to the tiny church in time for Mass - I was pinioned from behind by a pair of anonymous arms. It was Hansi. Seeing us passing, he had rushed out from the bar in which he was eating, to greet us all. It was good to exchange news and to compare notes on our respective journeys since Santiago. He told me that Roberto had found a flat down by the harbour and was planning to stay for a few days "to rebuild himself spiritually" after his journey. He would tell him I had arrived. Then he went back to his lunch, and I went on to the church marvelling at the rolling friendships of the Camino; an hour later we began the long climb up to the rock below the lighthouse, which is the furthest point and the true finishing line.

And there at the world's end, I finally said goodbye to my Musketeers. They had brought me to the end of the path and had encouraged and nurtured my determination to finish. It was tempting to go back with them to Santiago, and continue on the train with them as far as Bordeaux. But quite apart from my dread of the bus it seemed better somehow to part company there, on the Cape, than in some noisy, crowded railway station. And somewhere deep down I felt that I should end my pilgrimage as I had begun it, alone.

I watched their backs disappearing down the hill as I had done on so many mornings, confident always that I would find them again in the evening. But this time there would be no reunion. No shouting and waving, no running to relieve me of my rucksack. What, I wondered, would I do without my daily morale fix of congratulation? How would my vanity cope with only my own esteem to bask in? But it was more than that, and it was only then that I realised how important they had all become. Left alone among the day-trippers I went and found a deserted rock high above the sea, where nobody could see my tears, and sat down to wait for the sunset. They had said it had been a privilege to walk with me. I wished I could have found the words - in any language - to tell them how much it had meant to me.

"Remember O Cebreiro. It will give you strength." Vital had whispered as he had hugged me for the last time. In time he was right; the memory of that little, hilltop church, with its extraordinary energy, did bring a new strength to my life. At that moment though it only deepened the longing to run after them, to cling for a little while longer to the relationship that had been my life for almost a month. Always they had been there for me. No matter how late I had arrived, the welcome had always been the same. Always they would congratulate me, hug me, and always they would recoil politely and push me towards the showers - though lately I had noticed Vital passing on the hug and going straight to the push. And always, cleaned up and smelling sweeter, I had had the delight of their collectively irrepressible sense of humour at dinner. I had expected it to feel strange watching them go, but I had not expected this searing sense of loss.

As the sun began at last to dip towards the horizon, Roberto and Hansi arrived to ease the aching loneliness and to share the sunset. Intuitively, Roberto had waited until the evening, giving me time to come to terms with the confusion of emotions; and guessing that I might not have eaten for several hours they had brought food. Hansi had also brought stores for my walk back to Santiago; torn between gratitude and apprehension I watched him as he stuffed my rucksack with tins of this and bottles of that, how on earth was I going to carry it all?

Roberto had been told that the sunsets at Finisterre were among the best in the world, and certainly this one was spectacular. As we watched the sky turning red above the sea, fading upwards to gold and finally to aquamarine we discussed the pilgrims we had met, and he told me something of the background to the Little Breton's journey. Having worked all his life in the asbestos industry, the Breton had been recently diagnosed with Cancer. He had wanted to make the pilgrimage before he became too weak to do so, and it was for that reason that he had planned to spend his Silver Wedding walking into Santiago all alone - well, at any rate without his wife beside him, to ask Saint James for help. So that sort of faith still existed then. I hoped he wouldn't be alone, though. I hoped he would have found someone kinder than I had been to walk with him.

Remembering my less-than-charitable exasperation as he had walked with me I could feel my face turning as crimson as the sun.

We watched that sunset for what seemed like hours, until it was completely over and the night wind began to whip across the Cape. Roberto and Hansi stayed until the first stars came out, then hitched a lift back to the village with the last of the day-trippers. Left alone I spread my bivouac in the lee of a rock, out of the wind, whilst far below, the sea moved gently like silver silk in the dusk. I pulled my mosquito net over my head and fell asleep as the light faded. Waking in the dark some hours later, there didn't seem to be many stars about; I could only see half a dozen which was a bit of a let down as this part of the journey had always seemed rather important.

Eventually I got fed up with the mosquito net and pulled it to one side - and caught my breath. There they all were. The stars of the Milky Way. Thousands and thousands of them, stretching back to eternity.

It was also absolutely freezing. Bernard had given me an aluminium survival blanket as a last minute present, and now I rummaged for it in my rucksack, my fingers turning to ice in the dark. With difficulty I stuffed it inside the bivouac bag, there seemed to be an awful lot of it, and wrapped it round myself like a lumpy cocoon. Uncomfortably, I dozed off again. The next time I woke the sky was streaked with the grey of dawn, and a fleet of tiny fishing boats was chugging past the rocks below the lighthouse.

Sitting up I turned my head and saw, beyond the hills across the bay to the east, the red of the sunrise bringing the new life that Antonio had talked about. Hastily I stuffed everything into my rucksack (no need to pussy-foot around trying to be quiet out here) and went to stand on the spot where I had said goodbye to my Musketeers the day before. All alone this time I watched as, with a sudden and colossal burst of light, the brilliant yellow orb appeared above the skyline.

How my Mum would love this, I thought. She had a lot of time for symbols. When I had left her she had been so excited for me, buoyantly looking forward to my coming back and telling her all the things only a pilgrim would have seen. With a pang of guilt I reflected that I hadn't rung her as often as I could have. I'd written her a couple of letters though, and I would go to England just as soon as this was over, and tell her all about everything. She was going to love this story.

It was another three hours before I learned that she was dead.

And so I never walked those last few days alone. My pilgrimage ended at a bus stop in a tiny fishing village on a remote corner of the Galician coast. I had come to the Camino expecting to encounter loneliness and fatigue, and I had done. I had never expected to have to deal with grief, and yet here it was in double measure.

The pilgrimage had at last come to be about letting go.

Suddenly the walking pace which had been my life for nearly fifty days changed to a frenetic one of racing taxis and barely caught planes. As so often happens, the grief and bewilderment were overlaid by farce, with me going in one direction and my rucksack in another, trains which didn't stop when they said they would and armed guards searching my filthy belongings for contraband. All of this culminated in the noisy chaos of Toulouse station in the early hours of the morning, where I was buttonholed by a disturbingly unkempt woman, apparently homeless, who insisted I take her home with me.

I had been sitting, slumped with exhaustion, on my rucksack outside the station, wondering what to do next, when I heard her voice.

"Hellooo?" Followed by a question in French. I took the easy way out, which wasn't entirely a lie.

"I'm sorry, I am English. I don't understand much French." It didn't work.

"Oh zat is no matter, I speak excellent English!" She said, settling herself down beside me.

She was enormous. Two bulging carrier bags contained her belongings and she wore a long, grubby cardigan and skirt, beneath which poked an immense pair of Doc Martins. Her dyed black hair was piled on her head in a huge beehive which would have put Marge Simpson to shame and she smelt, if it were possible, even worse than I did. She was on her way to Carcassonne, she said, but could not get a train until the next day.

"What will you do now that you cannot take your train?" She asked. She must have been hanging around the ticket office when I had rushed in to buy a ticket, insisting tearfully that there must be a train which stopped this side of Paris before tomorrow. Wearily, I told her that a friend was coming to fetch me. Ever dependable, Bernard had not hesitated when I had rung him. He would come right away, he had said, but I knew that it would take him at least two hours to get there.

"Ah! When your friend comes, perhaps he can give me a lift to Cahors," she suggested. "The hospital here is full of jerks. They threw me out this afternoon. The hospital in Cahors is much better. They will let me stay."

It was perhaps a measure of my exhaustion that alarm bells didn't ring, this sudden reversal of her destination, from a tourist resort in the south to a medical institution in the north, not even appearing strange. Instead, remembering how much the kindness of strangers had meant to me over the past few weeks, I said I was sure he would; after all, it couldn't be that hard to find the hospital in Cahors. But why had she been in hospital? I asked. She had difficulty walking, she said, and she also had a problem "Here!" grabbing my hand and thrusting it energetically into the space between her thighs. I was grateful that her skirt was a long one and difficult for her to heave up in order to demonstrate further.

"Perhaps the hospital will be closed though." She went on.

"If you will take me home with you for tonight, you could take me to the train in the morning." Still the alarms didn't ring. Instead, I merely reflected that it would be perfectly possible to do that on my way to England, though it would be in the wrong direction for Carcassonne. Her mind, meanwhile, had moved on.

"I am sure the hospital will be closed." She decided. "It will be better if I stay with you. I could come and live with you. I am sure you have room. And if you let me live with you I will not need to go to Carcassonne."

It was surreal. I sat with my head hunched over my knees, wondering if this was the ultimate test of the pilgrimage. So much seemed to have been taken away and now this unlooked-for presence had apparently been added, and I who had been a homeless wanderer too over the past weeks, couldn't bring myself even to get up and move away. For over an hour we sat there on the edge of the pavement, our feet in the gutter, whilst she shouted obscenities at passers by - interspersing these with reminders of my 'promise' to take her home with me. The fact that I was to go to England immediately for my mother's funeral was no deterrent either, she could think of nothing she would like better than to come too.

"But you said you wanted to go to Carcassonne." I protested feebly. "My home is in completely the wrong direction."

"No, I don't want to go there anymore!" She announced cheerfully. "Your home will be much nicer, and I was in England before."

Perhaps it was the disjointed unreality of this conversation, or the realisation of the imposition I was placing on Bernard, who had uncomplainingly got out of bed after a full day's work to come and rescue me, and whose point of view – not having been a pilgrim for the past six weeks would doubtless be rather different, but I was at last galvanised into some sort of action. Fumbling in my pocket for a handkerchief, I felt the two twenty euro notes I had extracted from the cash machine at the airport, hoping to pay for a train ticket, and scrambled to my feet.

Hauling her onto hers, I dragged her off across the road to the hotel opposite where I handed over all forty for a room with a bath (at least she'd be able to wash) and left her in reception with the key, fleeing back to the anonymity of the station concourse; there to hide among the travellers, the addicts and the urine-soaked drunks of one of France's principle cities. And it was as I stood there, dazed and bewildered, jostled by passengers far more assured of their destinations than I was at the time, that I finally found the solitude to take stock of what had happened, and of the coincidence of it all. Coincidence almost too close to be so.

The stroke which had killed my Mum in mid-sentence had happened less than twenty-four hours after I had arrived in Finisterre, the end of the path. I thought of all the mornings I had crawled off my bunk in the dark to keep up with the Musketeers, and of all the sweltering afternoons through which I had trudged on blindly just to arrive exhausted at their designated refugio. The compulsion I had felt to do all that at last made sense - my Musketeers really had got me to the end of the path. If I had not worked so hard to keep up with them I would have been somewhere a long way short of Santiago by now.

Eventually, too, I was able to make sense of the frustrating delays caused by my injuries. At her funeral, a week later, I learned that the two letters I had written her had been treasured possessions during the last weeks of her life. She had read them over and over, to everybody who would listen. With a stab of shame I had to admit that had I not been forced to stop in St. Sever and in León, I would never have written them. It was Ignes who had made the suggestion.

"Use the time constructively!" He had called over his shoulder as he was cycling away across the square. "Write some letters!" Never again, I vowed, would I ignore my instincts or kick against what seemed to be inevitable.

From the station doorway I saw the car arrive and Bernard climbing out. But as I emerged from the crowd I heard a joyful shout. "Soozee! I have found you! I don't want to stay in that hotel, the people there are jerks. I am going to come with you - and so are my friends!" I turned and saw her waddling towards me, followed by three shambling men. From across the road Bernard was waving. Coward that I was, I summoned a last ounce of energy, picked up my rucksack and ran towards him.

There is something especially powerful about the Camino, and one would have to be very sceptical indeed to remain impervious to it...

Chapter Twenty Three
The Camino

It is difficult now to find the reflective, mystical atmosphere the Camino must have had when it was less well used - in the days Ignes spoke of, when refuges were huts with dirt floors, and pilgrims only there because they were committed to finding a more spiritual dimension. If Shirley Maclaine had sat down under a tree to meditate when I was there, half the world would have tramped by before she had got midway through her mantra. But modern motivation is every bit as diverse as it was in the days of the mediaeval ancestor whose steps I had set out to follow. Now, as then, the path is populated by the curious, the mystical, the religious; by seekers who are sceptical, sincere, devout or merely hopeful. There are also a good few people who are simply walkers, rather than pilgrims, there to complete a strenuous programme of exercise, though if I were looking for a good walk I think I'd agree with Log-Cabin-Frank, there are far more beautiful places to choose from.

The mystics are right, though. There is something especially powerful about the Camino and one would have to be very sceptical indeed to remain impervious to it; even Tim Moore was moved by it in the end. With the exception of the very religious ones (who presumably have sorted it all out before they go) every pilgrim I spoke to had arrived, at some point, at a spiritual crossroads - a point where curiosity or scepticism had given way to something deeper.

For most people this had happened well before their arrival in Santiago. As Vital said, the goal is in the journey, not in the destination. It was perhaps this common shift in perspective, as much as the shared hardship, which created the extraordinary bond of trust which makes the Camino so special; a magic which no amount of overcrowding and competition for beds, showers or anything else can completely erase.

Of course, in any spiritual search one grows unusually close to one's fellow seekers. But whether it is its proximity to the stars, as

Ignes believed, or whether, as Albert maintained, it has to do with the spirits of pilgrims past or even the depth of the belief of pilgrims present - the Camino offers the opportunity to form relationships far closer than one would expect to find anywhere else. For me, to have started out alone and to have forged such a close bond with three complete strangers in only a matter of days was certainly out of the ordinary.

Shirley Maclaine wrote that the Camino offers everyone who walks it an affair, and that it is up to them whether or not to accept it. Well if it did I never noticed, which I suppose proves the point.

I can't imagine that an affair on the Camino would be a straightforward thing to arrange, in any case, in dormitories of between twenty and two hundred people. Certainly you couldn't call the chivalrous attention of three men who adored their wives anything approaching an affair; and yet I had walked for twenty-nine days in the sort of happy, affectionate bubble normally associated with one. Feminism notwithstanding, it could hardly fail to be endearing to have arrived at late middle age, through all the aggravation of bringing up stroppy adolescents, and to find oneself addressed as 'Little One' or even, on one wonderful occasion, as "Sheeken Bébé".

It wasn't as if sex, or even physical attraction, had anything to do with it; for all their encouraging compliments it was only ever my spirit they praised; in fact my appearance was only mentioned once, when we were discussing my bus skive to León. Looking me over critically, Vital had remarked in that way they had of talking about me as if I wasn't there, "She could do something about her hair too, while she is about it, just look at her!" The other two had eyed me disparagingly and nodded in solemn agreement. It was an easygoing camaraderie, which would not have been out of place among the original Musketeers or on the original Camino. Nor did it end with the path; feeling raw and hollowed out by the news of my mother's death, and longing for the comfort of their sympathy, their understanding - their involvement - I had sent them each a message to tell them. Their reactions had been entirely in character. Albert had responded immediately and energetically, his voice message full of warmth and concern. He and his wife embraced me very strongly, he said, they were thinking of me all the time and willing me strength for the days to come. Vital and Xavier, on the train to Bordeaux, had simply got off at the next stop and gone to find a church where they could light a candle and say a prayer.

"Don't worry, Little One, your Musketeers do not forget you." Vital had said later, when he phoned back.

If the story of my lone walk became in the end their story, it was because of that generosity of spirit. It was also because that close relationship which sprang out of nowhere, and returning to nowhere still retained its purity and its joy, so completely embodied the essence of a path trodden by centuries of pilgrims. Above all, it had been driven by something far deeper than I had been able, at the time, to understand; and that, I believe, was the gift of the Camino.

~

Sitting in the garden of my cottage one evening three months later, talking to Regine and a rapidly recovering Frits, I looked up to see a man with Messianic hair and blue eyes smiling at me from the gateway, his bike propped up beside him.

"Ignes!"

He stayed for three days. He did his laundry, he washed his hair, he ate his first proper meal for days and he talked almost without stopping. Listening to Ignes was like living out the plot of a novel by Umberto Eco. In the years that he had been cycling the Way of St. James he had steeped himself in the legends of the Knights Templar, the order which had spawned the Knights Hospitaller and the Knights of Santiago. As he talked he leaped back and forth between myth and fact, whisking me across the credibility gap between them by the sheer force of his passion for the subject.

According to him, the roots of the Camino and the Knights who first traced it lie way back - even before the days of the Celts, and long before the body of Saint James was supposed to have been discovered. The Templars, he believed, had links with the Celts which ran far deeper than any they might have had with the Catholic church - hence the significance of the ultimate destination of Finisterre. He was interested in my experience at Finisterre because he had lived there for several months and knew it well. It appeared that the rock from which I had watched the sunset, and gazed at the stars, had been one of two sacred rocks in the days of the Celts; I hadn't been looking for it - I hadn't even known it existed - I had just gone to find somewhere quiet to sit and think.

210

He talked of his adventures during the months which had passed since St. Sever. After Assisi he had cycled on by a similarly circuitous route to Bosnia, to see the shrine at Medjugore where the Virgin Mary still pops in to visit the villagers once a week. She originally appeared, so they say, to six children forty years ago. Apparently it is still only those children - now grown up - who can see her and interpret her messages, but the whole village goes along to watch all the same.

Returning to France via Italy, and having had enough of pedalling against the wind, Ignes had decided to follow it instead. It had blown him first towards the coast of Provence, but before he had got there it had changed and blown him towards the Pyrenees. In fact it had blown him right into the path of the storms which had swept across the South of France that summer.

Images of the flooding and devastation had been broadcast across the news networks of the world and Ignes had been there, alone with his bike. On the night of one of the worst storms, where in St. Gilles the sewers had overflowed, he had with difficulty found shelter in a refuge; everyone had been too preoccupied with baling out their cellars to attend to a pilgrim. Worse was to come. Moving on the next day he had found all his familiar routes blocked by floods. Again and again he changed his plans, but each time it was the same story; he seemed to be imprisoned by water. Finally he had come to a huge roundabout where only one exit was open and he had had no choice but to take it, though it didn't appear to lead to anywhere he recognised. Along that road though, he saw a sign to a village through which he had passed several years ago. He remembered striking up a conversation with a local artist in the bar there. It was getting late in the day by now, and threatening another storm. He needed to find shelter and soon. Would she perhaps take him in? Would she remember him? Would she even be there? He could only try. In the village he had made enquiries, arriving eventually at her door with some trepidation. When she opened it she didn't even say hello.

"Why didn't you come yesterday, before the storm?" She demanded. "Look! I left the key for you in my letter-box!"

"But how did you know I was coming at all?" He asked.

"I saw you in a dream." She shrugged, as if it were the most natural form of communication in the world. He had stayed a week, until the storms had passed, before moving on to arrive eventually in my village. Could the story have been embellished? Possibly, but then again possibly not. After all, this was Ignes the Mystic.

"You should always travel without plans." He concluded. "Because then the Other World will guide you." Remembering the Camino and my mother, I had to agree that he might have a point. As he prepared to leave again, I remembered something he had said months before, as he was leaving St. Sever.

"You never need to say goodbye on the Camino." He had told me, "You are bound to meet again before the end."

At the time I hadn't really believed him, but now I did; I reminded him of it and said that I hoped we would meet again some day.

"Of course we will," he replied, as he mounted his bike.

"The Camino never ends."

Bibliography

The Pilgrimage to Santiago – Edwin Mullins – *Signal Books*
The Pilgrimage Road to Santiago – David M. Gitlitz and
 Linda Kay Davidson – *St. Martins Press*
The Badge of St. James – Christopher Hohler - *Shell Publishing*
Britain, France and the Empire – Margaret L. Kekewich
Susan Rose – *Palgrave Macmillan*
Priez Pour Nous à Compostelle – Barret /Gurand – *Hachette*